Bullying
Beyond the
Schoolyard

Bullying
Beyond the
Schoolyard

Preventing and **Responding** to **Cyberbullying**

Sameer **Hinduja**
Justin W. **Patchin**

CORWIN PRESS
A SAGE Company

For information:

Corwin Press
A SAGE Company
2455 Teller Road
Thousand Oaks, California 91320
www.corwinpress.com

SAGE India Pvt. Ltd.
B 1/I 1 Mohan Cooperative
   Industrial Area
Mathura Road, New Delhi 110 044
India

SAGE Ltd.
1 Oliver's Yard
55 City Road
London EC1Y 1SP
United Kingdom

SAGE Asia-Pacific Pte. Ltd.
33 Pekin Street #02-01
Far East Square
Singapore 048763

Printed in the United States of America.

Library of Congress Cataloging-in-Publication Data

Hinduja, Sameer, 1978-
Bullying beyond the schoolyard: preventing and responding to cyberbullying/Sameer Hinduja, Justin W. Patchin.
     p. cm.

Includes bibliographical references and index.
ISBN 978-1-4129-6688-7 (cloth)
ISBN 978-1-4129-6689-4 (pbk.)

  1. Cyberbullying. 2. Bullying. 3. Computer crimes. 4. Internet and teenagers.
I. Patchin, Justin W., 1977- II. Title.

LB3013.3.H566 2009
371.5′8—dc22   2008028870

This book is printed on acid-free paper.

     09   10   11   12   10   9   8   7   6   5   4   3   2

Acquisitions Editor:	Debra Stollenwerk
Editorial Assistant:	Allison Scott
Production Editor:	Eric Garner
Copy Editor:	Paula L. Fleming
Typesetter:	C&M Digitals (P) Ltd.
Proofreader:	Theresa Kay
Indexer:	Kathy Paparchontis
Cover Designer:	Rose Storey

Contents

Resources for Cyberbullying Prevention and Response

Preface

Though I know life has its challenges, it seems this new generation is faced with a whole new challenge brought about via cyberbullying and related technology-based assaults.

—Mother of a 14-year-old victim
of cyberbullying from Hawaii

For the past several years we have been studying how adolescents use and misuse computers and the Internet. Often, when someone asks us about our research and we mention the term *cyberbullying*, they usually chuckle and wonder aloud, "How can someone be *cyber*bullied?" We have heard this comment with such frequency that we decided to write a book to inform others about what cyberbullying is and why it merits recognition and response. After a few minutes discussing issues relating to cyberbullying with those who are willing to listen, most begin to realize clearly the unique challenges that this novel form of adolescent aggression presents. Our hope is that many more individuals will listen and understand after reading this book.

PURPOSE OF THE BOOK

The purpose of this book is to bring you up to speed about the kinds of hurtful behaviors youth are experiencing online and to equip you with the knowledge and resources necessary to do something about them. Many adults still lack basic knowledge when it comes to computers, the Internet, cell phones, and other electronic devices. This book will help usher you into the 21st century by describing the technology that youth are using, and in some cases misusing, every single day. The point is not to scare you into pulling the plug and abandoning all technology but to educate and empower you to take certain proactive steps to protect youth and prevent and respond to inappropriate behaviors that involve technology.

While this book is primarily concerned with cyberbullying among students, it is important to note that we also touch on what should be done in situations where students employ technology to harass educators. In fact, many of the lessons learned about how a school can and should respond to cyberbullying come from several cases where students were disciplined for cyberharassing staff (Chapter 5 covers these issues in depth). Given the similarities, the methods discussed in this book for the identification and prevention of, and response to, cyberbullying among adolescent peers can also be applied to incidents of staff harassment.

APPROACH

Rather than acting solely on what is heard in the popular media concerning a new phenomenon, educators, parents, and others concerned about youth need to examine the problem of cyberbullying responsibly to learn how best to address it. The alarmist headlines in the national news may grab our attention, but they do little to inform or teach us about the actual scope, prevalence, frequency, causes, and consequences of electronic aggression among teenagers. Research does.

Much of the information reported throughout this book stems from our own original research conducted over the last several years. Most recently, we gathered and analyzed data from a random sample of approximately 2,000 middle school students in one of the largest school districts in the United States. In great detail, we asked these youth about their experiences with traditional and cyberbullying as well as a number of other related factors (e.g., computer proficiency, stressful life events, self-esteem, and suicidal ideation). We wanted to systematically and scientifically illuminate the problem of cyberbullying to better inform those who work most closely with youth.

Moreover, these data are supplemented by information collected from thousands of youth who have corresponded with us over the years. We wanted them to tell us about their cyberbullying experiences *in their own words*. We found out that many of the targets of cyberbullying were scared to talk about online bullying with their parents because they didn't want to be blamed and/or lose their computer privileges. We learned that some incidents lasted for years and that youth felt helpless and didn't know where to go for help. Adolescents in our research had a great deal to say about cyberbullying and wanted their voices to be heard. We wrote this book in part for that purpose: to tell their stories. And, as you will see, these stories are rich, colorful, eye-opening, and even heartrending as they provide a very personal, vulnerable perspective.

The chapters that follow also include accounts from adults who are at the forefront of Internet-based behavior issues. We have spoken to teachers, school administrators, counselors, law enforcement officers, parents, and many other youth-serving adults who have been grappling with the complications that arise from cyberbullying incidents. Most of these folks simply improvised and did their best, because not much was known about how to handle these unique cases properly. Since there are so many "gray areas" in terms of responding to cyberbullying, their interpretations and actions are important to consider because they contribute toward building a body of knowledge over time that can consistently provide meaningful guidance. It is hoped that the "best practices" we have collected and now share in this book can capably inform the actions of those in the trenches so that their prevention and response strategies have utility and value.

THE IMPORTANT ROLE OF EDUCATORS

When considering our audience, we decided specifically to target educators with this information, since they are on the front lines in dealing with many forms of adolescent aggression. In many cases, youth are spending more direct time each day with their teachers than they are with their parents. As a result, school personnel may notice when something isn't quite right by picking up on subtle cues. Teachers, school counselors, administrators, and others who work with adolescents on a daily basis also tend to be more proactive in informing themselves about issues facing youth today. Finally, we believe they can also serve as the conduit through which this important information reaches the parents of their students, as well as others in the community who need to learn about cyberbullying.

Even though the vast majority of cyberbullying behaviors take place off school grounds, they very often make their way back into the school. In fact, many adolescent problems these days either begin at school and progress online or are initiated online and continue at school. Like it or not, educators will frequently have to deal with repercussions of disagreements or problems that began or escalated a great distance from the schoolhouse doors. Thankfully, you will see that there are many things educators can and should do with respect to the online behaviors of their students—even if most of those online actions and interactions occur outside of the confines of the school.

IMPORTANT FEATURES OF THE BOOK

This book includes a number of special features that will help you identify, prevent, and respond to cyberbullying incidents. In addition to incorporating personal voices and viewpoints from youth affected by or involved in cyberbullying incidents, as well as educators and parents on the front lines dealing with online aggression, the book also contains several valuable in-text features to help reinforce the key concepts, including the following:

- Dozens of breakout boxes highlighting hundreds of important strategies to deal with cyberbullying
- Review of the latest research in this emerging area
- Illustrations that help to illuminate what cyberbullying looks like
- Summary of important legal rulings
- Warning signs to help identify cyberbullies and their targets
- Strategies for safe and responsible social networking
- Questions for reflection after each chapter
- Chapter summaries
- Index

Along with the special features in the text, the book also includes a number of tools in the Resources section that can assist you in understanding and addressing cyberbullying. These resources can be reproduced and distributed to other educators, parents, and students to help inform and educate your community about cyberbullying. They include the following:

- Glossary
- Recommendations for Further Information
- Cyberbullying Scenarios for Discussion
- Internet Use Contract
- Family Cell Phone Use Contract
- Cyberbullying Assessment Instrument
- Cyberbullying Report Card for Schools
- Cyberbullying Crossword Puzzle and Word Find
- Supplemental Staff Development Questions

ORGANIZATION OF THE BOOK

This book has been organized in such a way that will allow for easy retrieval of important information, depending on the issues you currently face. We do not expect you to remember everything you read, so we structured the book to serve as a handy reference or resource for you. While there is some necessary overlap between chapters, each part is largely distinct in its examination of a particular topic relating to cyberbullying and online harassment.

Chapter 1 introduces the problem of cyberbullying with an illustrative story that highlights the harm that can result from the misuse of computers and other technology. It continues by exploring how the intersection of teens, technology, and traditional bullying has birthed the problem.

Chapter 2 discusses in detail what cyberbullying is and how you can identify it. Here, a number of real-life examples are described to highlight the nature of online harassment. While the particular tactics and techniques employed by adolescents are always evolving, this chapter will provide the basic information necessary to recognize most (if not all) cyberbullying behaviors in a variety of settings.

Chapter 3 summarizes our research and that of others who have systematically studied the problem. The findings from this research can help depict the scope and gravity of online harassment and be used to inform policy and programming as we move forward. Also, we are often asked, "Why exactly do kids bully other kids online?" While there is no simple answer to this question, a number of developmental, behavioral, psychological, and sociological explanations can help us understand the possible causes of this type of harassment.

In Chapter 4, the popular phenomenon of online social networking is explored with particular focus on MySpace. A number of youth related to us cyberbullying experiences carried out using MySpace or other similar online environments, and these are presented as hard-hitting illustrations of the problem. This chapter also covers the positive aspects and potential risks inherent in Web-based interactive communities and describes some of our recent research in this area.

Chapter 5 presents a comprehensive discussion of the legal issues confronting school administrators who are attempting to define the parameters of their role in responding to cyberbullying incidents. School officials are in a difficult position because they don't want to overstep their legal authority in disciplining student behavior that occurs off campus. We argue that they can (and should) intervene in specific situations—in incidents that ultimately impact students or the learning environment at school. We review a number of court cases that support this argument and detail the essential components of a well-developed and structured cyberbullying policy for school districts.

Chapter 6 provides a number of practical recommendations for preventing cyberbullying and online harassment. Specific emphasis is placed on early education and guidance from school personnel, as appropriate online habits must be instilled and reinforced before youth are extensively using the technology. Furthermore, we discuss how a coordinated effort by teachers, administrative staff, counselors, law enforcement, parents, and other stakeholders is necessary to encourage positive and productive Internet use among adolescents.

Finally, Chapter 7 explores constructive ways in which to respond to cyberbullying. When appropriate, educators must step up quickly to identify and then discipline harmful behaviors in cyberspace by their students. We argue that informal response strategies will prove most useful for the majority of cyberbullying behaviors but also discuss when formal disciplinary action must be pursued. It is once again essential that educators, parents, and others in the community present a unified front against all forms of online aggression. Adolescents must learn that bullying in any form, wherever and whenever perpetrated, will not be tolerated.

> *. . . bullying will never be eliminated unless teachers and children become partners in this crusade against cruelty.*

> —SuEllen Fried and Paula Fried
> *Bullies and Victims* (1996, p. 107)

Acknowledgments

This book would not have been possible without the assistance of a number of important individuals in our personal and professional lives. First, we are both grateful to have supportive families who have cared for, encouraged, and inspired us over the years. Their love and affirmation has sustained us through the long hours of research and writing. We gratefully acknowledge the support of the Office of Research and Sponsored Programs at the University of Wisconsin–Eau Claire and the Division of Research at Florida Atlantic University for their support of our research presented throughout this book.

We would also like to convey appreciation to our professional colleagues who stand alongside us on the front lines of online safety issues among youth. We are most indebted to those who provided valuable counsel throughout the preparation of this book, including Kim Mazauskas, Mike Tully, Mike Donlin, and Jace Galloway. We would also like to thank John Halligan, Debbie Johnston, Mark Neblett, and Tina Meier for allowing us to share the stories of Ryan, Jeffrey, Rachael, and Megan with our readers. For them, and for all who have been affected by cyberbullying, we offer this book as well as our commitment to continue this vital work. Finally, we would like to thank God for giving us the opportunities and abilities to study this problem and contribute to its understanding.

We would also like to thank the staff at Corwin Press and Sage Publications for their expert guidance throughout this process. We are indebted to Deb Stollenwerk, Allison Scott, and Eric Garner for helping us to bring this project to fruition. We also thank Paula Fleming for clarifying the meaning of our words while keeping our respective voices. We were also fortunate to have several blind reviewers whose suggestions contributed to a tighter and more comprehensive work.

Corwin Press gratefully acknowledges the contributions of the following individuals:

Melissa Albright
Teacher
Springfield Public Schools
Ozark, MO

Carries Ames
Teacher
Gallup High School
Gallup, NM

Sheri Bauman
Associate Professor
University of Arizona, Educational
   Psychology
Tucson, AZ

Margarete Couture
Principal
South Seneca Central School
   District
Interlaken, NY

Jolene Dockstader
Teacher
Jerome SD #261
Jerome, ID

Richard Hazler
Associate Professor and
   Coordinator of Elementary
   School Counseling Program
Pennsylvania State
Bellefonte, PA

Carol Holzberg
Technology Coordinator
Greenfield Public Schools
Shutesbury, MA

Jude Huntz
Teacher
The Barstow School
Kansas City, MO

Joyce Stout, PhD
Counselor, 2006 ASCA Counselor
   of the Year
Alta Vista Elementary
Alta Vista, CA

Barbara Trolley
Professor, Counselor Education
St. Bonaventure University
St. Bonaventure, NY

About the Authors

 **Sameer Hinduja, PhD,** is an assistant professor of criminology and criminal justice at Florida Atlantic University. He received his PhD in criminal justice from Michigan State University.

 **Justin W. Patchin, PhD,** is an assistant professor of criminal justice at the University of Wisconsin–Eau Claire. He also earned his PhD in criminal justice from Michigan State University.

For the past several years, Dr. Hinduja and Dr. Patchin have been exploring the online behaviors of adolescents, including social networking and cyberbullying. They travel across the United States training teachers, parents, and others on how to keep their kids safe online. They administer a Web site (www.cyberbullying.us) that serves as an information clearinghouse for those interested in learning more about cyberbullying.

1

Cyberbullying

The New Adolescent Aggression

Being bullied besides over the Internet is worse. It's torment and hurts. They say sticks and stones may break my bones but words will never hurt me. That quote is a lie and I don't believe in it. Sticks and stones may cause nasty cuts but those cuts and scars will heal. Insultive words hurt and sometimes take forever to heal.

—14-year-old girl from New Jersey

VADA'S STORY

Vada was a 14-year-old girl with strawberry-blonde hair and bright blue eyes. She was both beautiful and intelligent but kept largely to herself. She had a best friend named Ali, with whom she discussed schoolwork, popular culture, and boys. At the beginning of the seventh grade, a new boy named Jim arrived in their first-period class. Jim had just enrolled in the school and immediately caught the eye of both Vada and Ali due to his charming good looks. It turned out that Jim had two classes with both of the girls and thereby got to know each of them through group projects and afterschool study sessions. Both girls developed crushes on Jim, but Ali was more forthcoming about her feelings, while Vada—who was much more introverted—kept silent and just allowed Ali to gush about how cute, funny, and cool Jim was.

This went on for several weeks, and Ali began to get excited about the upcoming Homecoming Dance, confident that Jim was going to ask her to go with him. For three hours one night, Ali discussed with Vada her plans for the dance: what she would wear, how she would do her hair, what they would talk about, and how she would respond if he tried to kiss her. Vada was graciously able to feign enthusiasm and joy for Ali, even though deep down her heart was breaking because she wanted to go to the dance as well—with Jim.

Two weeks before the grand event, Ali and Jim went out for ice cream. While sharing a banana split, Ali subtly attempted to determine Jim's interest in going to the dance. Very cautiously, Jim demonstrated a desire to go but didn't reveal whom he might ask, even as Ali made very clear about how much she would like to go if only "some guy" would ask her. Their evening ended in awkward silence, leaving Ali crushed in spirit and hope. After she was dropped off at home, she rushed to her room, turned on her computer, and instant messaged Vada to share of her disappointment and pain. Vada felt awful for her friend, and tried to console and comfort Ali with encouraging words. Unfortunately, they did not help much because Ali had fallen hard for Jim.

After about an hour of instant messaging, it was time to call it a night. Before shutting down her computer, Vada reminded Ali that she was her best friend and would always be available if she wanted to talk some more. All of a sudden, Vada's doorbell rang. Wondering who it could be at this late hour of the night, Vada heard her Dad call out that "someone is here to see you." So she rushed out of her room and down the stairs and was shocked to see Jim with a rose in his hand, waiting for her in the foyer. After Vada's dad left the two of them alone, Jim said hello with a nervous smile and gave the rose to Vada. "What's this for?" she asked. "Well, it's for you . . ." stammered Jim, doing all he could to avoid eye contact with the girl in front of him. "I wanted to see if you might want to come to the Homecoming Dance with me."

"But I thought you were going to ask Ali?" said Vada, thoroughly confused and taken aback.

"I don't want to go with her . . . I want to go with you."

Before she knew what was happening, Vada said yes to Jim's request and hugged him goodnight. She rushed upstairs and jumped onto her bed and began staring at the ceiling, clueless as to how she was going to explain all of this to Ali.

At school the next day, Vada pulled Ali aside and told her that after they talked online last night, Jim had come over to ask her to go to the dance with him. And that she had said yes. Ali burst into tears and began to accuse Vada of going behind her back and stealing Jim away from her. Vada tried to calm her down and explain logically how that wasn't the case at all, but Ali simply wasn't willing to listen. Not only did the friendship abruptly crumble at that moment, but within a few hours, Vada noticed that other girls in their classes were treating her differently—staring at her, being standoffish, and even refusing to acknowledge her presence in the room. Apparently, Ali had told everyone what she believed had happened, and now everyone was talking about it. Already quite timid and unsure of herself, Vada was devastated because of the whispers and rumors that were now flying around. She couldn't concentrate for the rest of the day in her classes, even though she had exams to deal with and really needed to do well on them. She just wanted to get out of there. She just wanted to avoid Ali and Jim and everyone else and go home.

That evening, unbeknownst to Vada, Ali set up a Hotmail e-mail account in Vada's name and sent messages to all of their friends with insults, derogatory comments, and demands in an attempt to get the entire seventh-grade class to hate her. When Vada checked her e-mail before calling it a night, she was surprised to find horribly mean e-mail messages from a number of boys and girls in her class who were upset over what she had apparently e-mailed them. Not only was she inundated with cruel and hurtful words, she also was shocked when opening three "anonymous" e-mails that all said the same thing: "vada, if you go the homecoming dance with jim, you're gonna regret it!!!!!!!!!!" Completely exhausted, she crawled into bed, buried her face in her pillow, and cried herself to sleep.

The next day at school, Vada walked into her homeroom before the bell rang to find ten or so girls gathered around the computer workstations, staring and pointing and laughing at the computer screens in front of them. As soon as they saw her, though, they immediately quieted down and scurried away from the computers. When Vada got to the computers, she found herself staring at a Web page created with pictures of herself that she knew that Ali had taken. But parts of these pictures were clearly different: They had apparently been doctored to make it look like Vada was smoking marijuana and drinking beer. Another picture on the site had Vada's head attached to the naked body of an extremely overweight woman. And scattered around the page were horrible words in huge font sizes: "F*** Vada!" . . ."Vada is a bitch!" . . ."Vada is a whore!"

Immediately, she burst into tears as she thought how everyone in the world could get on the Internet and see this Web page. She then left homeroom and ran through the crowds of students getting ready for class in the hallway straight toward the front office, so she could call her mom to pick her up from school and take her home. But then out of the corner of her eye, Vada caught a glimpse of the same horrible Web page on . . . a locker? And there it was, on another locker, and another locker. The Web page had been printed out and photocopied and then taped to locker, after locker, after locker, up and down the halls of the school.

And then the first bell rang, signaling the beginning of classes, but no one vacated the hallways. There was complete commotion all around as everyone was staring at the printouts and talking loudly about them, laughing about them, passing them around. Some teachers had noticed them as well and were yanking them off of lockers and out of students' hands, barking orders at everyone to help tear them down and throw them away. "GET TO CLASS!" could be heard from several teachers in the hallway. But no one was listening—they had completely lost themselves in the contents of the Web page: talking loudly, and staring, and pointing, and laughing. It was absolute chaos in the school hallway. With tears streaming down her face, Vada ran past a couple of teachers who tried to grab her and slow her down and finally got to the front office, where she called her mom to come rescue her from this middle school nightmare.

❖

Vada's story raises a number of important questions. Why didn't Ali just bully Vada in traditional ways, spreading rumors through word of mouth? Why did she use her computer and the Internet? And what is it about this bullying instance that makes it so serious, resulting in such painful and disruptive consequences? How could this incident be prevented? Can or should the school respond? If so, how? What factors bring the situation within the jurisdiction of the school's disciplinary reach, even though Ali orchestrated the e-mail exchanges and created the disparaging Web site at home?

Although the students in Vada's story are fictitious, the story is very real and aptly illustrates the psychological and emotional harm that can result from *cyberbullying* (see Box 1.1 for other terms used to describe this phenomenon). You may think it is somewhat far-fetched, but as noted in the Preface, every story in this book is either real or based on real events. They help to reinforce important principles and guide us in the direction of appropriate prevention and response strategies.

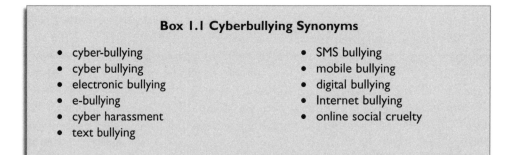

Box 1.1 Cyberbullying Synonyms

- cyber-bullying
- cyber bullying
- electronic bullying
- e-bullying
- cyber harassment
- text bullying

- SMS bullying
- mobile bullying
- digital bullying
- Internet bullying
- online social cruelty

The primary goal of this book is to illuminate the best ways to interpret and deal with these complexities, equipping you with the tools necessary to confront instances of cyberbullying. If you have previously faced some of these issues, you know how difficult it is to navigate this largely uncharted terrain. If you haven't encountered any instances of online aggression among the youth you serve, sooner or later you will. Regardless, we hope this book becomes your favorite resource when dealing with cyberbullying.

I would like my story to be anonymous. I am a 14-year-old girl who has been called fat online for many years. One day I was talking to my friend [and told her] that I was pregnant. She sent the conversation to everyone and soon enough everyone called me pregnant. I got kicked out of school and I started to cut myself. I was admitted to a hospital and spent 5 months in intensive care until my baby was born. Cyberbullying ruined my life.[1]

—Submitted anonymously

WHAT EXACTLY IS CYBERBULLYING?

In general, we define *cyberbullying* as "willful and repeated harm inflicted through the use of computers, cell phones, and other electronic devices."[2] (See Box 1.2.) We developed this definition because it is simple, concise, and reasonably comprehensive and it captures the most important elements. These elements include the following:

- *Willful:* The behavior has to be deliberate, not accidental.
- *Repeated:* Bullying reflects a pattern of behavior, not just one isolated incident.
- *Harm:* The target must perceive that harm was inflicted.
- *Computers, cell phones, and other electronic devices:* This, of course, is what differentiates cyberbullying from traditional bullying.

In the chapters that follow (particularly Chapter 2), we will further clarify this definition and provide numerous examples to help you understand the behavior and its potential consequences.

Perhaps you are familiar with some of the more commonly cited examples of cyberbullying reported in the media in recent years (see Box 1.3). Such stories have captured the attention of teachers, counselors, school administrators, law enforcement officers, parents, and other adults as they seek to understand this emergent form of youth violence. Moreover, the stories speak to the real, harmful nature of some forms of Internet-based communication and serve as a warning to adults who fail to prevent or respond to inappropriate Internet-based behaviors.

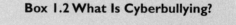

Box 1.2 What Is Cyberbullying?

Cyberbullying is willful and repeated harm inflicted through the use of computers, cell phones, and other electronic devices.

Box 1.3 Recent High-Profile Examples of Cyberbullying

In 2002, 17-year-old David Knight, a Canadian high school senior, became aware of a defamatory Web site that had been online for months. It accused him of being a pedophile and labeled him gay, dirty, immature, and strongly disliked by everyone. He became isolated and withdrawn and could not return to school due to the humiliation and embarrassment he experienced (Leishman, 2005).

In 2003, 13-year-old Ryan Halligan committed suicide after months of torment from classmates. Ryan's father John is clear about the causes of his son's untimely death: "We have no doubt that bullying and cyber bullying were significant environmental factors that triggered Ryan's depression" (Halligan, 2006, ¶ 22).

In 2004, a hate-filled Web site was created by students naming an Allendale, New Jersey, school's "top five biggest homosexuals" and the "top 20 gayest guys and gayest girls" (Cooper, 2004, ¶ 4).

In 2005, 15-year-old Jeff Johnston committed suicide after "relentless bullying that followed him home from the classroom and onto his computer" (Apollo, 2007, ¶ 6). As Jeff's mom, Debra Johnston, pointed out before the Florida senate committee, "Young children are killing themselves because taking their own lives is preferable to the pain of continuing" (Carson, 2007, ¶ 13).

In 2006, a 12-year-old seventh grader and her older sisters received hateful and threatening e-mails referencing their race and the KKK and threatening physical violence against them. One line from an e-mail stated, "All I got to say is that you better watch every move you make N***** and you can tell all of your older sister(s) the KKK will be after them (too) B****" (D. Williams, 2006, ¶ 4). According to the family, the youngest daughter has been in counseling, dislikes school, has suffered from a great deal of emotional stress, and wishes she could just disappear (D. Williams).

In 2007, national and international news covered the story of Megan Meier. The 13-year-old eighth grader from a small town in Missouri committed suicide in 2006 after being harassed on MySpace by someone she thought was a 16-year-old boy named Josh Evans (Jones, 2008).

In 2008, six teenaged girls were arrested for kidnapping and assault after videotaping themselves beating a female classmate. They intended to upload the video to the Internet. Allegedly, the victim had made comments about the girls on MySpace ("Teens Arrested," 2008).

Despite these recent high-profile incidents, some still view cyberbullying among teens as inconsequential. They likely haven't experienced it on a personal level. And they likely haven't spoken to John Halligan, Debra Johnston, Mark Neblett, or Tina Meier, who each lost a child to suicide after the child was cyberbullied. Some other stories from youth who have contacted us emphasize similar devastating implications:

> *I get bullied every day and I just want to hang myself. . . . I'm thinking about it but I doubt I will. . . .*

—Submitted anonymously

My friends don't want me around and I have invaded their privacy by Bebo and found out that they hate me but feel sorry for me and bitch about me. Everything I say to them goes around my school. They have taken over my Bebo account more than once and sent messages around saying that I had a sex change when I went on holidays. They are the only people in my class that I hang around with and I don't want to lose them but I have become depressed and suicidal and am afraid that if I'm pushed over the edge then it will be too late.

—Submitted anonymously

One of the reasons why cyberbullying is not taken seriously is that there remain a number of adults who continue to perceive traditional bullying as simply "a rite of passage among adolescents," as "boys being boys," or even as an inevitable and instructive element of growing up. If you experienced bullying during your formative years, perhaps you share those beliefs. However, we believe that if emotional, psychological, and potentially even physical harm stemming from online aggression can be reduced or prevented, it is definitely worth the effort. Our conversations with bullied youth around the world corroborate that sentiment. This book represents our effort to educate school personnel about cyberbullying so that they are better equipped to address, prevent, and respond to electronic harassment in meaningful and productive ways. Before delving deeper into how to identify, prevent, and respond to cyberbullying, it is important to understand its component parts: teens, technology, and bullying.

TEENS AND TECHNOLOGY

Just as the telephone revolutionized interpersonal interaction in the 20th century by enhancing our ability to "reach out and touch" others, and as the automobile provided us the means to transcend space and time constraints previously insurmountable, information technology has dramatically altered and expanded the way in which individuals communicate. According to market research, 1.26 billion people accessed the Internet in November 2007, accounting for just over 19 percent of the world's population and a growth of 249.6 percent since 2000. Approximately 335 million of those are in North America (where Internet access has penetrated over 70 percent of the population, Miniwatts Marketing Group, 2008). These numbers will continue to grow as computer systems and telecommunications capabilities reach farther and deeper into the countries of the world.

As a result of this rapid expansion of technology, kids are now being raised in an Internet-enabled world where blogs (Web logs), social networking Web sites, and instant messaging are competing with face-to-face and telephone communication as the dominant means and methods through which personal interaction takes place. Teenagers today have truly embraced Internet technology and online communication, and more youth are going online than ever.

According to the Pew Internet & American Life Project's *Teens and Technology* report, 93 percent of youth aged 12 to 17 used the Internet as of November 2006, with 61 percent going online daily (Lenhart, Madden, Rankin-Macgill, & Smith, 2007). Internet-enabled computers allow youth to conduct research for schoolwork, communicate with friends from afar, play games, and engage in a myriad of other positive, prosocial activities. In many ways, computer proficiency has become critical for personal and professional success, and it is largely demanded that adolescents in the current generation have an adequate level of computer proficiency before they enter the workforce.

Interestingly, most teenagers do not struggle with being computer proficient. It is the adult population that has had some difficulty keeping up with the profound transformations that technological advances have introduced into our culture. The terms *digital natives* and *digital immigrants* have been used to describe how youth have grown up with computers, cell phones, and the Internet and use them as seamless, complementing extensions of their real-world behaviors, while adults have largely been induced to adopt them into their lives as supplements to their normal activities (Prensky, 2001). Most adolescents these days have not known a time when they were not able to search the Internet or communicate with others electronically. Being raised in the Information Age has given adolescents a natural ability to understand how electronic devices can and must be used for a vast number of purposes.

Research by the Pew Internet and American Life Foundation (Lenhart et al., 2007) from November 2006 found that teenagers between ages 12 and 17 are involved in various Internet-based activities (see Table 1.1). Most teens regularly explore the Internet for information about movies, TV shows, music groups, sports stars, or other news. Many teens also frequently use the Internet to communicate and interact with others.

In addition to computers and the Internet, many teens religiously carry a cell phone with which they communicate both verbally and textually. As of November 2006, 63 percent of teens have cell phones, 35 percent of teens use their phones to talk to friends every day, and 27 percent send text messages every day (Lenhart et al., 2007). Many have become extremely comfortable (if not obsessed with) communicating with their friends by way of short text messages sent and received via cell phone. Chart 1.1 on page 10 shows the various online activities of middle schoolers.

As you can see, many youth are embedded in an online culture that is largely inseparable and indistinct from their offline world, and most adults cannot comprehend this lifestyle practice. Adults generally use computers and cell phones to accomplish a specific task (e.g., purposed communication, checking on news or stocks, or making travel arrangements), while these devices have become an integral part of almost *all* of the day-to-day activities of many youth. Young people often log onto

Table 1.1   Teen Internet Activities (Online Teens; $N = 886$)

Do you ever . . .	Percent
Go to Web sites about movies, TV shows, music groups, or sports stars	81
Get information about news and current events	77
Send or receive instant messages (IMs)	68
Watch video sharing sites	57
Use an online social networking site like MySpace or Facebook	55
Get information about a college or university you are thinking of attending	55
Play computer or console games online	49
Buy things online, such as books, clothes, and music	38
Look for health, dieting, or physical fitness information	28
Download a podcast	19
Visit chat rooms	18

SOURCE: Pew Internet & American Life Project Survey of Parents and Teens, October–November 2006. Margin of error for teens is ±4%.

the Internet immediately after returning home from school to check messages or comments left on their social networking profile page(s) (further discussed in Chapter 4) and use their cell phones to send text messages to friends at all hours of the day (including, in some cases, while at school).

Apart from the obvious benefits of information at one's fingertips, entertainment value, and speed of correspondence, online interaction can be very useful to teach youth various social and emotional skills that are essential to handling life. For example, cyberspace provides a venue to learn and refine one's ability to exercise self-control, to relate to others' viewpoints with tolerance and respect, to express sentiments in a healthy and normative manner, and to engage in critical thinking and decision making (I. R. Berson, Berson, & Ferron, 2002; M. J. Berson, 2000). In addition, adolescents are at a stage where they are negotiating beliefs, boundaries, roles, and goals as they discover, develop, and refine their self-identity (Calvert, 2002; Erikson, 1950; Turkle, 1995), and online socialization and interaction can assist tremendously in that regard.

Chart 1.1   Online Activities Among Middle-Schoolers

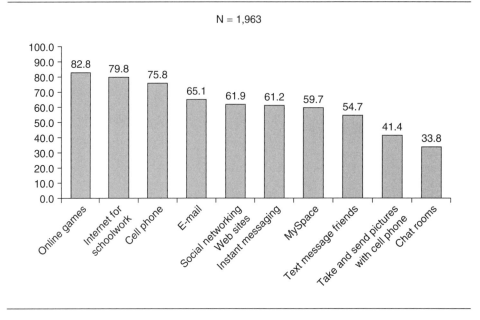

N = 1,963

These benefits, however, cannot be effectively internalized if the learning environment is unwelcoming or inhospitable to those who venture online. Indeed, if adolescents are uncomfortable using or unwilling to explore the Internet and take advantage of its positive attributes, they will be sorely lacking in certain developmental qualities that others who do embrace cyberspace will naturally obtain. Youth hesitate in social situations in part because they fear mistreatment, harassment, aggression, and rejection. The possibility of facing these challenges is seemingly augmented when considering Internet-based interactions, as cell phones, computers, and the Internet have created an environment conducive for those with malicious intent to cause harm to others.

While computer-based communication has been studied extensively in a variety of fields, victimization through cyberbullying is a relatively new area of research that has only recently been explored. Butterfield and Broad (2001) state that

> social change always provides opportunities for the predatory behavior that is characteristic of a small number of people. With the new technologies which support the Internet, those who cannot adjust rapidly, and that is almost all of us, are at risk from those who can and will deploy technology as a criminal weapon. (p. 5)

Thanks to the increased prevalence of these electronic devices, would-be bullies are afforded technology that provides additional mediums over which they can inflict harm. As instances of bullying are no longer restricted to real-world settings, the problem has become more complex and harder to address. Before delving deeper into these complexities, however, it is essential to provide some foundational information about traditional bullying as a point of reference and comparison.

TRADITIONAL BULLYING

If you let a bully come in your front yard, he'll be on your porch the next day and the day after that he'll rape your wife in your own bed.

—Lyndon B. Johnson

The specific impact of bullying on young people has been studied at great length in the disciplines of counseling, education, sociology, psychology, psychiatry, and criminology. Most generally, the term *bullying* is equated to the concept of harassment, which is a form of unprovoked aggression often directed repeatedly toward another individual or group of individuals (Manning, Heron, & Marshal, 1978). However, bullying tends to become more insidious as it continues over time and may be better equated to "violence" rather than "harassment." Accordingly, Roland (1989) states that *bullying* is "longstanding violence, physical or psychological, conducted by an individual or a group directed against an individual who is not able to defend himself in the actual situation" (p. 21). Johnson, Munn, and Edwards (1991) refer to *bullying* as a willful, conscious wish to hurt, frighten, or threaten someone. Finally, we like Nansel and colleagues' (2001) comprehensive definition of *bullying* as aggressive behavior or intentional "harm doing" by one person or a group, generally carried out repeatedly and over time and involving a power differential.

As is evident, different researchers interpret the meaning of *bullying* in similar yet slightly different ways, though certain dominant themes are pretty obvious. First, the behavior is intentional and purposed rather than accidental or inadvertent. Accidents happen all of the time on the playground, and some of these result in physical harm. Still, most people recognize that accidental or unintentional behaviors do not constitute bullying.

Second, bullying necessarily involves maliciousness on the part of the aggressor, and that maliciousness is one type of *violence.* Researchers have attempted to categorize various types of bullying violence in multiple ways. Some have focused on differentiating between direct aggression and indirect aggression (Besag, 1989; Ericson, 2001; Leckie, 1997; Limber & Nation, 1998; Olweus, 1978; Tattum, 1989). Direct aggression involves physical violence (hitting, kicking, taking items by force) and verbal violence (taunting, teasing, threatening; Hawker & Boulton, 2000). Indirect aggression includes more subtle, manipulative acts such as ostracizing, intimidating, or controlling another person (van der Wal, de Wit, & Hirasing, 2003). Others have focused on distinguishing between overt and relational forms of aggression. Overt aggression might involve name-calling, pushing, or hitting, while relational aggression includes gossip, rumor spreading, social sabotage, exclusion, and other behaviors destructive to interpersonal relationships (Prinstein, Boergers, & Vernberg, 2001; Simmons, 2003; Wolke, Woods, Bloomfield, & Karstadt, 2000).

Third, one instance of aggression is not sufficient to qualify as bullying; behavior must occur on a repetitive basis to be considered bullying. This is one of the features that distinguishes bullying from other forms of peer harassment. The repetitive nature of bullying creates a dynamic where the victim continuously worries about what the bully will do next. Indeed, the target often alters daily behavior patterns to avoid personal contact with the bully, because it is assumed that something bad will happen if they interact. Do you personally remember choosing to go down different hallways or to show up to class right when it began instead of early to avoid spending unnecessary "quality time" with someone who always harassed you? We vividly recall instances from our middle school days that taught us the art of skillfully dodging any run-ins with the bullies in our respective lives.

Fourth, inherent in any conception of bullying is the demonstration (or interpretation) of power by the offender over the target. If both parties were equal (socially, physically, or otherwise), one might think that neither has the proverbial upper hand. With differential levels of power, though, bullying as it is typically conceived can occur. Many characteristics can give an offender perceived or actual power over a victim, including popularity, physical strength or stature, social competence, quick wit, extroversion, confidence, intelligence, age, sex, race, ethnicity, or socioeconomic status (Olweus, 1978, 1993; Olweus, Limber, & Mihalic, 1999a; Rigby & Slee, 1993; Roland, 1980; Slee & Rigby, 1993). To summarize, there appear to be four distinct components of bullying, which are displayed in Box 1.4.

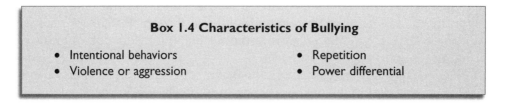

Box 1.4 Characteristics of Bullying

- Intentional behaviors
- Violence or aggression
- Repetition
- Power differential

While the harassment associated with bullying can occur anywhere, the term *bullying* often concerns the behavior as it occurs between adolescent peers in some proximity to school. This includes at or around school bus stops, in school hallways and bathrooms, on the playground, or otherwise close to or inside the school setting. Bullies can also follow their targets to other venues, such as shopping malls, restaurants, or neighborhood hang-outs, to continue the mistreatment. Nevertheless, because of the prominence of the school in the lives of youth, these behaviors and interactions often reveal themselves at or near that environment. Of course, this means that teachers, school counselors, and other school officials are on the front lines when it comes to bullying prevention, identification, and response. While many school districts have been relatively proactive in dealing with bullying incidents at school, others are lagging behind.

Though we exhaustively cover the various types of cyberbullying and their causes and consequences later in this book, it is essential first to briefly examine the problem of traditional bullying to provide some context. This backdrop should help readers fully appreciate the harm that often stems from bullying and appreciate how cyberbullying can do the same. Perhaps you have a conception of bullying based on your personal experiences, news headlines or stories, television and movie scenes, or other sources. However, those are all largely anecdotal, high-profile, or isolated examples that may not represent the majority of bullying experiences. Over the last few decades, a number of scholars have actively researched bullying to identify trends and patterns across the personal experiences of thousands of youth. We now turn to three major themes that can be extracted from this body of knowledge.

Prevalence of Bullying

A number of research endeavors in recent years have clarified the proportion of youth who have experiences with bullying. To begin, a nationally representative study of 15,686 students in Grades 6 through 10 identified that approximately 11 percent of respondents were victims of bullying each year, while 13 percent were bullies and another 6 percent were both victims and bullies (Nansel et al., 2001). Similarly, the U.S. Department of Justice's Bureau of Justice Statistics reported that of those youth between the ages of 12 and 18, 8 percent had been victims of bullying in the previous six months (Devoe et al., 2002). Other studies have suggested that the prevalence of bullying in American elementary schools is between 14 and 19 percent, while the secondary school rate is between 3 and 10 percent (Dake, Price, & Telljohann, 2003; Kaltiala-Heino, Rimpelä, Rantanen, & Rimpelä, 2000). Overall, conservative estimates maintain that *at least* 5 percent of those in primary and secondary schools (ages 7–16) are victimized by bullies *each day*—but the percentage may well be much higher (Bjorkqvist, Ekman, & Lagerspetz, 1982; Lagerspetz, Bjorkvqvist, Bertz, & King, 1982; Olweus, 1978; Roland, 1980).

Emotional and Psychological Consequences of Bullying

Consequences of bullying victimization identified in previous research include psychological and psychosomatic distress and problematic emotional and social responses (Borg, 1998; Cowie & Berdondini, 2002; Ericson, 2001; Natvig, Albrektsen, & Quarnstrom, 2001; Rigby, 2003; Roland, 2002; Seals & Young, 2003). For example, eating disorders and chronic illnesses have affected many of those who have been tormented by bullies, while other victims have run away from home (Borg; Kaltiala-Heino, Rimpelä, Marttunen, Rimpelä, & Rantanen, 1999; Striegel-Moore, Dohm, Pike, Wilfley, & Fairburn, 2002). According to an Office of Juvenile Justice and Delinquency Prevention fact sheet on juvenile bullying, victims of bullying often felt lonely, humiliated, insecure, and· fearful going to school; experienced poor relationships and had difficulty making friends; and struggled with emotional and social adjustments (Ericson).

Borg (1998) discovered that victims also regularly experience feelings of vengefulness, anger, and self-pity. Indeed, depression has been a frequently cited consequence of bullying and seems to continue into adulthood—demonstrating the potentially long-term implications of peer mistreatment during adolescence (Hawker & Boulton, 2000; Olweus, 1994b). Bullying victims have generally demonstrated more depression and distress than nonvictims (Hawker & Boulton; Kumpulainen & Rasanen, 2000; Mills, Guerin, Lynch, Daly, & Fitzpatrick, 2004; van der Wal et al., 2003).

Finally, research based in the United States has found that being a victim of traditional bullying frequently increases the likelihood of experiencing suicidal thoughts by 10 percent in boys and by more than 20 percent in girls (van der Wal et al., 2003). Generally speaking, victims tend to consider suicide and attempt suicide more often than nonvictims (Cleary, 2000; Eisenberg, Neumark-Sztainer, & Story, 2003; Mills et al., 2004).

Behavioral Consequences of Bullying

As briefly mentioned in the preface, students who are bullied at school may attempt to avoid that environment as much as possible—which may lead to tardiness or truancy ("Girl Tormented," 2001; Rigby & Slee, 1999). While truancy on its face may not seem too alarming, the behavior has been identified as often leading to delinquency, dropping out, and other undesirable outcomes (Farrington, 1980; Garry, 1996; Gavin, 1997; T. R. Nansel et al., 2001). Bullying victimization has also been linked to vandalism, shoplifting, dropping out of school, drug use, and fighting (Ericson, 2001; Loeber & Disheon, 1984; Magnusson, Statten, & Duner, 1983; Olweus et al., 1999a; Patchin, 2002; Rigby, 2003; Tattum, 1989).

As a final cautionary tale, consider the Columbine High School tragedy in Littleton, Colorado, in 1999. The educational system was challenged to address bullying because Eric Harris (age 18) and Dylan Klebold (age 17)—the two teenagers who carried out the massacre of 12 students and a teacher, while wounding 24 others, before committing suicide—were reported to have been ostracized and bullied by their classmates. Additional research of 37 school shooting incidents involving 41 attackers from 1974–2000 discovered that 71 percent of the attackers "felt bullied, persecuted, or injured by others prior to the attack" (Vossekuil, Fein, Reddy, Borum, & Modzeleski, 2002, p. 21). It was also determined that being bullied played at least some role in their later violent outburst (Vossekuil et al.).

To review, consequences of bullying victimization identified in previous research are both subtle (emotional and psychological) as well as tangible (physical and behavioral). We have felt it crucial to detail and group together these findings, because traditional bullying has been studied for many years while cyberbullying has only recently begun to be explored. We believe the consequences are—or will prove to be—quite similar. Next we point out the age of youth that we are targeting with this book.

TARGET POPULATION

It is important in this introductory chapter that we define the age range of youth to which we are referring in this book. In short, we focus our discussion on adolescents. That said, we realize that the terms *adolescent* and *adolescence* mean different things to different people. Most researchers identify three distinct developmental periods: early adolescence (usually between ages 10–13), middle adolescence (ages 14–17), and late adolescence (18 through the early 20s; see Smetana, Campione-Barr, & Metzger, 2006). We are most concerned with those under 18 and in their early and middle developmental stages, so the majority of stories and data in this book originate from this population—especially those of middle school age (Grades 6 through 8).

While this is not to suggest that the cyberbullying experiences of older adolescents and adults should be ignored, we have chosen to focus on an age group that is most susceptible to cyberbullying and least likely (comparatively speaking) to have acquired the skills to cope positively with it. In addition, we believe that it is easier to identify and intervene in experiences of online aggression among this population, which is still under the watch and care of parents and educators.

SUMMARY

By now, we have considered how teens have embraced new electronic devices and communications platforms. We have also considered the interpersonal conflicts that invariably exist during adolescence. Taken together, they create a volatile combination that has left many educators and parents shaking their heads, wondering how cyberbullying became so pernicious and pervasive so quickly. This book will attempt to clear up many of these issues. The next chapter will comprehensively cover the reasons why cyberbullying has flourished and describe the mediums over which it occurs and the forms that hateful or humiliating content posted or sent online can take. We will also explain exactly how intangible textual, aural, or visual content sent through cyberspace from a computer, cell phone, or other electronic device can significantly harm a person on an emotional, psychological, social, and even physical level.

QUESTIONS FOR REFLECTION

1. How do we define *cyberbullying*? Is this definition comprehensive enough?

2. Why do you think computers and cell phones have become such an ingrained part of the lives of many adolescents? What problems may result from this dependence?

3. What are some of the most popular Web sites among youth today? What makes them so popular?

4. Why do we focus on adolescents in this book?

5. How does cyberbullying differ from traditional schoolyard bullying? How are the two forms similar?

NOTES

1. Some of the quotes used in the book have been edited for spelling and distracting grammatical errors. The substance of the quotes, however, has not changed.

2. The astute reader will notice this definition is different from that in our previous research, where we defined *cyberbullying* as "willful and repeated harm inflicted through the medium of electronic text" (Burgess-Proctor, Patchin, & Hinduja, in press; Hinduja & Patchin, 2007, 2008a; Patchin & Hinduja, 2006). Over the years, cyberbullying has evolved to take additional forms, so we have accordingly updated our definition.

2

Cyberbullying Basics

I was talking to 2 girls who used to be my friends. Then [they] went on a chat I was also talking on and started saying horrible things about me. They used my screen name and everything. They even told one of my guy friends that I liked him since the day we met and he stopped talking to me. I was both depressed and angry. I wanted to die. I wanted to leave everything behind. I blocked them and signed off the Internet.

—13-year-old girl from West Virginia

The school is recognized as an important social and physical context within which adolescents develop. As discussed in Chapter 1, traditional bullying—an all-too-common form of youthful violence—has historically affected children and teenagers only while at school or while traveling to or from school. While bullying also occurs in other public places (such as neighborhoods or malls), the term *bullying* is widely associated with the school setting. Modern technology has enabled would-be bullies to extend the reach of their aggression beyond these physical settings through *cyberbullying*, where they are able to harass others regardless of space and time using various technological devices and mediums.

In Chapter 1, we defined *cyberbullying* as the intentional and repeated harm of others through the use of computers, cell phones, and other electronic devices. Cyberbullying, like traditional bullying discussed in the previous chapter, involves malicious individuals who seek implicit or explicit pleasure or profit through the mistreatment of another individual. Based on the research we have reviewed, the constructs of *malicious intent, violence,* and *repetition* are highly relevant when constructing a comprehensive definition of traditional bullying and are similarly appropriate when attempting to understand this new variety.

To be sure, cyberbullies seek pleasure or perceived social benefits through the mistreatment of another. Violence is often associated with aggression and corresponds with actions intended to inflict injury or harm (of any type). Through electronic means, cyberbullies commonly convey direct threats of physical violence ("I am going to pound you at school tomorrow!!!") and manifest indirect psychological, emotional, or relational aggression ("UR gay and smelly and nobody likes you."). All of this is carried out with some measure of maliciousness, even if it is subtle and not patently visible.

It is also important to remember that, as discussed in Chapter 1, one instance of mistreatment cannot accurately be equated to bullying, as it must involve harmful behavior of a repetitive nature. Even though many people call one instance of harassment on the playground "bullying," that really isn't an accurate characterization. Most research makes a clear distinction between bullying and harassment, differentiating the two based on the former's recurrent quality. That is not to say that harassment or some other form of hurtful behavior done once is not harmful to the victim—it just isn't bullying. And while this distinction can be perceived as one of simple semantics or a matter for purely academic debate, we feel it is important . In fact, we believe bullying is actually harassment taken to the next level.

To be sure, part of the reason bullying can be so emotionally or psychologically damaging is *because* it is repetitive. Victims actually have a relationship with the bully, albeit a dysfunctional one. For example, targets of bullying often dread going to school because of what the bully might do that day. If the incident occurs/occurred one time, there is no such dynamic. We believe that the nature of cyberbullying makes it very likely that repetitive harm will occur. For example, imagine someone posts a particularly embarrassing picture of another person online in such a way that others can see it, link to it, and even leave public comments in reference to it. While the action of uploading the picture is a one-time behavior, others can view it or otherwise refer to it repeatedly, thereby resulting in recurring humiliation and shame to the target. One person might see it, or millions of people might see it.

Though not explicit in our definition, there is usually an imbalance of power in cyberbullying situations. We choose not to include it as a definitional component, because the type of power being exerted in cyberspace is somewhat amorphous and often shifting. While power in traditional bullying might be physical (stature) or social (wit or popularity), online power may simply stem from proficiency with or the knowledge or possession of some content (information, pictures, or video) that can be used to inflict harm. Anyone with any of these characteristics or possessions within a certain online context has power, which can be wielded through some form of cyberbullying. Indeed, anyone who can utilize technology in a way that allows them to mistreat others is in a position of power—at least at that moment—relative to the target of the attack.

Also, as noted in the previous chapter, we focus our attention on adolescents when we refer to cyberbullying. Many people use the term *bullying* to refer to a wide variety of behaviors between individuals of varying ages. We feel, though, that it is more appropriate to reserve the term *bullying*, and therefore also *cyberbullying*, for the kinds of behaviors we describe below as they occur between adolescent peers. While these behaviors often occur among adults as well, it is not usually proper to call the incidents bullying. We acknowledge that there is some debate about this distinction, but we want to be clear who and what we are discussing in this book.

TOOLS AND TECHNOLOGY OF THE CYBERBULLY

Young bullies employ a number of electronic devices to harass their victims from afar, and these are becoming more and more ubiquitous. First, using an Internet-connected computer, a bully can send harassing e-mails or instant messages; post obscene, insulting, and slanderous messages to online bulletin boards or social networking sites; or develop Web sites to promote and disseminate defamatory content. Second, malicious text messages can be sent to the target via cell phones. As pointed out in the previous chapter, the vast majority of youth have their own personal cell phones and carry with them wherever they go. In addition to sending threatening text messages, most phones these days have picture-taking and video-recording capabilities. This functionality creates additional opportunities for would-be bullies to collect content (e.g., a picture) that could be used against someone else.

Finally, numerous other portable electronic devices have emerged on the market and are very popular among both adults and youth. Personal data assistants (PDAs) and smartphones (iPhone, Blackberry, Sidekick, Q, Dash, Blackjack, and Mylo) allow users to capture, store, and disseminate a variety of content (pictures, audio, and video) that could be used to cause harm to others. These are poised to replace the traditional cell phone, as component costs decrease and individuals increasingly look for just one device to perform a great number of functions that previously required multiple products.

The remainder of this chapter will describe the different forms of cyberbullying carried out using these devices and provide a number of specific examples to highlight their mechanics, content, and potential for harmfulness. First, though, we must consider the nuances and subtleties associated with cyberbullying that make it an attractive behavioral choice. Why not just bully and mistreat others in real life—using face-to-face interactions? Why use technological devices to manifest hate and aggression? The answer to these questions, as you will see, is quite intuitive. Very simply, the technology makes bullying much *easier*—in every sense of that word.

ISSUES SPECIFIC TO CYBERBULLYING

Some characteristics inherent in new technologies really add value to our lives. With personal computers, we benefit from being able to research certain personal subjects online with a measure of privacy since we are interacting with Web sites. With cell phones, we often appreciate the convenience of being able to call friends and family at any time regardless of their physical location and to be reachable by others in the same way. And we love having access to information and entertainment at our fingertips with portable electronics. Interestingly, these and related characteristics increase the likelihood that these devices will be exploited to harass and mistreat others.

Anonymity and Pseudonymity

First, electronic bullies can remain "virtually" anonymous. Temporary e-mail accounts and pseudonyms in chat rooms, instant messaging programs, and other Internet venues can make it very difficult for adolescents to determine the identity of their aggressors. An individual can hide behind some measure of anonymity when using a personal computer or cell phone to bully another individual, which aids in freeing the individual from traditionally constraining pressures of society, conscience, morality, and ethics to behave in a normative manner. A 14-year-old girl from an undisclosed location in the United States acknowledged the anonymous but harmful nature of these online interactions:

> *Just because you say it doesn't hurt you because they are online, it does. They call you names because everyone online is anonymous. So they think they can do whatever they want to you. But honestly it annoys me that everyone thinks they can do whatever they want because you don't know who they are.*

Further, it seems that bullies might be emboldened when using electronic means to carry out their antagonistic agenda, because it takes less energy and courage to express hurtful comments using a keyboard or keypad than one's voice. Malicious words and statements that an individual might be ashamed or embarrassed to use in a face-to-face setting are no longer off-limits or even tempered when that person is physically distant from the target. Anecdotal accounts from victims studied in our research point to extreme viciousness and unconscionable textual violence expressed by cyberbullies who try to be anonymous. For example, a 17-year-old girl from Washington reported:

> *The last time I was bullied online was when I got an e-mail from some anonymous person who said they went to my school, telling me that I was going to go to hell for dating girls. I have no idea who the messenger was.*

Bullies themselves find the benefit of anonymity appealing, as evidenced by a 15-year-old girl from New Jersey:

> *I didn't like this girl, so I said something to her and left nasty messages in her online journal signed "anonymous" saying "you're such a little slut" and things like that.*

With this said, though, it is important to understand that individuals are not completely anonymous when interacting in cyberspace. This is because a unique identifying address (Internet Protocol [IP] address) is assigned to each computer and computing device when it is connected to the Internet and all data and communications sent from it include that address. As such, the origination of any message can—with some effort—be identified. Furthermore, with traditional bullying, it is often "your word against mine," but with cyberbullying, there is always evidence of the behavior and almost always some indication of its origin (a "digital footprint"). Even though bullies often feel anonymous or think they cannot be detected, it is often much easier to investigate incidents of cyberbullying than traditional bullying because some evidence always exists. It can be found on the sender's or recipient's device, on the intermediary computers through which the message or posting or picture traveled en route, in computer activity logs, or in the form of screenshots and printouts. And as we discuss in Chapter 7, it is essential to find, collect, and preserve that evidence.

Disinhibition

Related to anonymity and pseudonymity online is the concept of disinhibition. To be disinhibited is to be freed from restraints on your behavior. In some venues, disinhibition can be a positive thing. For example, someone who tends to be socially restrained may be disinhibited and therefore more outgoing when attending a costume party. Hiding behind the safety of a mask, they can often interact more boldly with others. Alcohol also serves as a common disinhibitor: People who are inebriated often act out in very atypical ways. Disinhibition makes it more difficult to control impulsive behavior, because the consequences of inappropriate behavior are not instant or immediately clear to the actor.

Similarly, cyberbullies do not have to deal with the immediate emotional, psychological, or physical effects of face-to-face bullying on their victim. When a person expresses hurtful words to another in real life, there is often a clear and present danger of a fight breaking out or some other immediate consequence. If that doesn't happen, verbal violence will likely be volleyed back and forth between the two parties. In cyberspace, usually no swift or certain response clues in an adolescent to the inappropriateness of such words. Time, in fact, is sometimes rendered completely irrelevant, because the offending act can be discovered by the victim anytime in the future and even repeatedly in the future (as third parties discover it). Even if the communication occurs in real time over instant messaging, the spatial distance between the individuals insulates the aggressor from realizing the full meaning of what accompanies the typed-out words. Moreover, no immediate feedback loop visually (e.g., through body language) informs an aggressor that the victim is actually being harmed by what has been said. Such feedback in real life tends to induce most aggressors (unless they are sociopathic) to temper or qualify their words and to realize when "enough is enough."

I wasn't taking into consideration the fact that they might not think that my jokes were too funny. If they ask me to stop or showed signs of me wanting to stop, I do immediately. I was online and they didn't say for me to stop, so I had no way of knowing what mood they were in. I told them something that I regret now.

—17-year-old boy from Missouri

Lack of Supervision

Most everyone agrees that supervision is lacking in cyberspace. Chat room hosts or message board administrators sometimes observe dialogue and discussions in an effort to police conversations and evict those who post offensive statements. However, personal messages sent between users are viewable only by the sender and the recipient and are, therefore, outside their regulatory reach. That is, no individuals can monitor or censor offensive content in private communications through message boards, social networking sites, electronic mail, or instant messages sent via computer or cell phone.

Another contributive element is the increasingly common presence of computers in the private environments of adolescent bedrooms. Indeed, teenagers often know more about computers and cell phones than their parents and are therefore able to use the technologies without worry or concern that a probing parent will discover their participation in online bullying (or even their victimization). As a result, parents are left trying to deal with their child's participation in cyberbullying after the fact, which is always a headache and often a challenging endeavor. A teenage girl whose picture was taken at a concert and then modified and doctored in obscene and offensive ways (and subsequently posted online) shares her experience:

> *My parents came home and saw me distraught, I eventually told them what was going on. They flipped out, and were pretty pissed. I got word that one of my friends had already tried to talk to josh about taking the site down, and he wasn't having it. My parents wanted him to take it down, or they'd legally take it down. I don't blame them, if you came home and your kid was upset over the fact that, not a few but thousands of random people were making fun of him/her because of a Web site, you'd probably do the same. The situation was funny at first, I even laughed, but there was a line crossed, where cruelty came into play and I shouldn't have to be the one saying "please take them down."*

> —from www.moshzilla.com

Viral Nature

Another key feature that makes cyberbullying so problematic is the fact that hurtful or humiliating content can be sent to a large number of people in a short period of time. While spoken rumors seem to spread around a school like wildfire, this process is greatly expedited when utilizing technology. Text messages can be sent from one electronic device to a limitless number of recipients in a matter of seconds. If a student posts a humiliating picture of a classmate in the girls' bathroom, only those who venture there would view the picture. If the same picture were posted to a Web site or sent to "everyone" via e-mail, many more people would be drawn into the joke, thereby making the target feel even worse.

This, of course, ties into the concept of repetition or repeated victimization previously discussed. Cyberbullying can be a "viral" phenomenon, as certain content is spread from one person (the source or creator) to another and to another—all at dizzying speed due to the data-processing and sending capabilities of computers and cell phones. Malicious content often gains infamy in this manner and becomes practically impossible to control when everyone finds out about it. A student may attempt to cope with one or two classmates verbally or even physically picking on him or her, but when a large number of people are immediately in on the harassment, it can be overwhelmingly painful. This is compounded by the fact that online harassment is not confined or constrained to the school day or the school campus, which leads to protracted (and seemingly unending) suffering.

Limitless Victimization Risk

Electronic devices allow individuals to contact others (both for prosocial and antisocial purposes) at all times and almost all places. Many youth who are bullied by others in traditional settings, such as the school lunchroom, the playground, the hallway, at the bus stop, or on the bus, are generally able to escape continued victimization once their school day is over. Retreat into personal and protected environments, such as the confines of one's home, provides temporary relief for targets of bullying and perhaps allows them to be recharged and encouraged by loved ones before venturing out again into a potentially hostile world.

Sometimes bullies are forced to halt their attack because the target is no longer right in front of them. However, technological advances now provide bullies with the ability to utilize online applications to infiltrate the private spaces of victims by contacting them through electronic means. The fact that the vast majority of adolescents connect to the Internet from home indicates that online bullying can be an invasive, relentless scourge even when a person is away from school. A 16-year-old girl from Alabama writes:

> It's one thing when you get made fun of at school, but to be bullied in your own home via your computer is a disgusting thing for someone to do and I think anyone who gets kicks out of it is disgusting.

Furthermore, the inseparability of a cell phone from its owner makes that person a perpetual target for victimization. Individuals often need to keep it turned on for legitimate uses, which provides the opportunity for those so inclined to send threatening and insulting statements via text messages that can affect the target around the clock. There may truly be "no rest for the weary" as cyberbullying penetrates all possible confines, especially those places where victims might seek refuge. Indeed, we have heard cyberbullying described as being "tethered to your tormenter."

As a related point, the coordination of a cyberbullying assault from multiple aggressors can occur with more ease, because it is not constrained by the physical location of the bullies or victims. That is, a group of adolescents may decide to marshal an attack quickly or carefully on a particular individual through coordination over computers or cell phones. Moreover, these teenagers can be in the privacy of their homes, congregating in their neighborhood, hanging out in the mall, or in any other physical location away from their victim. And even if the target has been careful to avoid coming into contact with the bully, that doesn't prevent an onslaught of mistreatment. As such, cyberbullying greatly expands the reach and augments the intensity of interpersonal harm that occurs.

Finally, we must realize how intertwined real space and cyberspace have become when considering the ways in which youth socialize. Many teenagers spend days with their friends in school and nights with those same friends online through social networking sites, instant message programs, and chat rooms. That which occurs during the day at school is often discussed online at night, and that which occurs online at night is often discussed during the day at school. That is, face-to-face and computer-mediated interactions drift seamlessly between the two realms in contemporary adolescent culture. For many youth, there really is no clear distinction between life as lived in real space and in cyberspace; one social sphere is now a natural and complementing extension of the other. This is difficult to comprehend by an adult population who (1) has not grown up with Internet-based socializing and therefore is not naturally predisposed to it and (2) uses the Internet to supplement (rather than complement) life as lived in real space.

Anonymity and pseudonymity, the lack of supervision of youth online and offline, the viral nature of computer-based communications, and the limitless victimization risk on the Internet together work to increase the number of potential cyberbullying offenders and victims and increase the extent and scope of harm that can be inflicted. By now, we have covered the unique features that comprise cyberbullying and make it difficult to address. Next we discuss the mediums through which it occurs and the forms it may take.

MEDIUMS THROUGH WHICH CYBERBULLYING OFTEN OCCURS

E-mail

One of the earliest forms of cyberbullying simply involved sending e-mails to individuals that made fun of them or threatened their physical well-being. Still today, bullies use e-mail to distribute personal or scandalous information about the target to a wide range of people instantaneously. While e-mail bullying might seem like a relatively minor form of cyberbullying, it can still have devastating effects on the target. It used to take a day or two for cruel statements to spread throughout the school; nowadays it takes only a matter of seconds. An 11-year-old girl from California related this experience with e-mail bullying:

> I was surfing the Internet and decided to look at my e-mail. Kristina, a friend from school, in an e-mail said "tomorrow watch your back we are coming for you." It made me feel so bad I started to cry. Nobody likes me.

Apart from sending messages to the contacts in one's own e-mail address book, many school districts have mailing lists or other online repositories of contact information that can easily be mined and used to distribute hurtful information to others with very little effort. Some educators have also shared with us examples where youth create and exploit their very own master list of school-based e-mail addresses. This occurs because many school district networks use a standard format for e-mail addresses assigned to students and staff. For example, if Jane Smith worked for the Acme School District in Utah, her e-mail address would be jane.smith@acme.k12.ut.us. The domain (after the @) is the same for all school district employees, and the username (before the @) is simply a concatenation of a person's first and last name with a period (.) in between. Accordingly, cyberbullies can think of the first and last names of everyone within the school district they'd like to e-mail and thereby know their exact e-mail addresses. This provides an immediately accessible and relevant audience to receive defamatory or humiliating content about someone like those shown in Figures 2.1 and 2.2.

Figure 2.1   Cyberbullying in E-mail

hey

there is something i need to tell u

scroll down

keep going

nobody likes you because you smell
change your clothes once in a while
seriously |

Figure 2.2   Another Example of Cyberbullying in E-mail

!	🗋	🛇	From	Subject	Size	Received ▼
		🖃	Jimmy Franks	YOU CANT AVOID ME FOREVER!!!!!!!	2 KB	Sat 3/3/2007 9:53 AM
		🖃	Jimmy Franks	SMELLY BOY	2 KB	Sat 3/3/2007 9:51 AM
		🖃	Jimmy Franks	fag fag fag fag fag fag fag fag fag fag fag fag fag	2 KB	Sat 3/3/2007 9:50 AM
		🖃	Jimmy Franks	DON'T COME TO SCHOOL TOMORROW...OR ELSE	2 KB	Sat 3/3/2007 9:49 AM
		🖃	Jimmy Franks	GO TAKE A SHOWER	2 KB	Sat 3/3/2007 9:48 AM

Chat Rooms

Chat rooms are online environments where individuals with common interests congregate to discuss a particular issue or topic in real time. Because everyone in chat rooms is anonymous (to the extent that they don't reveal personal information through the chat profile associated with their chat username), these venues emerged as locations where people would say anything and everything that came to mind—irrespective of the consequences or impact it had on those present. It has also been common for "regulars" in the chat rooms to gang up on "newbies"—those who are unfamiliar with the usual protocol for participation and interaction.

> *I hate how AOL is a place for haters. I always go this certain chat room and I've been doing it since I was 14 years old. I don't know why I even started, because all I face is people who tease me, ex-boyfriends from online who side with my enemies, and people who criticize my looks. I'm often told in real life that I'm very pretty, but when I go online people tell me otherwise, like I have a big nose or other things wrong with me. I finally know that none of this is true, and that the person doing it has issues with themselves.*
>
> —Submitted anonymously

Early on, chat rooms gained a reputation for being havens for cyberbullies. Today, many teens are inclined to avoid them because pedophiles and predators tend to frequent these venues as well, trolling for their next victim. Moreover, most of the youth with whom we have spoken don't enjoy the free-for-all interactions where everyone is communicating at the same time and almost expect to be mistreated within minutes of entering a chat room (see the example in Figure 2.3). Finally, most adolescents have other public and private ways of communicating with their friends online (e.g., social networking Web sites) that do not have these same interruptions.

> *I have learned to not go into general chat rooms on IM. They're full of people who just insult each other and then you get tons of IMs from strangers telling you to check out their girls or porn.*
>
> —14-year-old girl from Illinois

Figure 2.3   Cyberbullying in a Chat Room

```
donnyjaley2407: sooo quit complaining
donnyjaley2407: moron
KeithMcK: big deal dipS*iT
mercuryman71: n
donnyjaley2407: ooooo callin me a dipsh*t hey
donnyjaley2407: your funny
KeithMcK: you're gay
donnyjaley2407: OMG he called me gay
```

Box 2.1 contains common acronyms used in chat room communication or text messaging. A more comprehensive list can be found at our Web site (www.cyberbullying.us). Many adolescents communicate in this form of code—partially to keep eavesdropping or shoulder-surfing parents out of the loop but also because it is much quicker. A newbie who is not aware of these common abbreviations and regularly asks for clarification may be targeted for harassment by regulars who don't appreciate the disruption in communication.

Voting/Rating Web Sites

Another relatively common form of cyberbullying occurs when the bully uploads a picture of the target to a Web site where visitors can rate aspects of that person's physical attractiveness. There are a number of these kinds of sites on the Internet, such as Babe vs. Babe, Pick the Hottie, and Hot or Not, and computer-savvy youth have even created similar sites specific to their school or community (see Figure 2.4 on page 29). Indeed, new sites have arisen where video clips can be posted and visitors can rate the attractiveness or appeal of another's voice, body shape, style, movement, or talent. The voyeuristic tendencies of humankind—and our almost obsessive desire to compare and judge physical appearances—contribute to the continued popularity of these Web sites.

Imagine how you would feel if someone sent you an e-mail with a link to a Web page with your picture on it that asked visitors to rate your "hotness" or how good-looking you are, as shown in Figures 2.5 (page 30) and 2.6 (page 31). We must remember that adolescence is a time when we cared a great deal about what others thought about how we looked and that most of us weren't yet very comfortable in our own skins and struggled with self-consciousness to some degree. If your peers are judging you to be "ugly" or "not hot" in sentiments expressed not just privately but publicly for the entire student body to see, it would be devastating. Self-assured adults may be able to shrug off this kind of negative feedback, but it is too much to ask of many adolescents when considering their stage of development.

Box 2.1 Common Chat/Text Acronyms

AFAIK	As far as I know
AFK	Away from keyboard
A/S/L?	Age/sex/location?
BBIAB	Be back in a bit
BF	Boyfriend
BRB	Be right back
BTW	By the way
CU	See you
CYA	See ya; Cover your ass
DWB	Don't write back
F2F	Face to face
FUBAR	F***ed up beyond all repair or recognition
FWIW	For what it's worth
FYI	For your information
GF	Girlfriend
IMHO	In my humble/honest opinion
JK	Just kidding
L8R	Later
LMAO	Laughing my ass off
LOL	Laughing out loud
M/F	Male or female
NIFOC	Naked in front of computer
NP	No problem
OMG	Oh my God
PAW	Parents are watching
PIR	Parents in room
POS	Parents over shoulder; Piece of sh**
ROTFL	Rolling on the floor laughing
RTFM	Read the f***ing manual
SNAFU	Situation normal, all f***ed up
TAFN	That's all for now
TMI	Too much information
TTYL	Talk to you later
WB	Welcome back
WTGP?	Want to go private? (into a private chat)
WTF?	What the f***?
WUF?	Where are you from?
YBS	You'll be sorry

Figure 2.4   Cyberbullying Via a Web Page

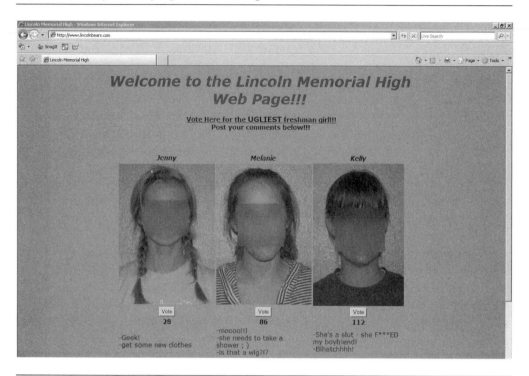

Figure 2.5   Cyberbullying Via a Polling/Rating Web Site

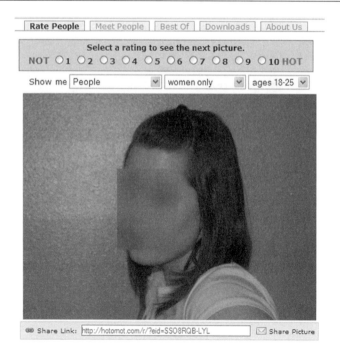

Figure 2.6   Another Example of Cyberbullying Via a Polling/Rating Web Site

Blogging Sites, Virtual Worlds, and Online Gaming

Also meriting discussion are a number of other venues in which cyber-bullying can occur. For instance, many adolescents have blogs on Web sites such as WordPress, Open Diary, Blogger, and LiveJournal and post frequent updates on their lives, experiences, perspectives, and interests (further detailed in Chapter 4). These have a commenting feature that may invite denigration or hurtful remarks from someone who reads the blogging posts and disagrees with the sentiments expressed or who simply wants to be a jerk.

Virtual worlds, such as There, Second Life, Active Worlds, Kaneva, and IMVU, are also environments in which online aggression can occur. These simulated realms involve individuals who interact and communicate through the use of avatars, or representations of themselves and their personalities. Avatars are typically three-dimensional models of those who are playing. Just as people in real life can speak or act in a way that harasses or otherwise hurts another, so can avatars. For example, there have been reports of virtual property theft (Holahan, 2006) and virtual sexual assault (Lynn, 2007) within the Web site Second Life. While we aren't aware of any documented case of cyberbullying on these sites, we assume that it occurs between virtual world participants to some extent and may become more common as these Web environments become more widely known.

Cyberbullying can also occur in environments such as World of WarCraft—a massively multiplayer online role-playing game (MMORPG). Additionally, increasing numbers of youth use their video gaming console (e.g., Nintendo Wii, Microsoft Xbox 360, Sony Playstation 3, and Playstation Portable) to connect to the Internet and play against opponents from other cities, states, and even countries. To add to the experience, many use headsets with microphones, which allow them to speak to (and hear from) others as if they were together in the same room. This technology (termed Voice over Internet Protocol, or VoIP) then allows adolescents to express excitement, displeasure, or anger vocally to others with whom they are playing. As such, they have the opportunity to verbalize malicious statements or insults, which can inflict emotional or psychological harm on the recipient.

Instant Messaging

Instant messaging programs, such as AOL (America Online) Instant Messenger, MSN (Microsoft Network) Messenger, Yahoo Messenger, Google Talk, and Apple iChat, allow individuals to communicate in real time with one another via typed text. Instant messaging is very popular among adolescents and adults alike, because it allows people who are geographically separate to communicate synchronously and instantaneously. Messages are sent and received almost immediately if the recipient is online at the same time. Messages can be answered when it is convenient, at that moment, at a later time, or not at all as long as the recipient's computer is turned on. Some programs also allow the use of microphones and webcams to complement the textual interaction with personal voice and streaming video, which allows participants to have a conversation in real time over the computer instead of in person.

Users can see who among their friends is currently online by looking at their "buddy lists." The buddy list, like the one in Figure 2.7, includes the screen names of everyone who is currently online whom the user has designated as a friend (or buddy).

Cyberbullies have embraced this technology, because it allows them to direct messages to specific individuals while they are online at the same time—and know that those messages were received by the target (since they are sent and received in real time). If aggressors do not care about disguising their identities, they can simply send a target numerous hateful messages or threats from their regularly used screen names. They can also hide behind pseudonymous screen names if desired. Multiple cyberbullies in disparate locations can gang up on and overwhelm a target over this medium—making it difficult for him to correspond with friends, browse the Web, or do schoolwork on the computer while trying to field, close, or block harassing instant messages.

We've also heard of examples where instant messages containing private information or personal content are forwarded by the original recipient and confidante to others for whom those messages were not intended. This covert, backstabbing form of cyberbullying can lead to great humiliation, shame, and pain—just as more overt, blatant malicious words would. While it is true that those who use instant messaging programs can block certain usernames from sending them messages, one can very easily create a new username to continue harassing someone.

Figure 2.7   Example Buddy List

Cell Phones

Cell phones have always been used for voice communications and, more recently, for electronic text messaging. Cell phones allow users to send short text messages to others who have cell phones, and it goes without saying that these messages can be hurtful, threatening, or otherwise upsetting. Figure 2.8 shows one example of this type of message. We even heard one example where a student orchestrated a lunchtime food fight by messaging other students via cell phone while at school.

Another way cell phone text messaging can be used to harm another is by sending text messages to users who do not have a cell phone plan that includes free messaging. We have heard examples where bullies have sent several hundred text messages to a victim who was required to pay 15 cents for each message received. Not surprisingly, the parents of the victim were not happy when the cell phone bill arrived; they immediately blamed their child and removed her cell phone privileges before asking any questions.

Figure 2.8   Cyberbullying Via a Cell Phone

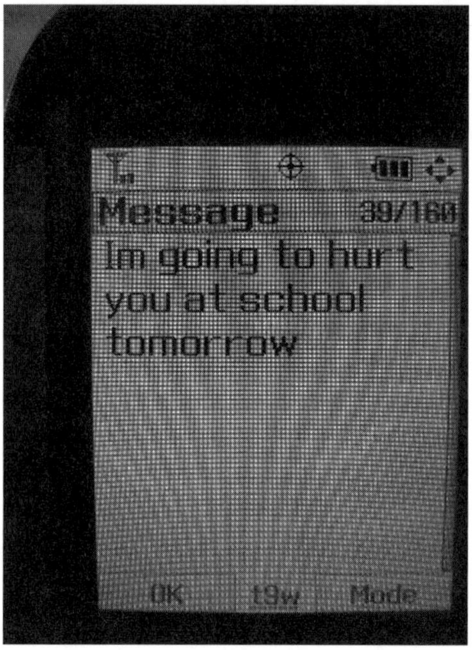

The vast majority of new cell phones can now take digital pictures and video—and these can be used to record embarrassing moments of others that are later posted on or sent across the Internet for the world to see. The small physical design of many cell phones also allows for their surreptitious use in places where individuals traditionally expect privacy, such as in locker rooms, bathrooms, saunas, and showers. Even in locations where a person is always fully dressed, someone else could be secretly recording your actions or interactions with others—waiting for or expecting you to do something that can later be used against you.

We have also heard of accounts where teenagers use voice-to-text services online from their cell phones to leave a harassing voice mail for another person, which is then transcribed to text and anonymized before being sent to the recipient. At this point, the victim receives a hurtful e-mail, instant message, or cell phone text message from an unknown number and location. A service that was designed so that individuals could communicate more easily with the hearing-impaired has been exploited to inflict harm online.

As technology continues to evolve, novel instantiations of cyberbullying of which we cannot currently conceive will become possible. We've therefore listed the tools or conduits through which online victimization can take place. But just as the medium can vary, the form that causes the harm can differ. Some types of mistreatment would not exist without the technology used to carry out the attack. Others simply involve traditional bullying carried out in cyberspace rather than the real world.

COMMON FORMS OF CYBERBULLYING

Photoshopping

Photoshopping is a neologism referring to one of the world's most popular image-editing software programs, Adobe Photoshop. However, the term applies to image or photo modifications or alterations made using any software program. While sometimes done strictly for clean or even flattering humorous intent, in cyberbullying instances, photoshopping generally involves doctoring images so that the main subject is placed in a compromising or embarrassing context or scene. One of the most widely known examples of photoshopping occurred when a boy named Alex posted online a picture of "Sam," a girl who was "moshing" (dancing in an aggressive, primal manner) at a punk rock concert in San Diego, California. The picture was then downloaded and altered hundreds of times in funny, humiliating, and even obscene ways, and each new version was redistributed across the Internet (see Figure 2.9). Recalling the incident, Sam later remarked (Katz, 2005):

> *You can't help but realize that you are being humiliated across the country. In a nutshell, I feel shitty.*

Many of these photoshopped images of "Moshzilla" are still available today and are retrievable using any Internet search engine.

Figure 2.9   "Moshzilla" Photoshopped Pictures

Rumor Spreading

Commonly perpetrated using e-mail, text messaging, or posts to social networking Web sites, gossip and hearsay about someone can be disseminated very easily among individuals over the Internet. Here is one story sent to us by a parent of a 16-year-old girl:

> *The bullying came from kids that were suppose to be her friends, other girls on her cheerleading squad. They had created a "MySpace" all about her, as though it was her "MySpace." It was vicious saying she had slept with all sorts of boys in her school, calling her names, using vulgar language too disgusting to even think about, sexual acts and more. Other teens in her school starting coming up to her asking her if she had slept with the boys, if she had really performed these sexual acts and more.*

Rumor spreading tends to be an activity performed by girls more often than boys, due to the relational aggression and social sabotage that occurs when rivalries arise among that gender (Simmons, 2003). That said, the following example aptly depicts how boys can also be harmed:

> *One time someone made me feel so bad that I wanted to kill myself because I believe those things that they said. My friends calmed me down and told me not to do anything dumb. I dislike it when people spread rumors online about you and it has happened to mostly everyone who chats.*

> —17-year-old boy from California

As we've discussed, the fact that technology allows messages to be sent very quickly and easily to a large number of people makes cell phones and computers a very attractive tool for those who would like to spread information about others. Within a matter of minutes, the whole school can learn of a rumor. And because these messages can be sent from fictitious e-mail addresses or anonymous screen names, it can be difficult (although still generally always possible) to determine the source of the rumor.

Flaming and Trolling

Flaming typically involves sending or posting hostile, angry, or mischievous messages intended to "inflame" the emotions and sensibilities of others. These comments or messages do not productively advance or contribute to the discussion at hand but instead attempt to wound another person socially or psychologically and to assert authority over others. Figure 2.10 shows one example of flaming in a chat room. Most often, flaming can be identified on Internet-based discussion boards, news-groups, and forums. We have also heard about instances of flaming on social networking sites like MySpace and within interactive virtual world environments such as Second Life. One person who contacted us sent in this example of a flame posted as a comment to another person's creative writing submission on www.fanfiction.net, a site where fledgling authors can share their works:

> *You have been chosen to be a recipient of the "Flame Writing Challenge for Flame Rising #2" flame for which I had to write a seething review for pieces of shit like yours using a list of random words given to me by people. What does this mean exactly? It means this story is still a piece of d.o.u.c.h.e.d-up excrement, and I got to use some big, fancy words to tell you so. Feel honored.* What is it that's wrong with you that makes you think you have actual talent as a writer, hm? Is it a calcium deficiency? Or perhaps you ate some rancid tapioca? You see, kiddo, you're being quite mendacious to yourself if you actually think you have what it takes to be a writer.*

Receiving such feedback after posting a piece of creative writing in the hopes of being encouraged by others can be quite damaging to the emotional state of an adolescent. If unable to shrug off the comment as a flame, the young person might even have a desire to pursue a dream to become a writer extinguished.

The concept of trolling is very similar to flaming, except that the latter is directed at another participant (or other participants) in the discussion, while the former is directed at the subject of discussion. Trolls attempt to

Figure 2.10 Flaming in a Chat Room

[01:34] Giggley(2): pigeon has ms sunshine offered to sleep with you yet?
[01:34] pigeonbra: how are u peps on this fine evening?
[01:34] Giggley(2): im good thnx pigeon
[01:34] pigeonbra: what?
[01:34] pigeonbra: lol no
[01:35] Giggley(2): well give it some time pigeon she will she offers to sleep with every guy
[01:35] Giggley(2): ms sunshine how many guys ya sleepin with now?
[01:35] cajuns_gator joined room #IntlFriendship, group is 'normal'
[01:35] pigeonbra: what are u on about really
[01:36] pigeonbra: come on its uncalled for
[01:36] solonley37 joined room #IntlFriendship, group is 'normal'
[01:36] Giggley(2): pigeon ms sunshine offers to sleep with any of the guys that will break couples up
[01:36] Giggley(2): pigeon its the truth though

incite arguments, controversy, and disruption in online social contexts. This is done by posting messages that are often cruel and insulting but other times are simply inaccurate, ridiculous, irrelevant, or obtuse. With all of this said, it is our belief that trolls are malicious or act maliciously, even if the content of their statements appears benign, because they intentionally attempt to provoke unproductive reactions from others.

Identity Theft/Impersonation

As will be discussed in Chapter 6, it is important for youth (and adults!) to keep their passwords and personal information secure and not to share them with others. If someone else knows your username and password to an online account, he or she can send out e-mail or instant messages that appear to come from you. The recipients of those messages will not know that your account has been hijacked. They may become very angry or upset with you and may respond in kind. We have also heard of cases where a bully has used another person's account information to log onto their online social networking profile and add incriminating or humiliating pictures, videos, or information. The password is then changed so that the target cannot log back in and modify or delete the problematic content—which extends the victimization.

In the example in Figure 2.11, we found an online picture of a teenage girl and created a MySpace profile page for "Jenni." We included some possibly truthful information—such as her age and her location—but also added content portraying her as a promiscuous, drug-abusing nymphomaniac who doesn't care about anyone except herself. We could then e-mail or message hundreds or even thousands of peers (or strangers!) to tell them of Jenni's recently updated profile page—much to her dismay.

In yet another example, a cyberbully can choose to post or reveal personal information with which you've entrusted him or her (another example of rumor spreading as discussed above). This might be the identity of a secret crush, a disclosure about personal or family problems, sensitive information you've overheard and then shared in confidence, or even contact information such as a cell phone number or home address. All of these can be used by others with malicious or perverse motives to inflict significant emotional, psychological, and even physical pain. As such, it is extremely important to protect against revealing username and password combinations, as well as privileged or private information about yourself or others.

> I do remember when someone went on my screen name and IMed all my friends and said things like, I hate you and you suck and you're the worst friend ever! And all my friends got mad at me.
>
> —14-year-old girl from Massachusetts

Figure 2.11   Cyberbullying Via a Social Networking Web Site

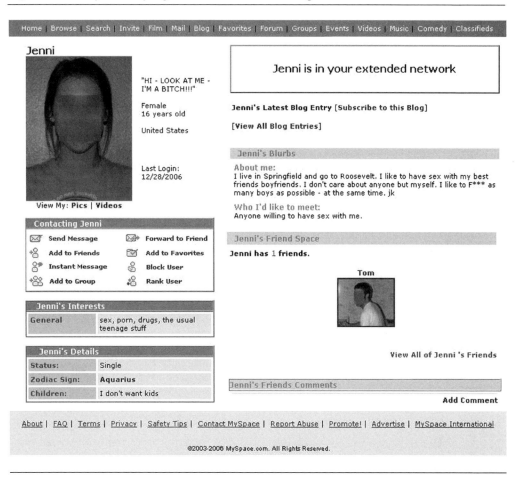

Happy-Slapping

Happy-slapping is a relatively recent phenomenon that links traditional bullying with cyberbullying. In happy-slapping incidents, an unsuspecting person is recorded being harassed or bullied in a way that usually involves some form of physical abuse, as shown in Figure 2.12. The resultant digital photo or video is uploaded to a Web site or otherwise sent around for

Figure 2.12   Happy-slapping

public viewing. With the growth of Flickr, Photobucket, YouTube, and other photo- and video-sharing sites whose content is user created, this form of cyberbullying gradually has become more common.

Physical Threats

With growing frequency, we are seeing instances of cyberbullying that involve threats to a person's physical safety and well-being. Of course, this type of cyberbullying warrants immediate attention and response by law enforcement to determine whether it is a threat with merit. It is important to remember that adolescents say things to one another quite frequently that may be construed as threats. For example, sometimes even youth who are the best of friends will e-mail each other saying, "I am going to kill you if you go out with her!" It is essential to determine the extent to which the language actually constitutes a threat or if it is simply adolescents being adolescent.

> It carried on with this disagreement between me and my mate. She was in the wrong team for PE. She was meant to be blue and me and my other mate were meant to be red, but my other mate kept saying I was just saying she was in blue so I could have the other mate to myself. And this argument was continued on the net, and she started calling me names and bullying me by threatening to get people on me!
>
> —Submitted anonymously

> When I was 13, I started dating a boy from the next town over and apparently a girl from that town had a huge crush on him and was very upset with me when she found out that I was dating him. She started yelling at me and threatening me over msn instant messenger. She scared me so much and when I would try to block her address, she would just create a new profile and continue where she left off. It got to the point where I was scared to go to see my boyfriend in his town because I was scared of running into her and what she would do to me. I am from Ohio.
>
> —Submitted anonymously

In the months leading up to the Columbine school shooting in Littleton, Colorado, in April 1999, a parent found a Web diary of Eric Harris (one of the shooters) where he threatened to "kill and injure as many of you pricks as I can" (Brown & Merritt, 2002, p. 84). The concerned parent reported this to law enforcement, but they were unable to find the Web site and argued that even if they could, there wasn't enough evidence that a specific crime had been committed. Because of the outcome, the Columbine incident has (hopefully) forced school officials and law enforcement to take seriously any threat articulated online.

Some may dismiss electronic bullying as normal behavior that does not actually harm anyone, unlike a punch to the face, for example. Others acknowledge the severity of the psychological and emotional wounds that are caused by insults or intentional embarrassment. In our research, 17 percent of students reported that threats made online are carried out at school, highlighting the relevance of cyberbullying in the real world. The concept of "harm" stemming from harassing online communications warrants attention so that we can accurately consider its gravity and severity. Fully comprehending that youth *are* negatively impacted by cyberbullying in tangible ways is essential to foster a strong and lasting motivation to combat it.

ONLINE HARM

> *That doesn't mean that you can't potentially hurt someone's feelings.*
> *Words can be just as powerful as fists.*
>
> —16-year-old girl from Michigan

Due to the widespread availability of electronic devices, there is no lack of participants in technologically assisted communication. This chapter has pointed out that such communication can easily take place through cell phone text messaging, electronic mail (e-mail), and instant messages; within chat rooms; and on personal Web sites, social networks, online bulletin boards, virtual worlds, and other Web-based environments. The ubiquity of technology provides a seemingly endless pool of candidates who are susceptible to being bullied or to becoming a bully. Though new technologies are intended to contribute positively to society, negative aspects invariably emerge. The negative effects inherent in cyberbullying are neither slight nor trivial and have the potential to inflict serious harm.

One particularly horrendous anecdotal account deserves mention. In May of 2001, viciously offensive messages making fun of a high school sophomore girl who suffered from obesity and multiple sclerosis were posted anonymously to an online message board associated with a local high school in Dallas, Texas (Benfer, 2001). In time, the bullying crossed over to the physical world as the victim's car was vandalized, profanities were written on the sidewalk in front of her home, and a bottle filled with acid was thrown at her front door—which incidentally burned her mother.

This example vividly depicts how bullying online can result in physical harm offline. Outside of physical harm (which also has collateral psychological and emotional consequences), cyberbullying can directly wreak psychological, emotional, and social havoc, because e-mails can be saved; instant messages and chat conversations can be logged; and Web pages can be archived for an offender, victim, or third party to read over and over again in the future.

Through our research, we have found that various types of harm result from cyberbullying. These include, but are not limited to, school problems such as tardiness and truancy, eating disorders, chronic illness, self-esteem problems, aggression, depression, interpersonal violence, substance abuse and other forms of delinquency, and suicidal ideation and suicide (as discussed in Chapter 1). We will cover some of these in further detail in the next chapter and will continue to study them as we move forward in our work with school districts across the nation.

SUMMARY

Though we've only brushed the surface of the subject matter, you can see how the ubiquity of communications technology in the lives of adolescents, coupled with the comparatively common occurrence of bullying, can lead to the use of various electronic devices to harass and mistreat others in various ways. While the specific type may differ, as might the medium over which it is perpetrated, cyberbullying is real and is occurring with frequency. Finally, it is clear that the repercussions of online aggression cannot be shrugged off as trivial or inconsequential. As they affect the vulnerable and impressionable population of adolescents, they demand our attention and response. In Chapter 1, we summarized the main findings of research in the area of traditional bullying. In Chapter 3, we turn our attention to the research that has been conducted regarding cyberbullying since the turn of the century to obtain a baseline on its causes and correlates.

QUESTIONS FOR REFLECTION

1. Describe the ways in which cyberbullying can be repetitive.

2. What was the most hurtful type of cyberbullying you have heard of or seen? How would it have made you feel if you were the target of that cyberbullying? What would you have done in that situation?

3. Why do you think adolescents like texting each other? Are there any popular chat or text acronyms that you know of that are not listed in Box 2.1?

4. Why would anyone create a Web page making fun of another person?

5. If you found out that a rumor was circulating around school about you, what would you do?

3

What Do We Know About Cyberbullying?

Cyberbullying sounds interesting and I wasn't aware of that until I learnt it in class so I did bully some kid because he had pissed me off. I didn't know the damages can be that severe but what I did served him right, keeping him on his toes as he seemed real tough and rude outside but inside he was nothing but a chicken and I did what he deserved although I personally don't support cyberbullying.

—14-year-old boy from an undisclosed location

Even though examples of cyberbullying and other forms of online aggression have attracted a modest amount of attention in the media in recent years, surprisingly little research has been conducted to explore its causes and consequences. As we discussed in Chapter 1, the specific impact of traditional bullying on young people has been studied at great length in a variety of academic disciplines, but bullying that takes place via electronic means has been largely neglected—perhaps because of the unique environment in which it occurs or the nontangible manner in which it is perpetrated.

When first exploring cyberbullying, we found a brief editorial published in 2003 in the *Journal of the American Academy of Child and Adolescent Psychiatry* that pointed to the lack of academic references on this topic despite its anticipated proliferation (Jerome & Segal, 2003). Now in 2008, an emerging literature base is helping to shed light on these behaviors. The *Journal of Adolescent Health* even recently published a special issue on youth violence and electronic media, highlighting some of the most recent cyberbullying research. This chapter will review that body of research with a particular emphasis on our own empirical work. We begin with a brief discussion of the research that we have conducted over the last several years.

OUR CYBERBULLYING RESEARCH

This book draws heavily on the research that we have conducted in recent years. We first explored cyberbullying through an online pilot survey in 2003. The primary benefit of utilizing an online survey is the ability to reach a wide number of online teenagers at an economical cost. We created a survey instrument that asked youth whether they had experienced online aggression or knew of others who had such experiences. From a very small sample, representing only those youth who visited the Web site that linked to our survey and volunteered to participate, we learned that cyberbullying was more of a problem than anyone at the time realized. We modified and replicated that survey in the spring of 2004 among a slightly larger sample and confirmed our earlier hypothesis that a significant proportion of Internet-using youth had experienced cyberbullying (Patchin & Hinduja, 2006).

We replicated our online survey one more time in the spring of 2005, seeking a larger and more diverse adolescent population. Several adolescent-oriented Web sites agreed to link to our survey, and we invited visitors to those sites to participate anonymously. Over 7,000 individuals completed the survey, which was actively linked for 30 days. We focused our analysis on the approximately 4,000 respondents who reported they were under the age of 18. Interestingly, in all of our online surveys, significantly more girls volunteered to participate than boys. To account for any potential biases, we constructed a subsample of approximately 1,500 youth that was evenly distributed across gender. Once again, the survey revealed important information about how adolescents were using and misusing computers, the Internet, and cell phones (Burgess-Proctor et al., in press; Hinduja & Patchin, 2007, 2008a).

In our online surveys, we also include the following question:

> *Please describe—in as much detail as possible—your most recent experience with **being bullied online**. Please tell us about the online activity in which you were participating, what you know about the others who were involved, how it made you feel, and what you did specifically in response.*

We expected short, one- or two-sentence summaries of respondents' recent bullying experiences. What we received instead were detailed stories about how online harassment has made their lives frustrating, miserable, and, in some cases and in their own words, "not worth living." Some youth wrote so much about their experiences that their responses overwhelmed our database; we had to modify the data fields to accommodate the lengthy responses. Many of the anecdotes included throughout this book come from these accounts.

Despite all of these important initial insights, the online survey methodology had certain limitations that leave it susceptible to criticism. While a complete discussion of these limitations is outside the scope of this book, interested readers are encouraged to consult our previous work cited above. To be sure, there are drawbacks in *any* research endeavor, and ideally several approaches should be utilized to analyze a problem from different vantage points. We therefore felt that our next project required an expanded survey and a more traditional research setting.

The result was a large-scale project in the spring of 2007 involving a random sample of approximately 2,000 middle school students from one of the largest school districts in the United States. These students were distributed across 30 middle schools and were in sixth through eighth grades. Since students were randomly selected to participate, results of the study should be representative of other students in that district and offer some insight into student online behaviors in other large districts of the United States as well. In the sections that follow, we present a detailed analysis of our work along with findings from other key studies of cyberbullying to depict who is affected and to what degree.

PREVALENCE OF CYBERBULLYING

Research suggests that a sizeable percentage of young people experiences cyberbullying as victims, bullies, or bully-victims. In one of the earliest studies (conducted between the fall of 1999 and the spring of 2000), online aggression and victimization were examined through a telephone survey of 1,498 regular Internet users between the ages of 10 and 17 along with their parents (Ybarra & Mitchell, 2004). In that research, Internet harassment was defined as "an overt, intentional act of aggression towards another person online," while victimization was defined as "whether anyone had used the Internet in the previous year to threaten or embarrass the respondent by posting or sending messages about him or her for other people to see" and "whether the respondent ever felt worried or threatened because someone was bothering or harassing him or her while online" (Ybarra & Mitchell, p. 1310).

Findings of this study indicated that 19 percent of youth respondents were on either the giving or receiving end of online aggression in the previous year. Specifically, 4 percent of regular Internet users were the victims of online harassment, 12 percent were aggressors, and 3 percent were both aggressors and victims. The vast majority of offenders (84 percent) knew their victim in person, while only 31 percent of victims knew who was bullying them (Ybarra & Mitchell, 2004). This suggests that cyberbullying is not typically a random event among strangers—in most cases, at least the cyberbullies know who they are targeting.

A subsequent study, conducted in 2001 by the National Children's Home, a charitable organization in London, surveyed 856 youth between the ages of 11 and 19 and found that one-quarter had been victims of cyberbullying. Specifically, 16 percent received threatening text messages via their cell phone, 7 percent had been bullied in online chat rooms, and 4 percent had been harassed via e-mail (National Children's Home, 2002). In a 2005 follow-up study of 770 youth in the same age range, 20 percent of respondents revealed that they had been bullied via electronic means. Almost three-fourths (73 percent) stated that they knew the bully, while 26 percent stated that the offender was a stranger. Another interesting finding was that 10 percent indicated that another person had taken a picture of them via a cell phone camera, consequently making them feel uncomfortable, embarrassed, or threatened (National Children's Home, 2005).

In our first study (data collected in the spring of 2004), we analyzed an online sample of 384 respondents 17 years of age and younger from around the world to determine their experiences with the following cyberbullying behaviors: bothering someone online, teasing in a mean way, calling someone hurtful names, intentionally leaving someone out of something, threatening someone, and saying unwanted sexually related things to someone. Overall, approximately 30 percent of respondents reported being the victim of cyberbullying, 11 percent reported bullying others while online, and almost half (47 percent) witnessed cyberbullying (Patchin & Hinduja, 2006). We subsequently replicated this initial study in 2005 among a larger sample (about 1,400 adolescents) and found that over 32 percent of boys and over 36 percent of girls have been victims of cyberbullying, while about 18 percent of boys and 16 percent of girls reported harassing others in cyberspace (Hinduja & Patchin, 2008a).

To provide some more context, another recent study completed in 2005, in conjunction with a statewide bullying prevention initiative in Colorado, assessed the prevalence of various types of bullying among 3,339 youth in 5th, 8th, and 11th grades. The researchers found that verbal bullying (70.7 percent) was most prevalent, followed by physical bullying (40.3 percent) and then Internet bullying (9.4 percent). No gender differences were found except for physical bullying, with males twice as likely as females to engage in that type (Williams & Guerra, 2007).

Yet another study conducted in 2005, this time of 3,767 middle school students from six schools, revealed that 11.1 percent had been cyberbullied in the last two months, 4.1 percent were cyberbullies, and 6.8 percent were both a cyberbully and a cyberbullying victim. The most frequently used mediums for cyberbullying were instant messaging (66.6 percent), chat rooms (24.7 percent), e-mail (24.2 percent), and Web sites (23.4 percent; Kowalski & Limber, 2007).

In our most recent classroom-based survey, we asked 1,963 middle school students whether or not they had experienced cyberbullying. At the beginning of the survey, we informed them that "cyberbullying is when someone repeatedly makes fun of another person online or repeatedly picks on another person through e-mail or text message or when someone posts something online about another person that they don't like." Note that this definition is slightly different from the one used in Chapter 1. We wanted to define it for the students in a way that they would easily understand.

When asked "Have you been cyberbullied in the last 30 days?" slightly less than 10 percent of students responded yes. When asked "Have you been cyberbullied in your lifetime?" slightly more than 17 percent of respondents said yes. When asked "Have you cyberbullied others in the last 30 days?" just over 8 percent responded yes. When asked "Have you cyberbullied others in your lifetime?" almost 18 percent of the students said yes. Finally, slightly less than 5 percent of students in our sample were both recent victims and cyberbullies (12 percent were both in their lifetime). Chart 3.1 summarizes the results of this survey.

Chart 3.1   Cyberbullying Among Middle-Schoolers

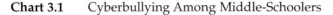

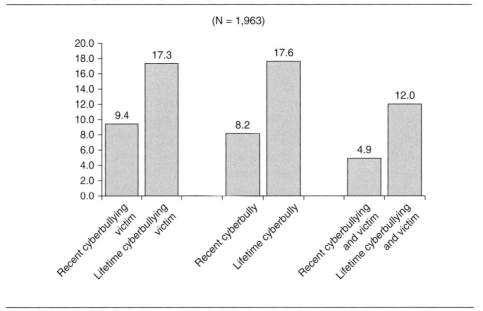

(N = 1,963)

When asked about specific types of online harassment and aggression, almost 43 percent of the students had experienced at least one of the following in the previous 30 days:

- Received an e-mail that made you upset.
- Received an instant message (IM) that made you upset.
- Had something posted on your MySpace that made you upset.

- Been made fun of in chat room.
- Had something posted on a Web site that made you upset.
- Had something posted online that you didn't want others to see.
- Been afraid to go on the computer.

While some of the above behaviors may not fit neatly under our definition, they may be considered cyberbullying if experienced by peers repeatedly over time. The point is that if you ask students if they have been cyberbullied and they say no, you may need to inquire further about the specific types of behaviors they have experienced while online.

As you can see from these select published studies and the others listed in Chart 3.2, estimates range widely as to how many youth have experienced online aggression. This is also true of the estimates of the proportion of adolescents who are cyberbullying others (see Chart 3.3). There are several explanations for the different statistics reported here. First, many of these studies target respondents of varying ages. As expected, the studies that focus on younger populations (middle school samples or younger) tend to report lower prevalence rates than those that target high school students.

Second, these studies employ different survey methodologies. That is, respondents could be asked questions through a phone interview, in-class survey, or Web-based survey. Those studies that used Internet-based samples tend to report higher numbers of aggressors and victims, because they are surveying those who are regularly online and therefore most likely to experience cyberbullying.

Third, some youth were selected at random, whereas others were selected deliberately because they were members of some larger group. Ideally, participants would be selected randomly from a known population so that the responses of the sample could be used to approximate how the population as a whole might respond.

Fourth, different studies utilize different reporting periods. When asking adolescents if they have experienced cyberbullying, some surveys asked about experiences over one's lifetime, while others focused on the previous year or just the last month.

Finally, one of the biggest differences among these research endeavors is the way that *cyberbullying* is defined. Researchers can't even agree on the appropriate spelling of the term (see Box 1.1 in Chapter 1), let alone what behaviors it constitutes. As noted above, we use a very specific definition of *cyberbullying* but also ask youth about their experiences with various behaviors that can be characterized as online harassment. We think this is the best approach to learn about the actual types of behaviors that youth are experiencing.

It is important to point out, however, that the one number you don't see listed in Chart 3.2 or Chart 3.3 is *zero*. We believe that even one child being cyberbullied or cyberbullying others is too many. Charts 3.2 and 3.3 also include trend lines that clearly illustrate that cyberbullying victimization and offending have increased over the years. We have to do our part to ensure these lines don't continue to increase in the next decade of the 21st century.

Chart 3.2   Select Published Cyberbullying Research

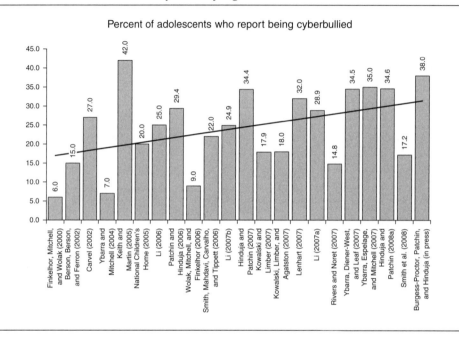

Percent of adolescents who report being cyberbullied

Chart 3.3   Select Published Cyberbullying Research

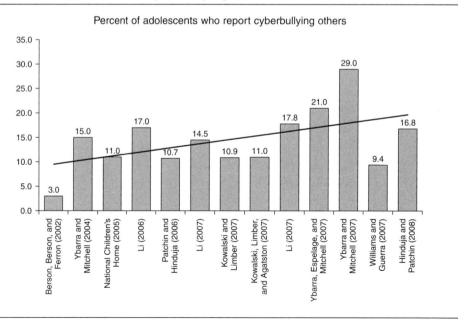

Percent of adolescents who report cyberbullying others

GENDER DIFFERENCES IN CYBERBULLYING

My most recent experience was with four girls, only one I knew in person (she goes to my school) . . . they kept dogging me and threatening me, laughing at me, and just constantly putting me down. Eventually I blocked them because I was getting so frustrated and felt so vulnerable. It took me months to get over feeling like that (even though it was online) and to finally getting to the point where I could just say F*** you guys and get over the whole thing.

—18-year-old girl from Canada

A significant body of traditional bullying research indicates that boys are involved in bullying more often than girls (Borg, 1999; Espelage, Bosworth, & Simon, 2000; Kumpalainen; Rasanen, & Henttonen, 1999; Seals & Young, 2003). However, research has also consistently noted that adolescent girls tend to participate in more indirect, less visible forms of bullying, including psychological and emotional harassment (e.g., rumor spreading and other forms of relational aggression; Bjorkqvist, Lagerspetz, & Kaukianin, 1992; Crick & Grotpeter, 1995; Owens, Shute, & Slee, 2000b; Simmons, 2003). Given the fact that the vast majority of cyberbullying behaviors involve these indirect forms of harassment, it makes sense that most research suggests that girls appear equally as likely to be active participants in cyberbullying as boys.

In all but one of the cyberbullying studies we have reviewed, teenaged girls appear to cyberbully (and be cyberbullied) as much as (if not more than) boys.[1] The nature of the cyberbullying behaviors, however, seems to vary. For example, girls were slightly more likely to be bullied via e-mail or social networking Web sites (more on this in the next chapter). Other studies have found similar results. After surveying 1,915 girls and 1,852 boys in sixth, seventh, and eighth grade from across the southwestern and southeastern United States, Robin Kowalski and her colleagues (2005) found that more girls than boys reported being bullied online (25 percent versus 11 percent) and bullying someone else online (13 percent versus 8.6 percent). When reporting on traditional bullying, however, this gender gap did not appear; similar numbers of boys and girls reported being bullied offline (12.3 percent versus 14.1 percent), while more boys than girls reported bullying someone else offline (8 percent versus 5 percent).

In an attempt to clarify some of these issues, we conducted further research to illuminate gender differences in experiences with cyberbullying. Data from 3,141 self-selected female respondents from around the world who were under age 18 were analyzed. Respondents ranged in age from 8 to 17, with most being between 13 and 17 (average age = 14.6 years). Over one-third (38.3 percent) of the sample responded positively to the statement "I have been bullied online" (Burgess-Proctor et al., in press).

The two online victimization behaviors reported most frequently were being ignored (45.8 percent) and disrespected (42.9 percent), both of which are relatively mild in nature (Burgess-Proctor et al., in press). It is important, however, to note that some girls did report more serious forms such as being threatened (11.2 percent) or being scared for their safety (6.2 percent). Finally, we also found that girls (15.6 percent) were just as likely as boys (18.0 percent) to report participating in these types of cyberbullying (Hinduja & Patchin, 2008a).

> *It has made me want to cut my wrists cause I couldn't cope with going back to school and the girls starting again. I just felt like throwing up.*
>
> —16-year-old girl from the United Kingdom

So why do girls seem to be experiencing and participating in cyberbullying more frequently than traditional bullying (see Charts 3.4 and 3.5)? There are a number of potential explanations. First, cyberbullying is text based, and girls tend to be more verbal while boys are generally more physical.

Second, girls partake in a different type of bullying—one that is more emotional and psychological (Owens, Shute, & Slee, 2000a; Underwood, Galen, & Paquette, 2001). Girls typically engage in "social sabotage" (gossiping and rumor spreading) much more frequently than boys, an activity that is well facilitated by the mediums of interaction in cyberspace (Owens et al., 2000a, 2000b; Simmons, 2003). Conversely, Internet-based communication does not facilitate bullying behaviors typical of boys (such as shoving and fistfights).

Third, girls are arguably less confrontational and more committed to maintaining balance and agreeability in their relationships—at least when face-to-face with another (Andreou, 2001; Miller, Danaher, & Forbes, 1986). Communicating online frees them to act out flagrantly from a safe setting behind a keyboard and monitor.

Fourth, girls have been culturally and socially constrained when it comes to manifesting violent or aggressive tendencies but are not bound by those constraints in cyberspace (Brown, 2003; Underwood, 2003; Zahn-Waxler, 2000). Even though vastly more males than females commit violent crime, which might lead one to believe that males are more violent than females, it is possible that females share the same tendencies toward hostility as males (Bjorkqvist & Niemela, 1992; Crick & Grotpeter, 1995). However, they have been historically entrenched in a social structure that forbids them to manifest violence in the same ways that men do because they are told it is not culturally appropriate to do so (Brown).

Finally, girls arguably often need social support to gang up on another girl, and this can be accomplished with ease through the marshaling of technology. Consider the story of Vada from Chapter 1; Ali was able to enlist the help of others in her peer group to bombard Vada anonymously with hateful and threatening e-mails. Such action could be quickly orchestrated and carried out with a mass message over a variety of electronic mediums (instant messaging, e-mail, cell phone text messaging, etc.), describing exactly what Ali wanted her peers to do to inflict the most harm.

Chart 3.4   Cyberbullying by Gender: Victimization

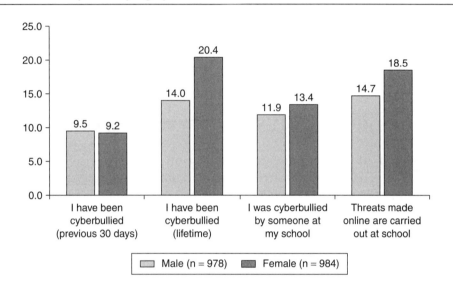

Chart 3.5   Cyberbullying by Gender: Offending

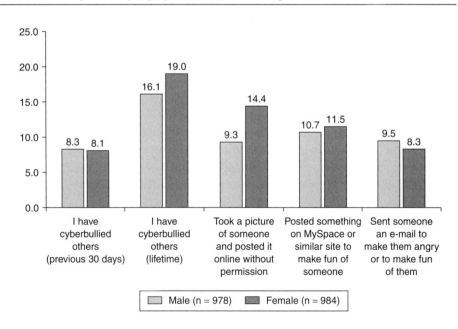

Interestingly, our research also found that female victims of cyber-bullying are significantly more likely to feel frustrated and significantly less likely to feel scared than males (see Chart 3.14 on page 63). This may be due to the nature of the cyberbullying behavior. Whereas boys may be more likely to threaten another boy physically online (which may lead to a feeling of fear), girls are more likely to spread rumors about another girl (which would lead to a feeling of frustration). To note, future research must clarify how these negative emotions (anger, frustration, sadness, embarrassment, fear) are related to negative behaviors in which youth might participate as coping mechanisms. Such research could markedly illustrate how aggression in cyberspace may have significant real-world implications.

RACIAL DIFFERENCES IN CYBERBULLYING

Studies that have examined traditional bullying across different racial groups have been largely inconclusive (Devoe et al., 2002; Graham & Juvonen, 2002; Nansel et al., 2001; Seals & Young, 2003; Siann, Callahan, Glissov, Lockhart, & Rawson, 1994; Sweeting & West, 2001). Generally speaking, in our most recent study we found that white students were *slightly* more likely to experience cyberbullying as a victim and offender—especially when they reported on their lifetime experiences (see Chart 3.6). In studies where there have been differences based on race, some have cited a so-called digital divide—where certain racial and economic groups have less access to technology (Norris, 2001). In our study, however, different races reported relatively similar rates of participation in other online activities (online games, e-mail, chat rooms, etc.), and no clear finding signaled differential levels of access to technology. Of course, that may be related to our particular sample.

Our findings are largely consistent with those of Michele Ybarra, Marie Diener-West, and Philip Leaf (2007), who studied 1,515 youth between age 10 and 15 in August and September 2006 and discovered that race did not significantly differentiate students' experience of online harassment. It may simply be that certain demographic characteristics, such as race and gender, are rendered less relevant in an environment where interpersonal communication occurs predominantly through electronic text.

An alternative explanation is that historically less powerful groups may be more powerful (or at least not disadvantaged) when online. Minority groups (irrespective of race or ethnicity)—while potentially unpopular at school—may not be exposed as marginal on the Internet. Moreover, youth who may not (or cannot) stand up for themselves at school may be more likely to do so in cyberspace if the perceived likelihood of retaliation is minimized.

Chart 3.6 Cyberbullying by Race

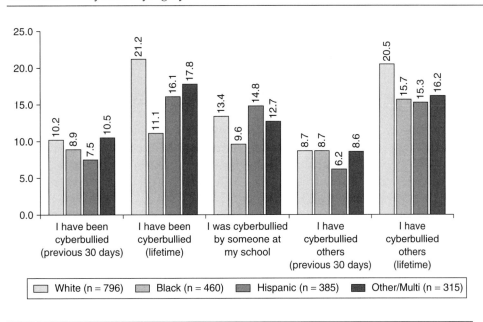

AGE DIFFERENCES IN CYBERBULLYING

Research has consistently indicated that traditional bullying tends to decrease as the student progresses through middle and high school (Seals & Young, 2003). With respect to cyberbullying, recent research has noted that electronic bullying tends to peak later in middle school (Williams & Guerra, 2007; Wolak, Mitchell, & Finkelhor, 2007) or in high school (Ybarra & Mitchell, 2004, 2007), a finding contrary to the age of youth commonly involved in traditional bullying (Nansel et al., 2001; Olweus, 1994a).[2] In our 2005 study, older youth, youth who spent more time online or who were more computer-proficient, and youth involved in offline bullying were all more likely to be involved with cyberbullying, both as victims and as bullies (Hinduja & Patchin, 2008a). This mirrors other research into online harassment, which has found that offenders (both those who have only offended, as well as those who have been both an offender and a victim) tend to use the Internet more frequently and with more proficiency than individuals who have only been victimized (Berson et al., 2002; Ybarra & Mitchell, 2004).

Findings from our most recent research also suggest that seventh grade seems to be an important transition point when it comes to online behaviors and cyberbullying specifically. When breaking the results down by grade, we see an obvious shift from sixth to seventh grade; Charts 3.7 and 3.8 clearly illustrate some of these changes. It is important to point out that our 2007 study only focused on sixth-, seventh-, and eighth-grade students and therefore misses any differences that may have occurred prior to sixth grade or following eighth grade. Furthermore, it bears mentioning that the methods of cyberbullying likely change as youth move through middle school. We would expect to see a greater variety of mediums being used as kids get older and more proficient with different technological devices and environments (Kowalski & Limber, 2007).

Chart 3.7   Cyberbullying Victimization by Grade

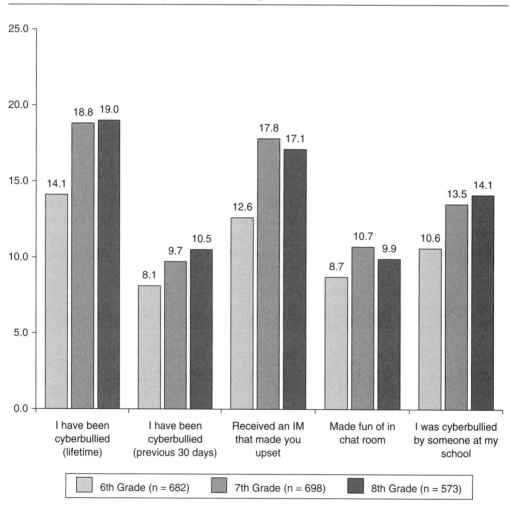

Chart 3.8   Cyberbullying Offending by Grade

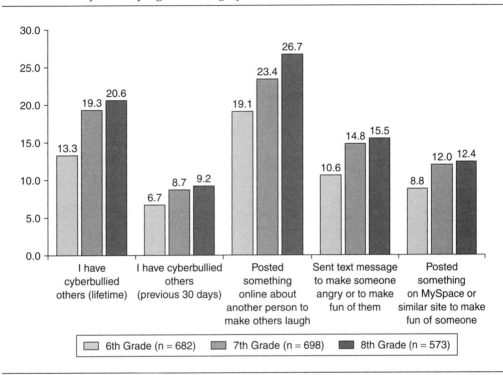

VICTIM/OFFENDER RELATIONSHIP IN CYBERBULLYING

The relationship between those who are victimized online and their aggressors merits attention, as bullying offline by and large involves adolescents who know each other—whether at school, in the neighborhood, or through some other social connection. Is cyberspace just another setting in which traditional bullying can take place, albeit without the immediate threat of physical harm and face-to-face interaction? Or is cyberspace emboldening individuals (for one reason or another) to harass and mistreat others with whom they have no previous relationship or contact?

Wolak and colleagues (2007) analyzed data from 1,500 youth between the ages of 10 and 17 from the Youth Internet Safety Survey (YISS) and found that 43 percent of Internet harassment victims knew their aggressor, while 57 percent suffered at the hands of online-only contacts. Victims were about five times more likely to harass others than nonvictims. Also, Kowalski and Limber (2007) found that almost half (48 percent) of cyberbullying victims did not know the identity of their aggressor. Also based on the YISS data, Ybarra, Mitchell, Finkelhor, and Wolak (2007) found that 12.6 percent of all harassed youth report that the same aggressor harms them offline and online, while 10.4 percent of victims report that different individuals mistreat them offline and online.

Our own research suggests that victims of cyberbullying overwhelmingly know (or at least think they know) who is harassing them (see Chart 3.9). Even though online bullying provides bullies with a veil of perceived anonymity, it appears that eventually, the target often figures out who is harassing them.

Chart 3.9   Victim/Offender Relationship

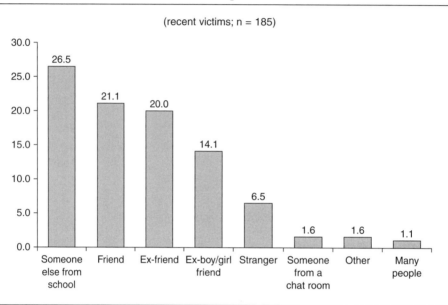

(recent victims; n = 185)

The person who bullied me online was an ex-friend whom I knew very well. She called me names and went behind my back and spread rumors about me. She heavily bullied one of my best friends to the extent where my friend could have been suspended from school. She tried to ruin my friend's reputation.

—16-year-old girl from Australia

It may be that in years past, cyberbullying was more often perpetrated by strangers but now tends to occur between youth who know each other in real life. Perhaps traditional bullies and cyberbullies were distinct, disparate populations in the past, but we are now seeing traditional bullies using computer-based communication to extend and expand their reach. This, of course, serves to increase the number of cyberbullying offenders and victims out there—which is in keeping with the news headlines and many of the academic research findings.

TRADITIONAL BULLYING AND CYBERBULLYING

Our research suggests that a strong connection exists between cyberbullying and traditional schoolyard bullying. While it is difficult to determine whether traditional bullying *causes* cyberbullying or vice versa, there is a clear correlation between online and offline victimization and offending (Hinduja & Patchin, 2008a). Youth who reported bullying others in real life in the previous six months were more than 2.5 times as likely to report bullying others online. Similarly, youth who were victims of traditional bullying in the previous six months were more than 2.5 times as likely to be victims of cyberbullying (Hinduja & Patchin).

> *I feel bad for the people being bullied, it's so rude to pick on someone and they are doing it online where they have proof of what they said and can print it out and pass it around school.*

> —15-year-old girl from Wisconsin

Charts 3.10 and 3.11 help further illustrate this relationship. For example, Chart 3.10 shows that 42.4 percent of youth who reported being cyberbullied also reported being bullied at school. This is compared to 16.1 percent who are cyberbullied but not bullied at school. Chart 3.11 demonstrates that 51.6 percent of those who report cyberbullying others also admit to bullying others at school. This is compared to 18.1 percent of youth who say they only bully online. These findings are instructive to the extent that they can help educators identify who is most likely to be involved in cyberbullying. Youth identified as bullies or targets at school should be counseled about other forms of bullying as well. Moreover, future research should focus on why some youth are targeted for bullying in multiple environments while others are not.

Chart 3.10   Victims of Cyberbullying

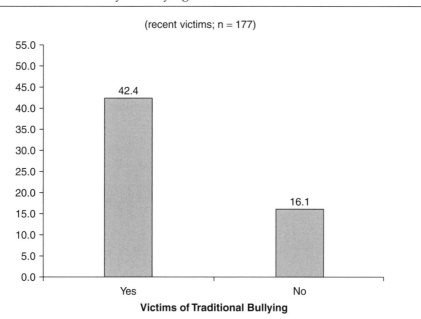

(recent victims; n = 177)

Victims of Traditional Bullying

Chart 3.11   Cyberbullies

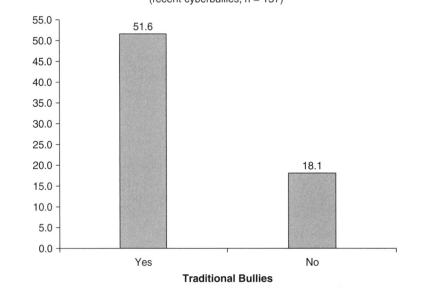

(recent cyberbullies; n = 157)

Yes — 51.6

No — 18.1

Traditional Bullies

I think its really dumb 2 bully someone online because some people go online because they think they won't be made fun of or anything unlike maybe at school or something.

—13-year-old girl from California

RESPONSES OF CYBERBULLYING VICTIMS

One of the first things we learned in our earliest cyberbullying studies was that victims were not telling adults about their experiences. Specifically, fewer than 10 percent of victims told a parent, and fewer than 5 percent told a teacher about their experiences with cyberbullying (Patchin & Hinduja, 2006). As displayed in Chart 3.12, these numbers have improved in our most recent research. It should be noted, however, that our earlier studies involved all youth under the age of 18, while our 2007 study only involved middle school students. So it may not mean that more youth are talking about their experiences; rather, it may simply suggest that *younger* youth are more likely to talk about their cyberbullying experiences than older, high school–aged youth. On the other hand, it may imply that messages about Internet safety are getting through to youth. More research is necessary to better understand the extent to which victims are confiding in adults.

Both boys and girls are unlikely to confide in others about their cyberbullying experiences, although girls are more likely to tell a friend (57 percent compared to 50 percent) and boys are slightly more likely to tell

Chart 3.12   Who Victims Tell

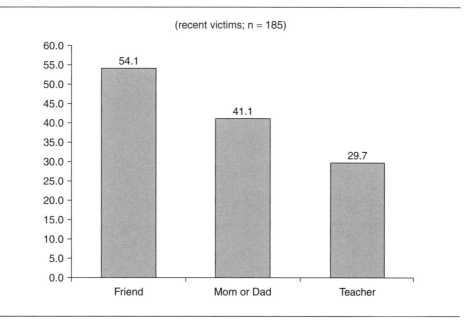

(recent victims; n = 185)

a teacher (39 percent compared to 21 percent). Even so, approximately 60 percent of recent victims of cyberbullying do *not* tell an adult about their experiences—which may be cause for concern.

There are several commonly stated reasons why many victims are not willing to discuss their cyberbullying experiences. First, victims don't want to be blamed for the behavior and are often afraid that parents will simply remove the source of the problem—the computer or cell phone. A 13-year-old girl from Virginia, for example, told us: "I wanted to tell my parents but I was afraid that they would never let me chat again and I know that's how a lot of other kids feel." The other concern that victims have is that adults are ill-equipped or unwilling to intervene on their behalf (and in a calm, rational manner) to resolve the situation. To be sure, many parents simply don't know what to do when confronted with a cyberbullying problem. It also seems that some teachers are gun-shy in responding to behaviors that happen away from school. Finally, law enforcement is unlikely to get involved unless a clear violation of the law can be articulated (which is uncommon in cyberbullying cases). So to whom can victims turn? For starters, we hope that after reading this book, you will make yourself available so that they will feel comfortable coming to you.

When it comes to responding to minor cyberbullying behaviors, many victims take matters into their own hands. As illustrated in Chart 3.13, over one-fourth of recent victims simply blocked the bully from communicating with them. This is an effective response to chat room, instant messaging, and e-mail bullying. Most electronic communication programs allow users to block certain screen names or e-mail addresses. Unfortunately, however,

Chart 3.13   How Victims Responded

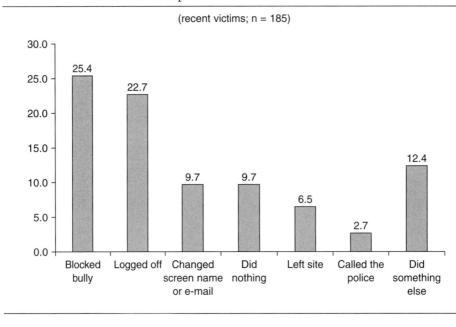

(recent victims; n = 185)

blocking can be a short-term solution, because the bully can always create new screen names or e-mail addresses and continue the assault.

Almost 23 percent of victims logged off their computer for a period of time. This can also be an effective way to counter many types of cyberbullying, because it temporarily removes the target of attack and source of amusement. Slightly fewer than 10 percent of youth were forced to change their own screen names or e-mail addresses, which can make communicating with friends or family difficult. Also noteworthy is the fact that 2.7 percent of victims thought their cyberbullying incident was so severe that they called the police. Incidents that involve a clear threat to the safety of an individual certainly warrant this response. Law enforcement officers are trained to investigate incidents to determine whether or not a true threat is imminent. Finally, over 12 percent of the victims took some other action, while almost 10 percent did nothing.

EMOTIONAL AND BEHAVIORAL CONSEQUENCES AND CORRELATES OF CYBERBULLYING

We have stated in previous chapters that although cyberbullying occurs in a virtual environment, the consequences of cyberbullying victimization are very real.

Emotional Consequences

Research has reported a variety of emotional consequences of traditional bullying, pointing to victims often feeling sad, anxious, and having lower self-esteem than those who are not victimized (Borg, 1998; Ericson, 2001; Hawker & Boulton, 2000; Rigby, 2003; Roland, 2002; Seals & Young, 2003), and Chapter 1 detailed some of these studies. Recent research of Internet-using adolescents specifically focusing on online harassment and emotional reactions suggests that victims of cyberbullying respond very similarly to traditional bullying victims in terms of the aforementioned negative emotions (Berson et al., 2002; Cowie & Berdondini, 2002; Ybarra & Mitchell, 2007).

In our own recent study, we found that many cyberbullying victims felt angry, frustrated, sad, embarrassed, or scared (see Chart 3.14). This is particularly noteworthy given that researchers have suggested that delinquency and interpersonal violence can result when these negative emotions aren't dealt with properly (Aseltine, Gore, & Gordon, 2000; Broidy & Agnew, 1997; Mazerolle, Burton, Cullen, Evans, & Payne, 2000; Mazerolle & Piquero, 1998). For example, if a victim feels scared about going to school because of cyberbullying, he may be tempted to bring a weapon to school for protection. Similarly, victims may feel so sad or depressed about the incident that they may hurt themselves.

Along similar lines, we wanted to ascertain how self-esteem might be related to online aggression. Within our survey, we included Rosenberg's

Chart 3.14   How Victims Felt

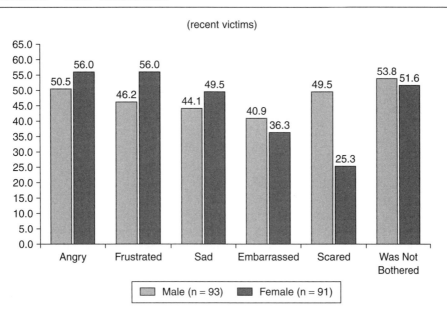

(1965) well-validated ten-item scale, which included the following statements:

1. On the whole, I am satisfied with myself.
2. At times I think I am no good at all.
3. I feel that I have a number of good qualities.
4. I am able to do things as well as most other people.
5. I feel I do not have much to be proud of.
6. I certainly feel useless at times.
7. I feel that I'm a person of worth, at least on an equal plane with others.
8. I wish I could have more respect for myself.
9. All in all, I am inclined to feel that I am a failure.
10. I take a positive attitude toward myself.

Response choices ranged from 1–4 and indicated higher or lower self-esteem, depending on the direction of the question wording. As noted in Chart 3.15, youth who have experienced cyberbullying have a significantly lower level of self-esteem. This was an expected finding with important implications, as lower self-esteem has been tied to a number of dysfunctional responses (see Leary, Schreindorfer, & Haupt, 1995). What we can't say, however, is whether experience with cyberbullying causes victims to have lower self-esteem or whether youth with low self-esteem are targeted for cyberbullying. Additional longitudinal research is required to clarify how self-esteem is directly and indirectly influenced by online harassment among youthful populations.

> I sometimes didn't want to go to school, my quiz scores went down, and I thought it was my fault.
>
> —13-year-old girl from Maryland

Behavioral Consequences

Chapter 1 also summarized the behavioral consequences associated with traditional bullying. Similar behavioral outcomes seem to be associated with cyberbullying—especially for those who are doing the cyberbullying. For instance, Ybarra and Mitchell (2004) found that cyberbullies were significantly more likely than youth who didn't cyberbully to be the target of offline bullying (defined as "being hit or picked on by another child during the previous year") and to display other problematic behavior (i.e., purposefully damaging property, police contact, physically assaulting

Chart 3.15   Cyberbullying and Self-Esteem

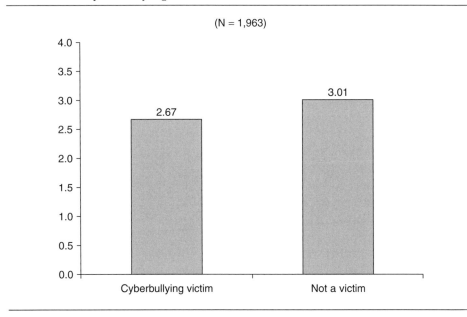

(N = 1,963)

a nonfamily member, and taking something that did not belong to the respondent within the previous year; p. 1310). Online aggressors were also found to have low school commitment and to engage in alcohol and cigarette use. In a more recent study, Ybarra and Mitchell (2007) also found that with increasing perpetration of online harassment comes increased aggressive and rule-breaking behavior among those youth. Ybarra, Diener-West, and Leaf (2007) found that online victims were eight times as likely as nonvictims to report carrying a weapon at school in the last 30 days.

Our own research identified a link between cyberbullying victimization and adolescent problem behaviors, such as recent school difficulties, assaultive conduct, substance use, and traditional bullying (Hinduja & Patchin, 2007). Some students were hesitant to go to school and did what they could to avoid attending and being victimized there. We also found that a significant proportion of victims removed themselves from the online venue in which the cyberbullying occurred, while one in five (20 percent) felt forced to stay offline completely for a period of time (Patchin & Hinduja, 2006).

This one time this girl that was a lot bigger than me made me cry when I talked to her online because she told me if she saw me in school she was going to stuff me in a locker and that no one was going to find me for a very long time. I faked sick for a week and a half until I found the courage deep inside me to go to school. Nothing bad even happened. I was really relieved.

—18-year-old boy from New York

CYBERBULLICIDE

People told me I was retarded, that I didn't fit in. This girl said that I was bitch and that she wished I was dead. I never did anything to her but I got really upset and depressed and started cutting myself and started seriously considering suicide. I just ignored them but it still really hurt.

—13-year-old girl from Australia

Another particularly upsetting outcome that we have seen in recent years has been the increase in suicides related to an experience with bullying or cyberbullying. As a point of reference, in 2004, suicide was the third-leading cause of deaths among those between the ages of 10 and 24. Even though suicide rates have decreased 28.5 percent between 1990 and 2004 among this age group, upward trends were identified in the 10- to 19-year-old age group in 2003–2004 (the most recent data available; Centers for Disease Control and Prevention, 2007). There have been several reported cases of suicide stemming from experiences with traditional bullying (Marr & Field, 2001), and we are aware of at least four cases in the United States and many others abroad where youth who were repeatedly harassed online took their own lives—in part because of that harassment.

We briefly introduced Ryan Halligan, pictured in Figure 3.1, in Chapter 1. You will recall he was just 13 years old in October of 2003 when he took his own life after months of being bullied online. He was teased, taunted, and called "gay" by classmates—both online and off. In the summer between his seventh- and eighth-grade years, he began an Internet friendship with a popular girl from his school. When school started back up again in the fall, he approached this girl in person with romantic gestures, but was rejected and mocked in front of others.

Figure 3.1   Ryan Halligan

SOURCE: Photo courtesy of John Halligan.

The main problem wasn't that Ryan was bullied or spurned by his adolescent crush; these things happen all the time in adolescence. Ryan's father suspects that because these behaviors carried over to the Internet, they were amplified due to the perception that "everyone" in the school knew of the incident. Apparently, the girl had forwarded or sent romantic-tinged excerpts from her instant message exchanges with Ryan to a number of classmates. It was hard enough to be humiliated in front of one or two peers, let alone to realize that the whole school seemed to be in on the joke.

Jeff Johnston, pictured in Figure 3.2, was a 15-year-old honor student in southwest Florida who loved computers and Japanese comic books. When a popular girl at school became his girlfriend, another boy seemingly became jealous and decided to send and post cruel statements and slanderous gossip through e-mail and Web site postings (Roemmick as cited in Johnston, 2007):

> *jeff is a fagget. he needs to die. a stalker of many sorts. he lies and says girls stalk him. BS.* ("Journal Entries: 2004 31 January")

One tormenter even hacked into a Web page hosting an online game that Jeff and his friends had designed and replaced it with a hate page in a type of "cybervandalism." As other kids joined in on the harassment, it became too much for Jeff to take. Six weeks before he took his life in June of 2005, he wrote a suicide note on his computer: "I'm just writing to tell you I won't be in school anymore. I decided to commit suicide because my life is too hard to live with" (Johnston as cited in Jurkowski, 2005, ¶ 18).

Figure 3.2   Jeffrey Johnston

SOURCE: Photo courtesy of Debbie Johnston.

In October of 2006, 17-year-old Rachael Neblett, pictured in Figure 3.3, committed suicide after experiencing bullying at school and online, mostly through her MySpace profile. She received threatening messages, including this one (Neblett, 2007):

> *I am not going to put you in the hospital, I am going to put you in the morgue.*

Even though the messages were sent anonymously, she knew the bully to be someone from school, because that person knew her daily movements and where and when she caught her bus. The situation was brought to the attention of school personnel, who subsequently kept a watchful eye over Rachael, but this failed to alleviate her concerns. Shortly after receiving the threatening messages, she committed suicide.

Figure 3.3   Rachael Neblett

SOURCE: Photo courtesy of Mark Neblett.

Like Ryan Halligan, 13-year-old Megan Meier, pictured in Figure 3.4, also began an online relationship with someone to whom she was attracted. For almost a month, Megan corresponded with this boy exclusively online because he said he didn't have a phone and was home-schooled. One day in October of 2006, Megan received a message on her MySpace profile saying,

> *I don't know if I want to be friends with you any longer because I hear you're not nice to your friends.* ("Parents," 2007)

This was followed by bulletins being posted through MySpace calling Megan "fat" and a "slut." Soon after, Tina Meier found her daughter hanging in her bedroom closet. Though she rushed her daughter to the hospital, Megan died the next day.

Figure 3.4   Megan Meier

SOURCE: Photo courtesy of Tina Meier.

Six weeks after their daughter's death, the Meier family learned that the boy with whom Megan had been corresponding never existed. He (and his online profile) was created by the mother of one of Megan's friends as a way to spy on what Megan was saying about her daughter. While some of the details are still unclear, some have suggested that the mother and her adult friends sent the harassing messages. Interestingly, the district attorney in the case refused to file charges and claimed that no criminal law had been broken. Despite that conclusion, a federal prosecutor from Los Angeles recently indicted Lori Drew, the parent presumed responsible, and those charges are still pending as of this writing. Legal advocates are mixed about whether or not the charge will stick. While most agree those responsible for Megan's death need to be held accountable, the federal indictment is really a last-ditch attempt to prosecute Drew criminally. These issues are explored in more depth in Chapter 5.

These stories point to the tragic consequences of ignoring cyberbullying. Our research has also uncovered a link between suicidal thoughts and online victimization. Middle school youth who experienced cyberbullying scored higher on a suicidal ideation scale than those who did not experience cyberbullying (see Chart 3.16). The scale included the following questions:

1. Did you feel so sad or hopeless almost every day for two weeks or more in a row that you stopped doing some usual activities?

2. Have you ever seriously thought about attempting suicide?

3. Did you make a specific plan about how you would attempt suicide?

4. Did you actually attempt suicide?

Chart 3.16   Cyberbullying and Suicide

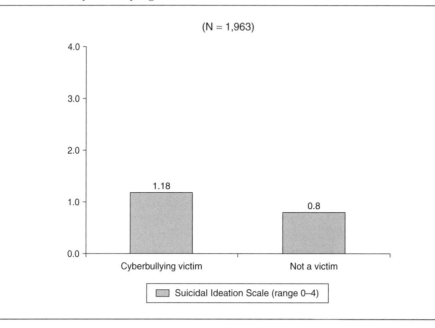

(N = 1,963)

Suicidal Ideation Scale (range 0–4)

Cyberbullying victim: 1.18

Not a victim: 0.8

Youth who responded yes to more of these questions scored higher on the scale. This finding suggests that youth who are bullied in cyberspace are at an increased risk for suicide and should be treated as such. It doesn't necessarily mean that cyberbullying *causes* suicidal thoughts—just that there appears to be a connection that we need to examine very closely.

It bears mentioning that in addition to the cyberbullying, many of these adolescents had other issues going on in their lives that may have contributed to their suicides. Ryan Halligan attended special education classes in elementary school and struggled socially and academically. Megan Meier suffered from low self-esteem and depression and was on medication when she took her life. From what we've seen, cyberbullying by itself doesn't lead to youth suicide. Rather, it appears that the toll that daily struggles, stresses, and relative hopelessness take on some adolescents is exacerbated when Internet-based harassment is added to the equation.

As displayed and discussed above, the extensive amount of data we collected in 2007, along with other key studies by committed researchers, have helped to inform our conception of the scope, prevalence, and frequency of cyberbullying among youth today. It has also clarified how gender, race, age, and victim/offender relationship is related to the behavior and lent insight into its emotional and behavioral consequences. Our findings, coupled with lessons learned from other, previously reviewed research on the topic, serve as foundational pieces in a growing body of knowledge. We hope this data-driven perspective provides context to the news headlines and can aptly inform educators who need to know the actual extent and depth of the problem before devoting their time, energy, and resources to addressing it.

In the next section, we briefly summarize our recent findings on why someone would engage in cyberbullying. This is a question that we are asked quite frequently and one that does not have a clear answer. Multiple theories from a variety of disciplines could be used to understand the phenomenon better, so we suggest some that seem relevant based on our discussions with adults and youth. As individuals increasingly recognize the seriousness of cyberbullying, more scientific studies will surface that explore the factors that prompt the behavior.

WHY DO YOUTH ENGAGE IN CYBERBULLYING?

The answer to this question is obviously very important to understanding the behaviors themselves. As depicted in Chart 3.17, the most frequent explanation given to us from youth who admit to cyberbullying others is that they were seeking revenge. Victims of traditional bullying may seek retribution through technological means (e-mail, instant message, or cell phone text message), thereby "turning the table" on their aggressors through the equalizing characteristics of the Internet and its ability to pre-empt the relevance of physical intimidation (Kowalski & Limber, 2007). Comments from a 17-year-old girl from Pennsylvania illustrate this:

> *I had recently picked on an old friend of mine [because] she had done something to me that was equally as wrong, if not worse. I was disappointed in her, and for that I decided not to be a friend any longer and spread her deepest secrets to everyone, which made her look like a complete fool. I felt somewhat guilty because I had known her for years, at the same time it was pay back and I think she learned from it when it comes to attempting to mess around with me.*

In addition to the 22.5 percent who were motivated by revenge, another 18.7 percent reported that the victim deserved it, while 10.6 percent said they cyberbullied because it was fun. It seems that among some adolescents, cyberbullying behaviors are easily justified.

In addition to these reasons, some cyberbullies simply just don't see the harm in their behavior and don't classify their actions as a form of bullying. "It was just text." "I didn't mean to hurt them." "I was just messing around." These are common replies when youth are asked about their cyberbullying activities. It is therefore important for adolescents to learn about the harmful consequences that befall victims. They need to hear the stories described above of Ryan, Jeff, Rachael, and Megan. One reason cyberbullying is so pernicious is that aggressors don't immediately see (and consequently internalize) the very real consequences of their actions—as we've discussed in Chapter 2.

Several developmental factors also make adolescents more susceptible to engaging in cyberbullying. A hallmark of adolescence is the

Chart 3.17   Reasons for Cyberbullying

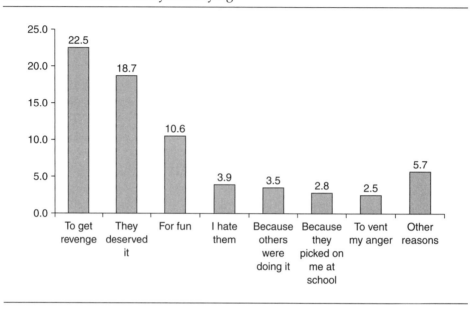

rapid cognitive, social, and emotional changes that youth experience. Gruber and Yurgelun-Todd (2006) note that "the developmental factors which influence decision-making in adolescents may result in choices which are suggestive of cortical immaturity, poor judgment, and impulsivity" (p. 322). That is to say that the brains of many adolescents may not have matured to the point where they can make the most prudent decisions or exercise self-control and restraint. As Malinda Wilson, a detective in the Seattle Police Department aptly points out: *The Internet and puberty do not mix!*

When presented with the opportunity to harass someone online, impulsive adolescents may be unable to hold back. Indeed, they often reflexively respond to the situation at hand and their emotions and attitudes at that moment, instead of carefully reasoning as to the acceptability or ramifications of their actions. Furthermore, since most activities in cyberspace are outside of the regular supervision of responsible adult authorities, impulsive youth are free to engage in a variety of inappropriate behaviors without concern about consequences.

Along these same lines, it is important to remember that adolescents are very "now" oriented. They are concerned with what is right in front of them at this very moment and rarely consider the long-term implications of their actions. Even though they may fundamentally know that cyberbullying is wrong, they engage in the behavior anyway, because they do not have to deal with any immediate consequences and do not witness its immediate emotional or psychological harm. In other words, usually no automatic or instantaneous cue indicates the unacceptability of online aggression to adolescents. If it is not detected and disciplined (in some informal or formal capacity) by parents or educators, the behavior may be reinforced and continue.

Determining why some youth are more prone to engage in cyberbullying than others is an important direction for future research. To that end, it may be wise to utilize existing criminological, psychological, sociological, or developmental theories to help contextualize cyberbullying behaviors. Since traditional and online aggression are deviant behaviors that society wishes to control, it may be instructive to explore the behaviors from a social-scientific perspective.

For example, cyberbullying behaviors may be learned from and reinforced by others (Akers, 1985; Bandura, 1969, 1973, 1977; Bandura & Walters, 1963; Skinner, 1953, 1971), or they could be passed down through culture and tradition and therefore viewed as acceptable behaviors (Brown, Esbensen, Finn, & Geis, 2001). They also may be a manifestation of some underlying personality trait, such as low self-control (Gottfredson & Hirschi, 1990). An adolescent may turn to cyberbullying others to cope with stressful life experiences (Hinduja & Patchin, 2007), or cyberbullying could result when the adolescent doesn't feel a sense of responsibility for her actions (Diener, 1980; Diener & Wallbom, 1976; Festinger, Pepitone, & Newcomb, 1952). Due to space limitations, we cannot elaborate upon these or other possible theoretical explanations for cyberbullying in this book. We simply wanted to mention a few that—based on our study of this phenomenon—appear relevant and merit deeper scientific inquiry and analysis.

SUMMARY

Within this chapter, we have covered a great deal of research in the hopes of thoroughly equipping you with the latest findings and statistics on the nature and extent of cyberbullying among youth today. While it is possible to get overwhelmed by so many numbers and so much data, we encourage you to remember that this book is a resource that you can continually consult when you are curious about some aspect of online aggression. Outside of research findings, we have addressed some of the reasons why youth might engage in this behavior. Deeper analysis of the motives and rationalizations used are necessary so we can better understand the mind-set of bullies at the moment in which they send or post harmful electronic content. As we move into Chapter 4, we open up a proverbial can of worms in discussing online social networking Web sites and the potential for cyberbullying that exists therein. With tens of millions of youth across the world interacting on these sites on a daily basis, it is crucial to understand their positives and negatives so that we can promote the former while dealing with the latter.

QUESTIONS FOR REFLECTION

1. Why are so many different statistics reported about how many youth experience cyberbullying?

2. Are any differences in cyberbullying victimization or offending based on gender, race, or grade?

3. What are some of the emotional, psychological, and behavioral consequences of being cyberbullied?

4. What is cyberbullicide?

5. Why do you think adolescents engage in cyberbullying?

NOTES

1. Ybarra and Mitchell (2007) analyzed the Youth Internet Safety Survey data of 1,500 youth between the ages of 10 and 17 in 2005 and found that boys were three times more likely to be "frequent perpetrators" of online harassment.

2. An exception to this is found in Rigby (2003) and the phenomenon of "relational bullying," which is more common among older students than younger and involves damage to the victim's relationship with peers.

4

Social Networking and Cyberbullying

My name is Logan. I have brown hair and brown eyes. I love to play sports. My favorite sport is football. I go to GNMS. I only like that school because all my friends go there. This probably sound weird but I like school. It is only fun cuz I get to see most of my friends.

—MySpace profile of "anonymous" middle schooler

W ith the growth of the Internet-based communication technologies, there are clearly numerous opportunities for youth to keep in touch with friends, family, and anyone else, regardless of geographical location and with minimal effort or expense. Communities of Internet users have sprung into existence and multiplied, as people around the world seek to share and receive information, ideas, and thoughts; obtain entertainment and diversion from the "real world"; and pass time (Flaherty, Pearce, & Rubin, 1998). Most importantly, the Internet is becoming an increasingly integral part of everyday social life. More users are going online primarily to satisfy their interpersonal and relational requirements and engaging in a form of more or less constant online interaction in fixed, inclusive settings.

MySpace, Facebook, Orkut, Bebo, Friendster, Xanga, and a host of other Web sites are Internet-based communities that have exploded in popularity in recent years. They allow those who join the ability to set up online representations of themselves, post personal updates or bulletins, share photos, create and facilitate topical discussions, send and receive one-on-one and communitywide messages, and develop relationships with other like-minded persons (explained further below). These Web sites where individuals are linked by certain commonalities or interests are commonly known as "social networking sites."

If you have never heard of MySpace or another social networking site, we can just about guarantee that your teenage children have. Of course, given the negative attention some of these sites have received in recent months, you likely have at least some familiarity with them. But what exactly are they? And why are they so popular among youth? A recent telephone survey of 935 teenagers between ages 12 and 17 found that 55 percent of online youth have created a personal profile page and 85 percent of those have done so on MySpace (Lenhart & Madden, 2007). It is also estimated that at least one-quarter of the approximately 230 million MySpace accounts created are registered to those under the age of 18 (Granneman, 2006; Hinduja & Patchin, 2008b). Moreover, even though youth represent only a relatively small proportion of overall MySpace users, they are among the most active. They often visit the site multiple times each day, and much of their socializing occurs through MySpace.

Given the popularity of social networking sites among adolescents, it should come as no surprise that they also provide opportunities for cyberbullying activities to occur. This chapter will discuss social networking in general, with a specific emphasis on MySpace because it has attracted the largest number of users and the bulk of the media attention. In the following text, we examine the potential benefits and risks of online social networking among youth and discuss in detail the ways in which these sites (and the content posted therein) have been used to cyberbully and otherwise cause harm to adolescents. We then provide recommendations about how to interact with others within these venues in a safe and responsible manner.

WHAT IS SOCIAL NETWORKING?

To understand social networking Web sites fully, it is essential first to comprehend a "social network" in the traditional sense and then consider how it has evolved into a cyberspace-based cultural phenomenon. Despite the fact that most people have only recently become familiar with it, social networking is not a new concept. Some scholars define a *social network* as a set of persons with whom specific types of support are exchanged (Wellman, 1981), as the set of relationships that is somehow important to a person (Kahn & Antonucci, 1981), or "interlocking structures in which supportive and non-supportive interactions both occur" (van Tilburg, 1995, p. 83). Others define a social network as "a collection of individuals known by a target person" and consider the network in terms of the "interdependencies that link partners to their kin, friends and other associates" (Surra &

Milardo, 1991, p. 2). Quite simply, a social network is a socialization frame-work that links individuals through some common purpose, interest, or characteristic.

Individuals can connect within a social network because they work together; go to school together; graduated from the same university; live in a particular city; or share an interest in a certain musician, television show, actor, technology, hobby, or lifestyle—the possibilities are endless. Regardless of the reasons for the connections, individuals are drawn to others with whom they can relate. Accordingly, social networks of persons naturally arise due to past and present life experiences and relationships and open up opportunities for future interactions. Because everyone is linked in some way or another to other individuals (e.g., a nuclear family is a very simple form of a social network), it is important to recognize that it is not enough to study an individual and that person's interactions with other people from a one-on-one perspective. Rather, it is essential to understand that each interpersonal relationship occurs within the context of many others.

ADOLESCENT ONLINE SOCIAL NETWORKING

Early on, teenagers embraced new communication technologies as quickly as they emerged (e.g., e-mail, chat rooms, instant messaging). In recent years, social networking Web sites have captured a lion's share of usage by adolescents in their quest to communicate and connect with others in cyberspace. The growth in Internet access, speed, and computer hardware and software availability—coupled with a population of youth that is increasingly being raised in front of a computer—has led to social net-works being replicated online.

An Internet-based social network can accordingly be considered a vir-tual community consisting of a number of characteristics. Generally, this involves

> using common language and ease of communication; public space; common interests, values, and goals; persistence of common mean-ing; use of information technology for interaction, not physical space; overcoming time and space barriers; and using digitized iden-tities as a substitute for physical being. (Wang & Chen, 2004, p. 4)

Without question, youth have embraced the concept of creating vir-tual presences and are the driving force behind the success of many online communities (Boyd, 2006).

At a basic level, these sites allow any individual quickly and easily to create a Web page or "profile" that serves as a digital representation of one's personal style, interests, affiliations, likes, and dislikes—and then connect with (link to) "friends" who have done the same. In addition, multimedia enhancements enable users to post and link to pictures, videos, and audio with relative ease. These profile pages have been equated to the highly decorated school lockers or bedrooms of youth (Boyd, 2007). Researcher Anne Helmond (2006) aptly describes this scene when she writes, "there are posters everywhere, the CD player is playing while the TV in the corner is also on . . . friends are dropping by and leaving notes . . ." (¶ 7). Indeed, stepping into a teenager's bedroom usually provides a significant amount of visual and auditory stimulation that gives the visitor more than a glimpse into current youth life and culture. On these sites, users create a public space that personally reflects who they are—or who they want to be (Boyd, 2006).

When individuals first log on to social networking sites, they generally check new comments posted, messages received, and requests to approve people who want to be considered their friend (and, as a result, linked to their social network). They might also modify or customize their own profile page, request new friends themselves, post a new blog, or join a group with others who have a similar interest. Additionally, individuals may browse the profile pages of friends or "friends of friends" (if publicly accessible) and leave comments indicating that they have visited. Some of these comments might be specific to a particular picture or video that the user had posted on his or her profile, for example. After perusing the pages of friends, the user may explore the profiles of those with whom they share something in common (e.g., same school, age, geographic location, or interests) or browse profiles created by musical artists—and consequently "friend" them (i.e., add them as members of their network).

The communication features within social networking Web sites facilitate easy interaction among a population that wants to receive or send information quickly while engaged in multiple other online tasks. On their profile pages, participants can post periodic blogs (short for "Web log") or journal entries. Returning to the bedroom analogy, teenagers' blogs are largely like diaries—but they are no longer secure in a locked drawer or hidden under the bed. Instead, they are often left out and open for all who visit to read. Visitors can also leave public "comments" on other profile pages or send private "messages" to other users, the content of which ranges from superficial greetings ("hey! what've u been up to?") to the expression of meaningful sentiments ("I already miss the talks we had at the beach. I learned so much from you guys.") to random observations or statements or questions about anything of interest ("zac efron is hot!"). If necessary, comments can be moderated and deleted by the owner of the profile page on which they are left.

All of these activities are done with the purpose of creating an online presence and interpersonal network that is socially appealing but also unique to the individual and representative of his or her likes and dislikes, inclinations, activities, and friendships. Indeed, the number of friends one has and the number of comments posted on one's profile are perceived as evidence of social success (i.e., popularity both online and offline; Boyd, 2006). Many youth go to great lengths to make their online profile pages stand out from the crowd by including as much information about themselves as they can. By updating and continually adding personal content, the profile creator attracts the attention of others in an effort to accumulate more "friends" and comments.

In addition, some adolescents enjoy filling out detailed surveys about themselves and posting that information on their profiles (see Box 4.1). These users may spend many hours describing every aspect of their interests and posting the information for everyone to read (Hinduja & Patchin, 2008b).

Box 4.1 Example Survey Found on MySpace

Name:	(removed)
Birthday:	8-12-91
Birthplace:	Virginia
Current Location:	uuh . . . my basement
Eye Color:	blue-grey
Hair Color:	blonde(dark and light)
Height:	???
Right Handed or Left Handed:	right handed
Your Heritage:	???
The Shoes You Wore Today:	hmmm flip flops
Your Weakness:	hitting in the boob
Your Fears:	bats,moths&spiders
Your Perfect Pizza:	???
Goal You Would Like To Achieve This Year:	hmmm . . . something dirrty you aint gunna kno
Your Most Overused Phrase On an instant messenger:	wow
Thoughts First Waking Up:	what to wear
Your Best Physical Feature:	hmmm dont ask me
Your Bedtime:	whenever i want
Your Most Missed Memory:	every time i was with the one i LOVE
Pepsi or Coke:	Coke
MacDonalds or Burger King:	fast food . . . ick
Lipton Ice Tea or Nestea:	Lipton Ice Tea
Chocolate or Vanilla:	chocolate
Cappuccino or Coffee:	cappuccino
Do you Smoke:	yes
Do you Swear:	haha . . . yah
Do you Sing:	hmmm . . . sometimes . . . mostly when i am DRUNK
Do you Shower Daily:	yess
Have you Been in Love:	yess . . . and i still am . . . but i dont want to be

(Continued)

(Continued)

Do you want to go to College:	of course
Do you want to get Married:	yess
Do you belive in yourself:	sometimes
Do you get Motion Sickness:	nop
Do you think you are Attractive:	depends
Are you a Health Freak:	not really
Do you get along with your Parents:	yess i doo
Do you like Thunderstorms:	yess i looooove them
Do you play an Instrument:	uuh sorry but no
In the past month have you Drank Alcohol:	ooh yess i have
In the past month have you Smoked:	mmhmm
In the past month have you gone on a Date:	nop
In the past month have you gone to a Mall:	yes
In the past month have you eaten a box of Oreos:	no
In the past month have you eaten Sushi:	nop
In the past month have you been on Stage:	nop
In the past month have you been Dumped:	nop
In the past month have you gone Skinny Dipping:	yepp
In the past month have you Stolen Anything:	nop
Ever been Drunk:	ooh baby yess
Ever been called a Tease:	yeah but i think every grl has been called that
Ever been Beaten up:	not yet . . . hahaha
Ever Shoplifted:	sadly yeah
How do you want to Die:	uuh i dont
What do you want to be when you Grow Up:	hmmmm . . . pornstar . . . hahahahahahahaha

Many adults simply don't understand why an adolescent would reveal so much personal information on a publicly accessible Web page. One possible explanation could be the fact that youth have grown up with reality television. Programs like *The Real World, Big Brother, Laguna Beach, The Hills,* and others have turned "normal" people into celebrities, in part because they were willing to share anything and everything about themselves to the public. Youth today receive the message that it is perfectly appropriate to tell everything about themselves to anyone who is willing to listen. Of course, this creates many potential problems that will be detailed below.

With this in mind, though, it is incorrect to assume that all of this personal information posted by youth online is accessible by *everyone* who might venture to their profile pages. All mainstream social networking sites allow individuals to set their profile pages to "private," thereby restricting viewing only to those who have been designated and accepted as "friends" by the user. Many adolescents have done this; as we'll discuss later, we encourage *all* individuals to take this prudent step. It serves as a line of defense by requiring that you specifically choose to allow some persons into your network of friends (and consequently into your online "life"). By default, it blocks everyone else.

To summarize, social networking Web sites enable people of all ages to represent themselves online in a creative way and to keep in touch with (and involved in) each others' lives. This is accomplished through each site's varied interactive characteristics, such as messaging; commenting; blogging; posting of multimedia content; and "virtual" scrapbooking of events, people, places, hobbies, interests, and ideas. While a number of popular social networking Web sites have been launched, MySpace has emerged as the most popular among them, accounting for as much as 80 percent of the social networking traffic in 2006 ("MySpace Gains," 2006). What exactly is MySpace and what makes it so popular among youth?

MYSPACE: THE MOST POPULAR SOCIAL NETWORKING WEB SITE

MySpace (see Figure 4.1) was founded in July of 2003 by Tom Anderson and Chris DeWolfe and quickly gained popularity among budding musicians who were looking for a place to promote their music (Boyd, 2007). Fans began to visit these profile pages, create their own profile pages to represent themselves, and interact with each other. The fans could also keep in contact with the artists, who would update their respective profiles with new tour dates and stories from the recording studio or from the road and otherwise attempt to cultivate more familiarity and intimacy with those who supported their work. These fans then introduced the technology to their friends, who in turn created their own profile pages and began to form small social networks around different interests. Accordingly, MySpace became a "one-stop shop" for individuals who wanted to connect and communicate with others with whom they had something in common.

Figure 4.1   Main MySpace Page

In short order, individuals signed up en masse, and MySpace's popularity grew exponentially from what is termed the "network effect"—where initial users invite multitudes of others to sign up and participate. Its population rose from 500,000 user-created accounts in early 2004 to 9 million in early 2005, 40 million in November 2005, 150 million in February 2007, and 212 million in December 2007 (see Chart 4.1).

As of March 2008, MySpace was the third-most popular Web site in the United States, the fifth-most popular English-language Web site in the world, and the most popular of approximately 200 social networking sites (Alexa.com, 2008). While recent numbers are not available, estimates in 2006 gauged its peak growth at 230,000 new accounts each day, largely because individuals wanted to be on the network that houses and supports the most number of users (with whom they could possibly connect and interact; Sellers, 2006).

It deserves mention that MySpace specifically "requires" users to be at least 14 years old and automatically sets the profiles of users who indicate they are 14 or 15 years old to private. This means that only those the user chooses to include in his or her network as friends are allowed to see the contents of that user's profile. Those who are 16 and 17 years old have their profile set to private by default but can choose to make it publicly

Chart 4.1   MySpace Growth

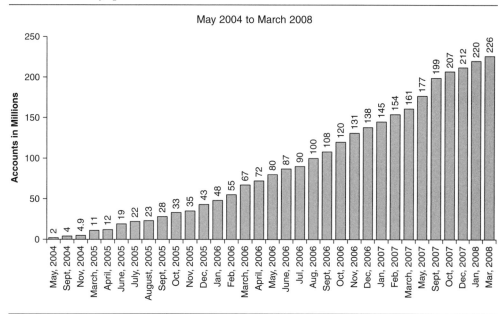

May 2004 to March 2008

viewable (Hempel, 2008). Additionally, users who are 18 or older (and indicate their age as such) are not able to add 14- or 15-year-olds into their friend network unless they know that youth's full name or e-mail address. Despite these restrictions—or maybe because of them—a number of children 13 or younger have lied about their age to create their profiles. Still others not yet 16 have lied about their ages so that they have the option to set their profile to be publicly viewable and accessible by all. MySpace and most other social networking sites have no way to ensure users are listing their actual ages, and the sheer number of profiles makes it practically impossible to police all of the pages to look for underage or otherwise misrepresented users.

OTHER POPULAR SOCIAL NETWORKING SITES

MySpace became more popular than its competitors in part because it integrated many of the online activities that other sites had popularized— blogging, synchronous (real-time) and asynchronous (delayed) messaging, the sharing of multimedia content (pictures, music, videos, etc.) in a very user-friendly, unrestricted, and self-expressive way. However, other online social networking sites continue to grow in popularity. They include, but are not limited to, Facebook, Bebo, Orkut, Friendster, and Xanga. While some differences exist, the reader will note that their structure and the manner in which they are used are virtually identical to those of MySpace. The motives behind participation and the manner in which participation occurs are constant across the landscape of these social networking sites.

Facebook is the second-most popular social networking Web site, with over 64 million active users and approximately 250,000 new accounts created each day (Facebook, 2008; see Figure 4.2). The aesthetic customization features are much more limited than those of MySpace, but the environment itself is feature-rich, as third-party developers have created fun, interesting, and useful applications that profile owners can implement at their sites. These range from small, interactive games to basic photo-editing functionality, horoscopes, music-recommending services, and camera-phone interactivity.

Chart 4.2   Facebook Growth

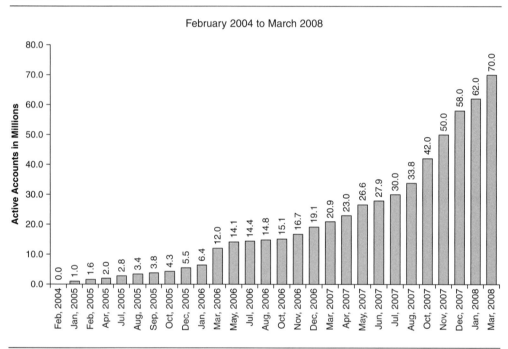

Bebo boasts more than 40 million users. It has significant market share in the United Kingdom and has also garnered growing usage in Ireland, Canada, and Australia ("Jangl," 2007). It appears to be frequented primarily by the 13- to 24-year-old group and has been lauded for its efforts and features to promote safe online practices (Smithers, 2008). For example, Bebo administrators have created numerous short videos and animations to teach online safety and have provided resources to aid schools in instructing students about responsible use of social networking sites (Durrani, 2007).

Orkut, which was created by a Google employee, claims 67 million users and is used predominantly in Brazil and India (Richmond, 2007). Friendster has over 50 million members, is used extensively in Asia, and was actually the most popular online social networking site until April 2004 ("Friendster Launches," 2007). At that time, its position was usurped by MySpace (Makki, 2007).

Xanga provides multimedia blogging features to a user population of around 40 million (Yu, 2007). Of note, Xanga has implemented a number of unique technological features to promote safe use. These include a flagging system that allows for quick and easy reporting of problematic pages, a ratings system that limits the viewing of material inappropriate for certain ages, and a Footprints facility that allows members to see the usernames of other signed-in members who have visited their pages (Xanga, 2007).

Again, the vast majority of these types of sites share standardized characteristics (blogging, messaging, multimedia, etc.) and purposes (to bring people together and build communities based on shared interests and activities). They also include various privacy controls that enable individuals to specify who can view the details of their online profiles and who can privately or publicly leave messages for them. These controls have been implemented in response to the risk of victimization that exists when an individual interacts with others in these venues. When considering these risks, no other social networking site has been under the microscope as much as MySpace. It is important to examine the scope of these risks and the resultant formal responses to appreciate the complexities of this significant component of youth culture.

REPORTED RISKS OF SOCIAL NETWORKING

One reason MySpace grew so quickly is the tremendous amount of media attention it received. Admittedly, most of the attention was negative—covering incidents where MySpace was implicated in some victimization or criminal behavior. This, of course, touched the sensibilities and emotions of many adults who have children or who work with youth. The media have specifically reported on instances where MySpace profiles have been linked to a variety of social maladies, including alcohol and drug abuse, hate crimes, planned or executed bombings, planned school shootings, suicide, and even murder (Edds, Lawhon, & Miller, 2006; Hoover, 2006; Matsuoka, 2006; "Soldier Found Dead," 2006; "Teens Arrested," 2006; "Teens Attracted," 2006; Usher, 2006). Figure 4.2 shows some of these headlines.

In addition, the biggest public concern centers on the potential vulnerability of youth to predators and pedophiles. For example, in Oregon in January 2007, two 21-year-old males were accused of having a sexual relationship with a 14-year-old girl after communicating with her through MySpace ("MySpace Predator," 2007). In Connecticut during February 2006, seven underage girls were fondled or had consensual sex with adult men whom they had met on MySpace and who had lied about their age ("MySpace.com Subject," 2006). Also in February 2006, a 26-year-old male from California was arrested for molesting a 14-year-old girl and a 27-year-old man in Maine was imprisoned for a sexual relationship with a 14-year-old girl; and in September 2005, a 37-year-old man from New York was

Figure 4.2   MySpace in the News

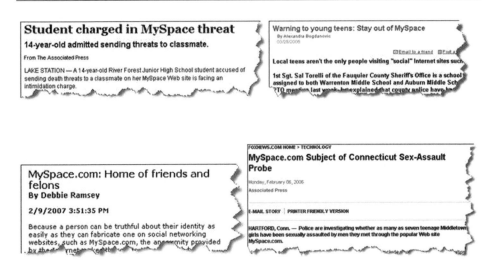

arrested for molesting a 16-year-old girl—all of these incidents reportedly stemming from MySpace-based interactions (Angwin & Steinberg, 2006; Poulsen, 2006). These cases have given credence to parents' worst fears, further contributing to an outcry and opposition from certain adult populations. Figure 4.3 shows one of the many headlines reflecting these concerns.

Figure 4.3   Social Networking Web Site Headlines

Interestingly, despite all of the concerns raised in the media about social networking Web sites, we rarely hear mention of cyberbullying. Adults are (justifiably) concerned about sexual predators and pedophiles, even though the likelihood that youth will be victimized in those ways is very small. There is a far greater likelihood that youth will experience cyberbullying in a way that emotionally or psychologically hurts them. We talk more about this specific risk later in the chapter.

In response to these and other examples of potentially dangerous situations facilitated through MySpace, the site has adopted a number of safety measures in an effort to protect users. For example, it began airing public service announcements in 2006 promoting online safety, as well as rotating online banner ads within its pages. It also hired a chief security officer and has increased and trained its staff to screen and remove problematic personal profiles more capably and to work with law enforcement more effectively on complaints of criminal behavior (Olsen, 2006). Partnerships between MySpace and the National Center for Missing and Exploited Children (NCMEC), as well as with the nonprofit organization WiredSafety.org, have also been initiated to further the safeguarding of youth who venture online (Olsen).

MySpace also recently added new technology designed to block known sex offenders from the site. Of course, this will only be effective if offenders use their real contact information when attempting to sign up for MySpace (see Figure 4.4). In addition, as of 2008, parents can submit their children's e-mail addresses to a database so that MySpace can disallow their use to create a profile page. In our opinion, this seems to be more a symbolic gesture than an actually useful strategy, since youth can simply open up a new e-mail account at a free Web-based e-mail provider within

Figure 4.4   MySpace Battles Sexual Predators

minutes and use that to sign up at a social networking site. MySpace is also in the process of developing free notification software that will inform parents as to the name, age, and location that their children are using to represent themselves within their profile (Angwin, 2007). Finally, as noted above, MySpace users who list their age as over 18 are not allowed to add friends who list their age as under 16, unless the adult knows the teen's full name or e-mail address. Again, these protections will only help if youth are completely forthright with MySpace when it comes to their original e-mail addresses, names, and ages.

> *I never realized how dangerous MySpace could be. . . . It was foolish of me to put that picture of me in my bikini up. One day a guy sent me a message saying that he wanted to "do it" with me, and if I didnt he would tell everyone at school that I'm a little whore . . . I called the police after crying all day and talking to my parents.*
>
> —15-year-old girl from Canada

It deserves comment that none of the safety measures described above is foolproof and all can be easily circumvented due to the unique nature of the Internet. Indeed, some critics would argue that they have very little merit apart from demonstrating to legislators, politicians, educators, and other members of society that "something" is being done and that MySpace and other social networking sites are doing their "best" given the current limitations of technology. With this array of potential risks and the real possibility of youth skirting the safety measures designed to prevent harm from those risks, is it even worth it for adolescents to participate in online social networking? We submit that there are a number of benefits for youth, despite what the popular media would have us believe. In our opinion, these benefits, discussed below, can in fact outweigh the dangers.

POTENTIAL BENEFITS OF SOCIAL NETWORKING

Research has shown that online interaction provides a venue to learn and refine the ability to exercise self-control, to relate with tolerance and respect to others' viewpoints, to express sentiments in a healthy and appropriate manner, and to engage in critical thinking and decision making (Berson et al., 2002). It also promotes self-discovery and identity formation and production among an age group whose self-worth stems largely from peer perceptions, popularity dynamics, and current cultural trends (Boyd, 2006; Calvert, 2002; Erikson, 1950; Leary, Haupt, Strausser, & Chokel, 1998; Leary, Tambor, Terdal, & Downs, 1995; Turkle, 1995). Additionally, online interaction provides a virtual venue in which to share Web-based cultural artifacts like links, pictures, videos, and stories and remain intimately connected with friends regardless of geographical location.

Some schools are even embracing social networking Web sites as instructional tools. Quite a few teachers have created virtual classrooms, which include supplementary information about the topics discussed in the brick-and-mortar environment. For example, an English teacher could have students post their writings online for other students to read and critique. A photography class might post their pictures on sites that allow for expeditious review and evaluation by others. Administrators could even use the site to send messages, newsletters, or other important information very quickly to all members of the school community (Appel, 2007). Some administrators are even exploiting the benefits of social networking Web sites to *build* a strong school "community" and facilitate connections among students across campus (Hass, 2006). In fact, some school districts are developing their own online social networking platforms so that only those directly affiliated with the school have access. This would seemingly alleviate some of the concerns about strangers contacting students or others using posted information to cause harm.

Social networking sites also serve as a largely uncontrolled, unregulated, unconstrained public space in which adolescents can "see and be seen" in ways that support youth socialization and the assimilation of cultural knowledge (Boyd, 2006). For generations, teenagers have sought out places where they can "hang out" without being constantly supervised by adults. It used to be at the malt shop, the skating rink, the neighborhood basketball court, or the local mall. Due to cultural changes and safety concerns in some cities and neighborhoods, these opportunities have gradually disappeared, and public spaces have become largely unwelcoming to adolescents who just want to spend time with friends outside of the home (Boyd, 2007). Many kids these days are only involved in activities that are directly supervised by adults, but they long for time alone with friends. As a result, many youth initially flocked to social networking Web sites because they were perceived to be relatively free from direct adult supervision and control.

In these settings, adolescents have found their socialization needs can be met—and perhaps even augmented due to the benefits that accompany computer-mediated communication. MySpace offered a virtual place where youth wanted to be—a place among friends where they could autonomously be themselves without the presence and intrusion of unwanted others. Indeed, MySpace might be equated to the bar in the 1980s comedy sitcom *Cheers*—a place where everybody knows your name and they're always glad you came (to interact with them). This is the environment that now exists online for youth, and they have fully incorporated it into their lives. Within this (and any) environment, though, there is always the opportunity for interactions to turn mean, ugly, or obscene. Just as cyberbullying evolved with other Internet-based technologies, so has it developed in the online social networking scene.

SOCIAL NETWORKING AND CYBERBULLYING

My daughter was devastated to discover a Web site called the "I hate [name removed] Web site" on Bebo. It took us 5 months for Bebo to acknowledge that the site was willful bullying because they have so many sites. As it was an overseas site her education dept in Queensland stated they could not order it to be removed. The contents were so disgusting that when Bebo kept asking for more details we pasted the entire Web page and sent it, within 28 hours it was removed. Why doesn't Bebo screen the contents of each page? Because there are too many, thus the bullies have found the perfect way to bully until someone dies over this (suicide or murder as my daughter wanted to do) then there'll be an enquiry! Why have these free Web sites anyway? What moral, ethical and uplifting purpose do they serve? Concerned mother from Queensland.

—Submitted anonymously

As previously noted, there are a number of potential threats to youth who expose too much about themselves on the Internet. Even if an adolescent uses the Internet responsibly, someone else could still use the technology to cause the young person harm. As we've mentioned, the likelihood that a sexual predator will contact your child online and exploit your child offline is extremely low. However, vulnerability to cyberbullying through social networking sites (or elsewhere) is much more likely and, therefore, must be addressed. These environments are ideal for online harassment because they are popular and easily and widely accessible and because users and visitors can remain virtually anonymous. Below are some examples of common cyberbullying behaviors that happen on or through social networking Web sites. These were broadly discussed in Chapter 2, and as we pointed out, some are more harmful than others. Nonetheless, it is important for readers to familiarize themselves with the types of cyberbullying that are most common in these specialized settings so they can identify them and then respond appropriately.

Anonymous Commenting

Due to the detached nature of posting messages online, many youth feel freed from the moral constraints of appropriate social behavior. Those who would not say mean things to another person to their face are more than willing to use their keyboard or keypad to type and then send or post these same sentiments. As such, it is quite simple to set up a fictitious account on a social networking site for the sole purpose of posting derogatory or hurtful messages (when those profiles are publicly available) on the profile pages of others. It takes very little time to post a comment on another's page and also requires little skill or forethought, so the potential consequences are often not considered at all (see Figure 4.5.).

Figure 4.5   An Example of a MySpace Comment

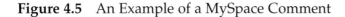

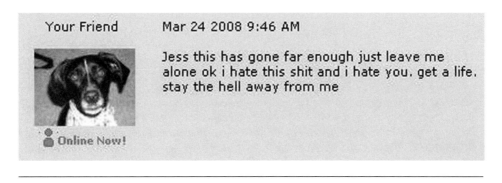

Your Friend   Mar 24 2008 9:46 AM

Jess this has gone far enough just leave me alone ok i hate this shit and i hate you. get a life. stay the hell away from me

Online Now!

Information Spreading

As discussed above, many youth disclose details about themselves online that they wouldn't necessarily share with others in real life. Perhaps they feel as though they are undetectable or untraceable or that adults or strangers won't stumble upon what they reveal. Whatever the reason, a number of adolescents include personal information about themselves on the Internet that can be powerfully used against them. Take, for example, a teenage boy who reveals on his MySpace page that he is gay. Perhaps he feels his site is anonymous enough that others will not be able to identify him. Unfortunately, this information could be potentially damaging to the young man if exposed and disseminated to other students at his school. Another example is shown in Figures 4.6 and 4.7—a young girl has posted a lot of personal information about herself on her MySpace page, which can be used by another to create a non-MySpace (and therefore completely accessible) Web page detailing ways to contact her. This renders her susceptible to victimization by those with ill intent (both cyberbullies and sexual predators). We discuss the issue of personal information disclosure in more detail below when describing the results of some of our recent research on adolescent MySpace use.

My daughter was informed that a Web site was developed about her. When we visited this awful site, I sent her out of the room and read all the horrible comments and untrue stories they had made-up about her. She is ten years old and a sweet person with a big heart. She is trying not to let this bother her, but honestly how does one do that?

It is difficult for me to understand how someone could be so hurtful. Why would you spend the time to create an entire Web page full of ugly things to hurt someone?

—Submitted anonymously

Figure 4.6   Too Much Personal Information Revealed on a MySpace Page

About me:
hey guys wuts up? n2m here jus thought id tell u bout mi self. my name is jeni. im 5'3 brunette brown eyes. i just turned 16 on january 3rd!!! i go to washington high – c/o 10 (yea i know i got a long way). im no longer a freshman im a sophomore baby WOOHOO LOL. i know im young but u know u luv me lol. i lived in florida my hole life. i have the best friends – sara and kelly – i luv you!!!!!! i absolutely love goin to tha beach dancing shopping singing (tho i am no good). i love watchin movies and basketball. i can be crazy hyper at times and i can be serious also. i hate fake bitches that talk shit then cant back it up! there really annoying!!! i also dont like stuck up concieted bitches even tho i get called concieted sometimes but hey its of to have self confidence LOL! i love my family especially my mom without her i dont know wut i would do i love her very much also! im single and lookin for that someone! i dont make the 1st move the guys gotta do it sorry just not my thing, if i do make the 1st move then consider urself lucky becuz it doesnt happen often LOL! i don't like it when guys move fast unless i want them too! if you wana know more leave me a comment or send me a message if you wana talk my cell phone is 588-██████.

Name: Jeni
Birthday: january 3
Birthplace: franksburgh
Current Location: britt
Eye Color: brown
Hair Color: brunette
Height: 5'3
Right or Left Handed: right
Your Heritage: white
The Shoes you wore today: black ballet flats
Your Weakness: boys LOL
Your Fears: my heart bein broke
Your Perfect Pizza: cheeze!
Goal You Would Like To Acheive This Year: get good grades and lose weight
Your Most Overused Phrase on an Instant Messenger: LOL
Thoughts First Waking Up: *someone*
Your Best Physical Feature: my boobs LOL

Figure 4.7   How Personal MySpace Content Can Lead to Cyberbullying

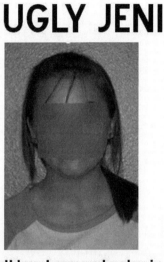

UGLY JENI

Tell her how ugly she is...
Washington High School
Britt, Florida
Phone: 588-****

Rumor Spreading

A common form of adolescent aggression, especially among girls, is directed at relationships and termed "social sabotage." This indirect and more subtle form of bullying has been popularized in recent years by the movies *Odd Girl Out* and *Mean Girls*. One approach is to spread harmful rumors about someone, and Internet-based communications have made this very easy. You'll recall the anecdote with which we began Chapter 1. When Jim decided to take Vada instead of Ali to the homecoming dance, this made Ali extremely jealous and upset. Lonely and distraught at home on the night of the big event, Ali might post a comment on the MySpace profiles of everyone at their school to let them know that just that weekend Vada had slept with the entire drum section of the school band. Indeed, it is common for girls to spread rumors about the promiscuity of other girls, while boys tend to spread rumors about the homosexuality of other boys (Duncan, 1999; Pascoe, 2005; see Figure 4.8).

As mentioned above, MySpace and other social networking sites allow individuals and their profiles to link together within a "group" or sub-community based on a shared interest. For example, everyone who likes the popular television show *American Idol* can belong to a group that

Figure 4.8   Cyberbullying Comment on MySpace

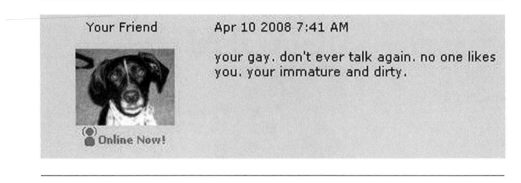

serves as a virtual place in which they can congregate, hang out, and interact. Here, they can send messages publicly and privately about the show to individuals who are also definitely interested in it (i.e., interested enough to join a group formally to talk about the show). Groups can revolve around any topic, interest, or commonality among people. This begs the question: How can cyberbullying occur in one of these subcommunities? An example underscores the very real possibility.

A group of adolescents belonging to a group created around a shared high school might decide one day to humiliate or disparage a girl from their class publicly by posting mean comments about her on the profiles of other students—profiles the girl would surely see when visiting the pages of her "friends" in this group. The aggressors likely wouldn't post comments on her own profile page, because she could delete malicious content before it was publicly displayed. Rather, it would probably appear on another student's profile page who condones or even encourages the bad-mouthing of the girl. Then, even more students who visit that profile page can read those messages and reply in kind with further verbal abuse or by sharing additional humiliating or harmful stories to fan the flame of harassment. When she visits these profile pages and sees the hurtful comments, she is victimized. When other students visit those profile pages—whether or not they actively contribute more to the disparagement—she is victimized again. The public nature of malicious posting and commenting on social networking profile pages easily leads to repeated harm being inflicted on the target.

> Sometimes, I believe, students use MySpace almost as a modern day "slam book" to gang up on other students and leave inappropriate or inconsiderate comments. In the majority of cases, students don't know what to do with their emotions.
>
> —School counselor from Florida

Identity Theft

One particularly debasing form of cyberbullying that occurs via social networking sites involves misrepresenting or stealing the identity of another person. This type of cyberbullying happens when a "friend" acquires access to another's e-mail address and password and uses the information to log onto that account and change the profile by adding embarrassing or false information. A similar strategy involves creating a profile for another without that person's knowledge, consent, or approval. Typically these fictitious profiles include actual pictures of the victim along with some factual details (city, school, age) but are supplemented with false, incriminating, or embarrassing information. You'll recall in Chapter 2, we mentioned the fictional MySpace page we created for "Jenni." That example aptly portrays the ease of impersonating someone else in cyberspace to inflict harm. Another illustration, from "Carolyn MT," was posted on www.blogsafety.com on December 29, 2006:

> *My teenager is also having a problem with MySpace. Someone made another account impersonating her and stole her "about me" and pictures of her friends that were on her site. They, impersonating my daughter, made racist remarks and terrible remarks about her friends. This is causing problems for her from people in her school and strangers responding to those remarks.*

As a final anecdote, two of our acquaintances recently went to a local pizzeria near Detroit, Michigan, for lunch. There were no tables free inside the restaurant, so they decided to take their pizza out to their car and eat lunch there. The next day, one received a harassing message through her MySpace page from someone she didn't seem to know. That message contained insults about her weight and said, "The next time you go with your fat friend to scarf down pizza in your car, you should be more careful because there are always people watching." The harasser then provided a link to a new MySpace page entitled "Lesbian Pig-Out Date" that had been created the day before. Some of the comments on this page—replete with images of pigs and pizza slices—included the following (see Figures 4.9 and 4.10): "I like to meet my even fatta friend for secret rendevoos behind the pizza shack," "We relentlessly shove in oodles of pizza and even more breadsticks," "eating and thinking no one is watching me while I down a large pizza and 42 breadsticks in 2 minutes flat," and "These 2 fat bitches came in to get sum pizza and breadstix the other day and I heard one of em say they was gonna go eat on the side of the building so noone would see their fat asses moosing down da food."

Our friends—who were in their early 20s—were initially appalled but were later able to shrug off the instance of cyberbullying as juvenile and irrelevant. However, if this occurred to a couple of teenagers, we believe they would have suffered greatly from the insults and embarrassment,

Figure 4.9   Cyberbullying Via a MySpace Profile Page

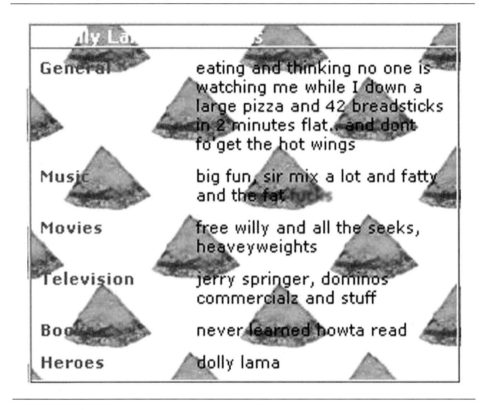

Figure 4.10   Cyberbullying Via a MySpace Blog Entry

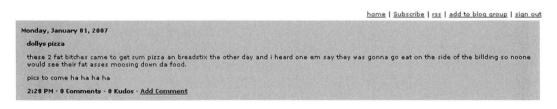

especially considering the comparative immaturity and impressionability of many youth.

Educators who are confronted with problems associated with a MySpace profile are encouraged to contact MySpace. They have become very educator-friendly and have even published "The School Administrators Guide to Understanding MySpace and Resolving Social Networking

Issues," which you can find with your preferred Internet search engine. MySpace also has contact information dedicated specifically to educators (see Box 4.2), and we applaud this and similar efforts that make it easier to resolve the online problems that affect schools and students.

OUR MYSPACE RESEARCH

We initially became interested in MySpace and social networking in general when we heard examples from kids about harassment carried out through various social networking Web sites. Additionally, like many concerned adults, we had heard many horror stories from the media about sexual preda-

Box 4.2 MySpace Contact Information for Educators

E-mail: schoolcare@myspace.com

Phone: (310) 969–7398

Fax: (310) 969–7394

tors and pedophiles who apparently use the site to lure victims. We first consulted the academic literature to see what empirical studies had been done about adolescent online social networking. We weren't surprised to see that there hadn't been any empirical research conducted about these online communities because they are so new.

Despite the lack of research, however, we still hear on a daily basis unsubstantiated claims about adolescent activities on MySpace that place them in harm's way. We recall reading a headline somewhere that said "millions of kids [were] at risk" on MySpace. And so we asked ourselves: Upon what information is this claim based? Where are the data that back up this statement? Interested in more thoroughly investigating the extent to which youth were rendering themselves vulnerable to victimization by what they revealed on MySpace, we analyzed the content of a random sample of approximately 2,500 adolescent profiles (Hinduja & Patchin, 2008b).

To be sure, we braced ourselves for the worst. Based on what we had heard from the media, we expected there to be widespread revelation of personal, private, and provocative information (see Figure 4.11). While we did see examples of profiles that included many of those things, the situation wasn't nearly as bad as we anticipated. In fact, almost 40 percent of the profiles that we randomly selected were set to private, thereby denying us access to the information contained therein. Of the remaining profiles (1,475), over 80 percent listed the creator's current city, about one-quarter indicated current school, and fewer than 9 percent included full name. Only 4 out of the 1,475 profiles included a phone number.

Of additional concern, though, were the reports of partying and experimentation with illicit substances. Over 18 percent of youth reported using alcohol, and 7.5 percent reported smoking cigarettes, while less than 2 percent admitted to using marijuana. Finally, about 1 out of 5 profiles (19.9 percent) included swear words, and 1 out of 20 (5.4 percent) included a photograph of the profile's creator in underwear or a swim-suit. While there is no way for us to substantiate the validity of the infor-mation contained on these profiles, it is reasonable to assume that the vast majority is truthful.

Figure 4.11   MySpace and Provocative Pictures of Youth

As previously explained, much of this information could be used to harm youth. Listing phone numbers and e-mail addresses provides would-be bullies with the means to contact targets and directly harass them. Posting provocative or incriminating pictures or information can also be used as ammunition to corroborate rumor spreading or verbal or textual abuse and may even foster additional informal and formal troubles from parents, teachers, administrators, and law enforcement. Pictures can also be manipulated by Photoshop or a similar program (see Chapter 2) or altered using digital imaging software to make it appear as though the user is doing something he or she wasn't doing. The well-known example of "Moshzilla" described in Chapter 2 is one example of this form of cyberbullying.

In the summer of 2007, we revisited the same group of profiles from 2006 to identify patterns in adolescent MySpace participation over time. Our hope was that the data would demonstrate an increasing trend towards safe and responsible Internet use, especially in the wake of online safety and security strategies gradually being implemented by adults and organizations. This was largely the case, although there were some inter-esting secondary findings. First, 10 percent of the profiles had been deleted between the times of our analyses. This means that either youth are abandoning MySpace in general or they are creating new profiles using different e-mail addresses or profile names. Also noteworthy was the finding that the most active users included significantly fewer swear words on their profiles and in their comments, suggesting that those who frequent the site most often are seemingly "cleaning up" their profiles.

With respect to identifying information, about the same number of profiles included the youth's current city, while significantly fewer revealed the school they attended. Two pieces of data—first name and full name—were disclosed more often in the 2007 profiles. To be sure, simply having a teenager's name, current city, picture, and school is all that someone might need to easily locate the individual (Hinduja & Patchin, 2008b). We were pleased to see that more youth were setting their profile page to private (a 13 percent increase), while only a small proportion (5 percent) changed their profile from private to public. As a final note, males were more likely to have their profiles viewable to the public, while females were more likely to restrict access to their profiles.

While our analysis indicated that a relatively small number of teenagers are still placing themselves at risk with the kinds of information they are revealing online, we believe that social networking sites are a *comparatively* safe place for youth to hang out. Overall, the data suggest that adolescents have learned to be more responsible and guarded with their information on the World Wide Web. And, assuming educators and parents teach their kids how to use the sites responsibly, any problems or added risks to their personal safety are unlikely. This is why we recommend that adults and kids engage in online activities together at times. Do you think kids would include curse words and discussions of parties and substance use on their profiles if they knew their parents were sometimes checking up on them? Of course not.

Some adults think they can simply forbid the children under their care from participating on MySpace, Facebook, Bebo, Orkut, Friendster, or any other site (or even worse, prohibit them from using the Internet at all!). The truth is, if children want to participate, they will find a way—even if access is banned at school and/or home. Even if putting up a unified front, teachers and parents cannot supervise kids 100 percent of the time. They will log on at the library, at a friend's house, or somewhere else. Why fight it? Why not instead teach teenagers how to use social networking sites (and other online environments) conscientiously? There certainly are more dangerous activities in which they could be participating.

That being said, we respect your authority as an educator or parent to "just say no." We encourage you, however, to discuss with youth the reasons why you do not want them interacting in a Web-based social environment. Simply banning the site isn't going to work. Discussing with them *why* it is potentially dangerous is the key—regardless of whether you allow them to participate.

It is true that predators troll social networking sites looking for victims. It is also true that victimization can happen at school any day of the week (via fights, shootings, sexual assaults, etc.). Just because these things might occur (even relatively rarely) at school doesn't mean we should ban students from going to school any more than we should ban students from using the Internet. Furthermore, most responsible adults would not allow children to explore a new or potentially dangerous neighborhood without supervision or guidance. The same sage approach should be used as we attempt to guide the online experiences of youth today.

> *I believe when information is presented to school staff, we need to investigate the allegation to protect the student(s). If I, as a Principal see anything [on MySpace] that would affect my school, then I will deal with it as I would any neighborhood issues affecting my school.*

> —Principal of an elementary school in Florida

BEING SAFE ON SOCIAL NETWORKING WEB SITES

Eliminating the possibility that the youth in your school will be cyberbullied on social networking sites is not as easy as simply preventing them from accessing such sites at school. Even though this strategy is often employed by school districts across the United States (and is an important first step) and even if the parents at home implement the same restriction, it doesn't necessarily insulate kids from the harassing behaviors that occur via the site. For example, as in the case of 17-year-old Canadian teenager David Knight, a hateful Web site that called him an immature, dirty pedophile was online and viewable for months before he became aware of it. When he found out about the site, it devastated him emotionally and psychologically to the point that he had to finish his senior year at home (Leishman, 2005). The point is that youth can be victimized online even when they are not online.

Most of the suggestions we give to educators about how to help keep their students safe in cyberspace are commonsense recommendations that they intuitively already know (see Chapter 6). Most importantly, clear rules must be set. Adolescents must know with certainty what they are and are not allowed to do online (see the sample "Internet Use Contract" in Resource D for direction in establishing important rules). When the opportunity presents itself, it is crucial to discuss the potential dangers and risks of online interaction. Instead of simply forbidding the use of social networking sites (or the Internet) altogether, it is extremely important that youth are able to internalize, learn from, and act on your guidance and wisdom. In addition, educators should not be afraid to ask students about their specific social networking practices. From that foundation, deeper inquiry into possible experiences with cyberbullying can be made.

We need to teach people about SNet-iquette (Social Network etiquette), and the positive and negative effects of their online "behavior" and how they are creating an online "digital footprint." I believe educational institutions should be "leading the way" in educating people about these things. Therefore, by encouraging staff and students to use these sites as educational tools, we are encouraging the conversations necessary for people to work out what is, and what is not, appropriate in an online environment.

—Sue Waters, Lecturer at the University of
Western Australia

Concerning adolescents, it is important to remind them that they would never leave a personal diary out in the open for an inquisitive sibling or parent (or complete stranger) to peruse. Similarly, they should take care not to expose themselves in an online environment—even if they think they know who has access to the information. Also, youth must understand the permanence of profile pages and any information shared in cyberspace due to page archives and search engine caches. Simply changing or updating one's profile page does not completely delete copies of older versions stored on other Internet-connected computers.

Box 4.3 lists several commonsense strategies for safe online social networking. In general, all who use these sites (or any publicly accessible site for that matter) should keep these guidelines in mind. As an educator, you share some of the responsibility in conveying this information to the youth you supervise. (See also the MySpace safety reminders in Figure 4.12.)

In addition, all youth should fully grasp that photographs and other personal data presented within profile pages may possibly be used against them—by cyberbullies, their parents, school administrators, potential employers, college admissions officers, and even the police. Educators must emphasize to their students the importance of setting profile pages to private so that the students can control who views their content. They should also inquire as to the level of familiarity that teenagers have with their online "friends" and caution youth that many real-world victimizations of youth happen at the hands of people that they "know"—but do not know well (Finkelhor, Turner, Ormrod, & Hamby, 2005; Hotaling & Finkelhor, 1990; Magid & Collier, 2007). And, as we've reiterated, the potential for cyberbullying and similar forms of peer harassment is great even if the possibility of real-world harm is rare (Burgess-Proctor et al., in press; Hinduja & Patchin, 2007, 2008a; Patchin & Hinduja, 2006).

Box 4.3 Strategies for Safer Social Networking

Assume that everyone has access to your profile (parents, teachers, future employers, and law enforcement), even if you have your profile restricted to "friends only." Don't discuss things you wouldn't want them to know about. Don't use language you wouldn't use in front of your parents. Even so, make sure you set your profile to "private" so that you can control who has easy access to your information.

Use discretion when putting pictures (or any content for that matter) on your profile. Your friends might think that picture of you acting silly at the party last night is hilarious, but how will your parents or a potential employer react? Also, remember that when your friend takes your picture, it may end up on your friend's profile for all to see.

Assume that people will use the information on your profile to cause you harm. Don't put anything online you wouldn't want your worst enemy to find out about. Also, don't add people to your friend or contact network unless you know them in real life. Even if you think you know them, be skeptical. Kids often think it is cool to accumulate and have a million "friends." Just remember that these people have open access to all of your posted content and information.

Assume there are predators out there trying to find you based on the information you provide on your profile. Think like a predator. What information on your profile identifies who you are, where you hang out, where you live? Never post this kind of information anywhere online. Your friends know how to find you.

You may be held responsible for inappropriate content on your profile that is in violation of the "Terms of Service" or "Acceptable Use Policies" of the Internet service provider or Web site(s) you use. Moreover, school districts across the country are revising their policies to allow them to discipline students for online behavior that can be linked to a disruption in the classroom environment—even if you wrote the content at home from your own computer.

Figure 4.12   Safety Reminder From MySpace

Hey folks a friendly reminder about Safety!

MySpace is a public space. Don't post anything you wouldn't want the world to know (e.g. your phone number, address, instant messenger screen name, or specific whereabouts). Don't post any nudity, violent, or offensive material, or copyrighted images. If you violate these terms, your account will be deleted.

People aren't always who they say they are. Exercise caution when communicating with strangers and avoid meeting people in person whom you do not fully know. If you must meet someone, do it in a public place and bring a friend or a trusted adult.

Harassment, hate speech, and inappropriate content should be reported. If you feel someone's behavior is inappropriate, react. Talk with a trusted adult, or report it to MySpace or the authorities.

If you ask them, most kids will think they don't reveal much personal or identifying information about themselves in cyberspace. It is critical, though, for concerned adults to *make sure* they are responsibly using the Internet. Remember Logan, the MySpace user quoted at the beginning of this chapter? A brief review of her profile gives the would-be bully a wealth of information about her that could be used to inflict harm. In fact, Logan filled out and publicly posted "getting to know you" surveys that revealed almost one hundred unique pieces of personal information. Her middle and last name is [removed], and she was born on November 11, 1993. She lists her age as 17 (although if she were born in 1993, she is actually 14 or 15). She was born and lives in [removed] and goes to "GNMS." A quick Google search indicates that "GNMS" is [removed]. As noted in her "About Me" section quoted above, she has brown hair and brown eyes. She is 4'11", has two siblings, likes cheese pizza, and prefers Coke over Pepsi and chocolate over vanilla.

While most of the information she includes on her profile is harmless, the fact that she includes her full name, city, school, and some identifying physical characteristics makes her susceptible to all sorts of harassment. Moreover, malicious youth can take the "harmless" information she includes and spin it in mean and nasty ways. For example, she lists her face as her "best physical feature" and her "biggest fear" as spiders. She also provides two pictures of herself that could easily be altered to make it look as though she is engaging in provocative behaviors. To be sure, Logan's profile is about as typical as they come. She doesn't include her personal e-mail address, instant messaging name, or cell phone number. Nevertheless, her profile is open for the public to view (including us as researchers). While we have no ill intent toward Logan, others may. In our opinion, she—and the adults in her life responsible for her—must do more to reduce her susceptibility to cyberbullying and other forms of victimization.

SUMMARY

With a particular focus on MySpace, this chapter has described online social networking—the latest major trend among adolescents. While we don't go into the details of how to set up a MySpace profile (others do a thorough job of this; see Magid & Collier [2007]), we do encourage educators and parents to explore the online environments that adolescents frequent to understand better what they are doing. For example, parents should enlist the help of their children in setting up their own social networking profiles and then become online "friends" with their children. We suspect that they will learn a great deal about what their children are into and can then point out inappropriate or potentially dangerous behaviors or content.

In closing, we would like to reiterate that while MySpace is currently the most popular online social networking site and, therefore, served as the central focus of this chapter, MySpace may no longer be as popular next month. Indeed, by the time you read this, another Internet-based interactive environment may have attracted the largest market share of youth. That said, the principles described throughout this chapter that reference MySpace are expected to be relevant when considering any online social networking platform. The potential for abuse, aggression, and interpersonal harm remains the same, and the issues that contribute to that potential are relatively constant.

Social networks are online services that bring together people by organizing them around a common interest and by providing an interactive environment of photos, blogs, user profiles, and messaging systems. When people of divergent viewpoints, backgrounds, traditions, and experiences are brought together, bullying can occur—just as in any real-world context. It is hoped that this chapter has served to clarify the positives and negatives associated with this new realm of interaction and will meaningfully assist educators in their efforts to promote safe participation and reduce victimization.

QUESTIONS FOR REFLECTION

1. Why are adolescents (and many adults) attracted to social networking Web sites?

2. Why does MySpace receive most of the attention?

3. Do you think the benefits of online social networking outweigh the risks? Why or why not?

4. What characteristics of social networking Web sites make them a popular environment of the cyberbully?

5. What advice would you give a younger student who is setting up a social networking Web profile for the first time?

5

Legal Issues

It's pretty difficult to figure out what to do. The law seems so complex. I just know that we have got to do something, because it [cyberbullying] is leading to other problems on my campus and under my watch.

—Administrator at Florida middle school

In 1998, a junior at Westlake High School in Ohio created a Web site from home that disparaged his band teacher as "an overweight middle-aged man who doesn't like to get haircuts" and who "'likes to involve himself in everything you do" (McManus, 1998, ¶ 2). When made aware, the school proclaimed that the Web site disrupted the school environment, undermined the teacher's authority, and violated a rule in the student conduct handbook, which stated that "students shall not physically assault, vandalize, damage, or attempt to damage the property of a school employee or his/her family or demonstrate physical, written, or verbal disrespect/ threat" (Hudson, 2000, § III.A).

The student was consequently suspended for ten days, but he countered that the suspension violated his constitutional right to free speech and sued the district for $550,000. The district court agreed with the constitutional violation, submitting that "the involvement by the school in punishing plaintiff for posting an Internet Web site critical of defendant . . . raises the ugly specter of Big Brother" (*O'Brien v. Westlake City School Board of Education*, 1988).

As a result, school officials had to expunge the suspension from the student's records and pay him $30,000 to drop the lawsuit. The superintendent of the school district also wrote a letter of apology, stating

> I wish to offer my sincere apology for the misunderstanding which resulted in the imposition of this disciplinary action. Please know that it is neither the Board's policy nor the administration's practice to abridge students' legitimate exercise of their constitutional rights. (Hudson, 2000, § III.A)

It was also acknowledged that "the Board recognized that this right [to freedom of speech] extends to students who, on their own time and with their own resources, engage in speech on the Internet" (Hudson, § III.A).

When considering the details of this case, many questions may arise. Could the school have restricted the student's speech if the Web site had been created on campus? At what point do insults and disparagement of another person posted online cross a threshold where the behavior can and must be punished? When does harm caused by cyberbullying warrant legal action? Why did the school district have to pay tens of thousands of dollars and issue such a humbling formal apology?

Before attempting to clarify some of these issues through the discussion of relevant case law, it is important to note at the outset of this chapter that we are not lawyers. Even those who are and who specialize in student speech cases struggle with the complexities arising from the rapid advancement of computer technology and the Internet. Because the law is continuously evolving and little crystal clear consensus has been reached regarding key constitutional and civil rights questions, school districts are given the task of addressing problematic online behaviors committed by students while attempting to protect themselves from civil liability.

Many school district personnel are reluctant to get involved in cyberbullying cases because they fear they will overstep their legal authority. Unfortunately, some school administrators seem too focused on protecting the status quo at their institutions rather than protecting the youth they supervise, educate, and mentor. Similarly, law enforcement officials are hesitant to get involved in cyberbullying cases unless there are crystal clear violations of criminal law (e.g., harassment, stalking, felonious assault). It is important to remember, however, that inaction *is* action. School administrators have a moral (and often legal) obligation to take action when harassment is brought to their attention (Shariff & Hoff, 2007). While specific strategies for responding to cyberbullying situations are detailed in Chapter 7, this chapter will help frame the later discussion by highlighting legal issues present in cases involving online or electronic behaviors.

The following text describes some of the critical legal questions faced by school administrators and seeks to illuminate the procedural and disciplinary issues related to electronic communication generally and cyberbullying specifically. We begin with a discussion of several foundational court rulings and legislative actions that have shaped the way schools intervene and discipline the behavior of students. These are important insofar as they have served as precedent in more recent cases involving electronic harassment. We then summarize a number of these court findings. This should equip you with an appreciation of the central issues upon which courts focus when deciding the outcome of such cases.

Finally, many states have proposed or passed legislation related to cyberbullying and the school's role in addressing and preventing its relevance among its student body. We have reviewed numerous legislative actions and policies with the intent of parsing out the most essential components. We have then worked to present them as a guiding framework for school professionals who need a helping hand in creating or modifying such a document. This framework encompasses what we believe is an ideal way to define *cyberbullying;* cover how it can result in formal discipline; and discuss how it should be investigated, reported, and prevented on a general, prescriptive level.

IMPORTANT JUDICIAL RULINGS AND LEGISLATIVE ACTIONS APPLICABLE TO THE SCHOOL

Harassment, Discrimination, and Civil Rights

Harassment has always occurred among individuals, but it has been explicitly outlawed for only about the last half century in the United States. The monumental matter of harassment (in the form of discrimination) and public education first arose in the Civil Rights Act of 1964. Among its other aspects, this law specifically outlawed segregation based on race in the school system but more generally led to the prohibition of harassment based on race, ethnicity, or religion in public places.

The Civil Rights Act was followed the equally important Title IX of the Educational Amendments of 1972, which involved the intersection of sexual harassment and public education in the United States. Specifically, Title IX states:

> *No person in the United States shall, on the basis of sex, be excluded from participation in, be denied the benefits of, or be subjected to discrimination under any education program or activity receiving Federal financial assistance.*

Collectively, these legislative rulings compel school administrators to take action when they observe or are made aware of behavior that is discriminatory in nature or that violates the civil rights of students or staff members.

Two recent Supreme Court rulings involving sexual harassment reinforce these principles. In *Gebser v. Lago Vista Independent School District* (1998), a student who had been in a sexual relationship with a teacher sued the school district for sexual harassment because the district failed to provide her with an avenue for reporting the abuse. The court ruled that school districts can be held liable for damages under Title IX if "an employee with supervisory power over the offending employee actually knew of the abuse, had the power to end it, and failed to do so" (*Gebser v. Lago Vista Independent School District*). In the end, the court ruled there was no evidence a district official with the authority to take corrective action knew about the misconduct and failed to respond. With the decision, though, the Court reaffirmed that if deliberately indifferent to harassment or discrimination by a teacher against a student, a school district could be held responsible.

The court supported this ruling in *Davis v. Monroe County Board of Education* (1999), where evidence demonstrated that school officials did in fact know of the sexual harassment of a student by another student and failed to respond adequately. Also noteworthy in the *Davis* ruling was the Court's reminder that "the common law, too, has put schools on notice that they may be held responsible under state law for their failure to protect students from the tortious acts of third parties" (*Davis v. Monroe County Board of Education*).

These two rulings have seemingly opened the door for federal and state courts to extend this standard broadly to issues involving other forms of harassment and bullying and, in principle, to cases involving cyberbullying that have implications at school. As such, school districts may be found liable and responsible for monetary damages if they become aware of discrimination or violations of civil rights and fail to take appropriate action (that is, if they are deliberately indifferent).

Educator's Ability to Restrict and Discipline Student Behavior and Speech on Campus

Court rulings have provided some direction to school districts in terms of when they can discipline students for their behavior or speech. A few landmark Supreme Court cases warrant discussion here. First, in *Tinker v. Des Moines Independent Community School District* (1969), the Court ruled that the suspensions of three public school students for wearing black armbands to protest the Vietnam War violated the Free Speech clause of the First Amendment. Specifically, Justice Fortas, writing for the majority, stated:

A prohibition against expression of opinion, without any evidence that the rule is necessary to avoid substantial interference with school discipline or the rights of others, is not permissible under the First and Fourteenth Amendments. (*Tinker et al. v. Des Moines Independent Community School District et al.*)

The key phrase in this opinion is "substantial interference," and because the school district could not articulate that such a disruption occurred, the students' behavior could not be restricted. According to the rule of law, then, for school district personnel to intervene in similar situations, they must demonstrate that such behaviors "materially and substantially interfere with the requirements of appropriate discipline in the operation of the school" (*Tinker et al. v. Des Moines Independent Community School District et al.*). Box 5.1 highlights a key legal principle involved in the *Tinker* case.

While the quiet, passive expression of a political viewpoint in the *Tinker* case was upheld by the Court, in *Bethel School District v. Fraser* (1986), the Court ruled that not all expressions are protected by the First Amendment. The Court considered the case of Matthew Fraser, a student who used "an elaborate, graphic, and explicit sexual metaphor" in a nominating speech at a school assembly for a friend who was running for student body vice president (*Bethel School District v. Fraser,*). The school responded by suspending Fraser for three days.

The District Court and Circuit Court of Appeals both sided with Fraser, citing the *Tinker* ruling. The Supreme Court, however, reversed the decision, arguing that there is a substantive difference between a nondisruptive expression and "speech or action that intrudes upon the work of the schools or the rights of other students" (*Bethel School District v. Fraser*). Moreover, the Court maintained that schools have an interest in "teaching students the boundaries of socially appropriate behavior" and therefore must play a role in restricting behavior and speech that is considered "highly offensive or highly threatening to others" (*Bethel School District v. Fraser*). Highly offensive or threatening material communicated electronically *from school grounds,* then, may fall under the *Fraser* ruling and, therefore, may be restricted.

Another classic Supreme Court case foundational for understanding whether schools can respond in contemporary incidents is *Hazelwood School District et al. v. Kuhlmeier et al.* (1988). Here, the Court reviewed the

> **Box 5.1 Important Legal Principle**
>
> "It can hardly be argued that either students or teachers shed their constitutional rights to freedom of speech or expression at the schoolhouse gate."
>
> —*Tinker et al. v. Des Moines Independent Community School District et al..*

extent to which school personnel may censor the contents of the school newspaper. The court first reiterated its earlier ruling in *Tinker:*

> Students in the public schools do not "shed their constitutional rights to freedom of speech or expression at the schoolhouse gate." They cannot be punished merely for expressing their personal views on the school premises—whether "in the cafeteria, or on the playing field, or on the campus during the authorized hours,"— unless school authorities have reason to believe that such expression will "substantially interfere with the work of the school or impinge upon the rights of other students." (*Hazelwood School District et al. v. Kuhlmeier et al.*)

Next, the Court restated its earlier ruling in *Fraser*—that the school environment is fundamentally unique and that school officials can in fact censor speech or behaviors on campus that the government could not necessarily interfere with outside of school. As such, the Court ruled that

> educators do not offend the First Amendment by exercising editorial control over the style and content of student speech in school-sponsored expressive activities so long as their actions are reasonably related to legitimate pedagogical concerns. (*Hazelwood School District et al. v. Kuhlmeier et al.*)

This case may be particularly appropriate when considering electronic material created and/or disseminated using school-owned computers or other technological devices or within or through content that is ostensibly or actually endorsed by the school. School districts have the authority to discipline students who misuse *school-owned* property, resources, or materials to cause harm to other individuals, as long as their policies clearly proscribe such behavior.

A recent case involving student expressions on or near the school campus, *Morse v. Frederick* (2007), has received a great deal of public and legislative attention. In 2002, a Juneau, Alaska, high school senior named Joseph Frederick displayed a banner that read "BONG HiTS 4 JESUS" during the Winter Olympics torch relay. Students were released from class and lined both sides of the street as the torch passed through the city. Frederick unfurled the sign with the help of other students across the street from the school (not on school property). Upon seeing the act, the school principal grabbed the banner and suspended Frederick for ten days. Frederick promptly sued, and the case was argued before the U.S. Supreme Court in 2007.

The majority opinion concluded that Frederick's First Amendment rights were not violated. This decision was based on the arguments that

(1) the banner was displayed during a school event, which made the expression "school speech" rather than "free speech," (2) the banner undeniably referenced illegal drugs and could be reasonably interpreted as advocating use of illegal drugs, and (3) that the government (and, by extension, schools) has an important and compelling interest in deterring drug use by students (*Morse v. Frederick*). As such, the Court reaffirmed the school's ability to discipline students for inappropriate speech. Even though the students were off campus, the court ruled that the activity was a school event (basically, like a field trip) and they could, therefore, be disciplined.

Several other cases have more specifically addressed the extent to which schools can discipline students for off-campus speech or behavior. Since the majority of cyberbullying behaviors occur away from school, it is important to understand what the school can and should do in these cases.

Educator's Ability to Restrict and Discipline Student Behavior and Speech Off Campus

> *In our district, we are seeing students using the Internet to deface teachers . . . writing ludicrous, hideous things about them and posting their pictures as well. And we are seeing students bullying other students, resulting in the victims taking their own life. It seems we do not have any recourse for these online student behaviors that occur off-campus.*
>
> —Principal from Florida

It is important to point out that each of the above-referenced cases involved behavior that occurred *on or near school property*. Traditionally, the courts have compartmentalized expressions by students on campus as appropriate for restrictions, while disallowing constraints on off-campus speech:

> When school officials are authorized only to punish speech on school property, the student is free to speak his mind when the school day ends. In this manner, the community is not deprived of the salutary effects of expression, and educational authorities are free to establish an academic environment in which the teaching and learning process can proceed free of disruption. Indeed, our willingness to grant school officials substantial autonomy within their academic domain rests in part on the confinement of that power within the metes and bounds of the school itself. (*Thomas v. Board of Education, Granville Central School District*, 1979)

This principle was clearly illustrated in the case of *Klein v. Smith* (1986), which involved student-on-staff harassment. In a restaurant parking lot after school hours in 1986, a high school student showed one of his teachers his middle finger. Upon hearing of the incident, the school administration suspended the student for ten days for "vulgar or extremely inappropriate language or conduct directed to a staff member" (*Klein v. Smith*). This promptly led to civil action by the student, who claimed that his First Amendment free speech rights had been violated.

In an interestingly worded opinion, the Court majority ruled that "the First Amendment protection of freedom of expression may not be made a casualty of the effort to force-feed good manners to the ruffians among us." The Court concluded that school officials failed to demonstrate that the vulgar gesture had negatively impacted the school environment or its orderly operation (see Box 5.2).

> ### Box 5.2 Important Legal Principle
>
> School officials cannot discipline students for off-campus speech or behavior with which they simply do not agree unless the school environment is significantly affected.

As is evident in the aforementioned rulings, several key issues surface when considering the ability of school districts to restrict off-campus student speech. While none of these cases involves cyberbullying or electronic communication specifically, you can clearly see how the principles raised can be applied to contemporary issues that educators face. We next turn our discussion to a few recent examples of cases that do involve school districts responding to the electronic behaviors of their students.

RECENT CASES INVOLVING ELECTRONIC HARASSMENT AND SCHOOLS

The first major case involving online harassment by a student was *Beussink v. Woodland R-IV School District* (1998). The case involved a junior in Marble Hill, Missouri, who created a personal Web site at his home that denigrated the school's administration using vulgar but not defamatory language. After being suspended for ten days, Beussink filed suit. The U.S. District Court ruled that his First Amendment rights had been violated and that the suspension was unconstitutional because the school district could not show that it "was caused by something more than a mere desire to avoid the discomfort and unpleasantness that always accompany an unpopular viewpoint" (*Beussink v. Woodland R-IV School District*). School administrators, then, cannot discipline students for off-campus behavior or speech simply because it is unpleasant. As articulated above, they must demonstrate that the behavior or speech resulted in a substantial disruption *at school.*

In *Emmett v. Kent School District No. 415* (2000), the U.S. District Court for the Western District of Washington reviewed a case where a senior created a Web page from home entitled the "unofficial Kentlake High Home

Page," which included mock obituaries of students and a mechanism for visitors to vote on "who should die next." Interestingly, it included a disclaimer that the page was not sponsored by the school and was for entertainment purposes only. Nonetheless, after an evening news story referenced the page as containing a "hit list," the student was placed on emergency expulsion (although this disciplinary action was later reduced to a five-day suspension) for intimidation, harassment, disruption to the educational process, and violation of school copyright.

The court ruled that the school had overstepped its bounds, because the Web site was not produced at school or using school-owned equipment. Even though the court recognized that the intended audience included members of the high school, "the speech was entirely outside the school's supervision or control" (*Emmett v. Kent School District No. 415*). Furthermore, the court ruled that the school district failed to demonstrate that the Web site was "intended to threaten anyone, did actually threaten anyone, or manifested any violent tendencies whatsoever" (*Emmett v. Kent School District No. 415*). That is, the school district was unable to show that anyone listed on the site was actually intimidated or threatened by the site or that the site resulted in a significant disturbance at school. With these rulings, the court reminded school districts to tread lightly when intervening in the off-campus activities of students.

Many courts have held that school districts are allowed to intervene in situations where off-campus speech is clearly harassing and threatening to students or staff and/or disruptive to the learning environment. For example, in *J.S. v. Bethlehem Area School District* (2000), the Commonwealth Court of Pennsylvania reviewed a case in which J. S. was expelled from school for creating a Web page that included threatening and derogatory comments about Kathleen Fulmer, an English teacher. The Web page included lists for "Why Fulmer Should Be Fired" and "Why Should She Die." Reasons listed included "She shows off her fat F—ing legs," "The fat f— smokes," and "She's a bitch." The writer of the Web page also added: " . . . give me $20.00 to help pay for the hitman" (*J. S. v. Bethlehem Area School District*).

Fulmer indicated she had been traumatized by the incident, which had led to physical problems (headaches and loss of appetite, sleep, and weight) and psychological problems (anxiety and depression) and to an inability to teach for the rest of the year. The school district also argued that the Web page "had a demoralizing impact on the school community" and "caused an effect on the staff . . . comparable to the effect on the school community of the death of a student or staff member because there was a feeling of helplessness and a plummeting morale" (*J. S. v. Bethlehem Area School District*). Based on these factors, the court upheld the expulsion of J. S. Fulmer also sued the family of J. S. in civil court and was awarded a $500,000 judgment (Conn, 2004). Furthermore, law enforcement got involved, as the local police and the Federal Bureau of Investigation conducted investigations to ascertain the validity of J. S.'s threat. They eventually determined it not to be credible.

Box 5.3 Important Legal Principle

"School officials [can] discipline students for conduct occurring off of school premises where it is established that the conduct materially and substantially interferes with the educational process."

—*J. S. v. Bethlehem Area School District* (2000)

In a similar case, eighth grader Aaron Wisniewski created a graphic icon of his English teacher's head being shot with a bullet from a gun along with the text "Kill Mr. Vandermolen" (*Wisniewski v. Board of Education of the Weedsport Central School District*, 2007). He then sent the icon via instant message to 15 of his friends, among whom it circulated for three weeks before the teacher was informed. After hearing from the distressed teacher, the principal of the school decided to suspend Wisniewski—an action that prompted a lawsuit from his parents. The district court found in favor of the school district, but the case was appealed by Wisniewski's parents to a higher court. In July of 2007, the U.S. Court of Appeals for 2nd Circuit upheld the lower court's decision, arguing that the icon represented a threat that the student should have known would cause a disruption to the school environment (*Wisniewski v. Board of Education of the Weedsport Central School District*).

The courts in the *J. S.* and the *Wisniewski* cases ruled that schools do have the authority to discipline students when speech articulated or behavior committed off campus results in (or has a high probability of resulting in) a clear disruption of the classroom environment (see Box 5.3). The appellate courts in these cases referenced the *Tinker, Fraser,* and *Kuhlmeier* cases to argue that student expressions can be suppressed if and when they materially and substantially disrupt the mission and discipline of the school or infringe upon the rights of others. This was again exemplified in a recent case in western Washington.

In June 2006, a senior at Kentridge High School posted a link from his MySpace page to a video on YouTube that made fun of a teacher's hygiene, organizational habits, body weight, and classroom conduct. The footage, covertly recorded in class, also involves close-up shots of her buttocks and a student making faces, giving her "bunny ears," and giving pelvic thrusts in her direction from behind. The students responsible were suspended for 40 days, with 20 days "held in abeyance" if a research paper was completed during the suspension. The court in *Requa v. Kent School District No. 415* (2007) upheld the suspension, pointing to the *Tinker* and *Fraser* cases:

> The school is not required to establish that an actual educational discourse was disrupted by the student's activity. The "work and discipline of the school" includes the maintenance of a civil and

respectful atmosphere towards teachers and students alike—demeaning, derogatory, sexually suggestive behavior towards non-suspecting teacher in a classroom poses a disruption of that mission whenever it occurs. (*Requa v. Kent School District No. 415*)

The crux of the argument in favor of the school district involved (1) that covert video recording in the classroom violated school policy and (2) that the video substantially and materially disrupted the work and discipline of the school. It is also important to point out that the sexually suggestive "pelvic thrusts" could be construed as sexual harassment and should, therefore, be disciplined based on the relevant district policy. A school resource officer from Minnesota told us that his own district successfully prosecuted a student for disorderly conduct when a video surfaced of him walking behind a teacher in a classroom making pelvic thrusts. Again, it is imperative that schools intervene and discipline students for behaviors that may constitute harassment based on sex or race. Failure to do so may open the district up to liability as discussed above.

Another recent case, *Layshock v. Hermitage School District* (2006) examined "whether a school district can punish a student for posting from his grandmother's home computer a non-threatening, non-obscene MySpace profile making fun of the school principal." While the court noted that the act of creating the profile page was in fact protected by the First Amendment, it became punishable by the school district when it resulted in an "actual disruption of the day-to-day operation" of the school. According to the school district, the page was repeatedly accessed by students at school and forced the school to shut down its computer system for five days. The district also argued that many school staff were required to devote an extraordinary amount of time to this particular problem, that many students were unable to use school computers for legitimate educational purposes, and that a number of classes had to be cancelled. Consequently, the lower court issued the following statement:

> Under these circumstances Plaintiffs' actions appear to have substantially disrupted school operations and interfered with the right of others, which, along with his apparent violations of school rules, would provide a sufficient legal basis for Defendants' actions. (*Layshock v. Hermitage School District*)

But that wasn't the end of the story. The U.S. District Court judge reversed himself in July 2007. The court found that multiple MySpace profile pages had been created of the school principal and that the school district could not specify exactly which profile led to the disruption on campus. Also, upon more carefully examining the facts of the case, the court found that the disruption was not substantial, nor did it undermine the school's basic educational mission. Finally, the school was not able to demonstrate that the profile created by Layshock—rather than the investigative response of administrators—led to the disruption at school. Essentially the school was unable to provide adequate evidence of the disruption and its cause.

The distinction between situations where a school district can intervene in cases involving off-campus and/or electronic speech or behaviors is important because the potential implications for schools can be significant. To reiterate, school districts cannot formally intervene in cases involving off-campus speech or electronic communication, unless it can be demonstrated that the speech threatens someone or otherwise substantially interrupts the learning environment at school. Some districts have even been required to pay significant sums to students who have sued them for overstepping the bounds of their authority in punishing off-campus, online speech. For instance, we mentioned the Westlake High School case at the beginning of this chapter. In another example, a high school student in Washington was suspended in 1999 for creating a parody Web page that ridiculed the assistant principal. Similar to the finding in the *Beussink* case, the courts ruled that the school district failed to prove that a substantial disruption had occurred and, therefore, the student's First Amendment rights had been violated. This led to the district agreeing to pay the student $52,000 in attorney's fees and $10,000 in damages (*Beidler v. North Thurston School District*, 2000).

Such outcomes have tended to undermine disciplinary action by school districts because the threat of civil litigation and bad publicity seems too great. This is unfortunate, because as noted above, there are a number of situations when it is completely appropriate (and necessary) for school officials to get involved. Table 5.1 at the end of this chapter neatly lists each of the cases we've covered and includes a statement of precedent stemming from the respective court ruling. We hope this serves as a quick and easy reference when you must consider the legal implications of certain school district actions.

WHEN CAN EDUCATORS INTERVENE?

To summarize, U.S. courts are generally oriented toward supporting First Amendment rights of free expression. However, certain expressions are *not protected* and allow intervention and discipline, including those that

- substantially or materially disrupts learning;
- interferes with the educational process or school discipline;
- utilizes school-owned technology to harass; or
- threatens other students or infringes on their civil rights.

Even though many school personnel are understandably hesitant to get involved in cases of cyberbullying that occur off campus (especially given the uncertainty of the current legal footing), as long as administrators can point to the aforementioned exceptions, their restrictive response is probably within the boundaries of the law (Shariff & Hoff, 2007).

> *There's always the legal discussion of "if it doesn't happen at school, can a district take action?" If a student is harassed for three hours at night on the Web and they come to school and have to sit in the same classroom with the student that's the bully, it may negatively affect that student's ability to learn in a safe, nonthreatening atmosphere. School districts that can document this connection may then be able to informally or formally address the matter.*

> —Joe Wehrli, policy services director
> for the Oregon School Boards Association

As stressed above, the current standard reached in *Tinker* and reflected in many subsequent cases regarding the extent to which schools can discipline students for inappropriate behavior is whether or not that behavior resulted in a substantial disruption at school. Actual, material disruption to the school environment—irrespective of where the behavior took place (on or off campus)—perennially seems to be the primary issue in these cases.

From a cyberbullying perspective, it is clear that many forms of electronic harassment carried out off campus would impact the learning environment, at least for the individual who is the target of the harassment. However, the question remains: At what point does such behavior "materially and substantially" disrupt the school environment as a whole? The Arkansas state legislature has attempted to articulate more clearly what this might look like in cases involving bullying and cyberbullying (see Box 5.4).

Box 5.4 Definition of Substantial Disruption

According to Public Act 115 of the Arkansas Legislature ("An Act to Define Bullying," 2007), "'substantial disruption' means without limitation that any one or more of the following occur as a result of the bullying:

(i)   Necessary cessation of instruction or educational activities;
(ii) Inability of students or educational staff to focus on learning or function as an educational unit because of a hostile environment;
(iii) Severe or repetitive disciplinary measures are needed in the classroom or during educational activities; or
(iv) Exhibition of other behaviors by students or educational staff that substantially interfere with the learning environment" (§ 1.a.3.D)

On its face, we believe the approach taken by Arkansas is well conceived and detailed and, therefore, should be used as a model to provide clarity to an otherwise vague clause or concept. Perhaps students are constantly chattering about a mass e-mail filled with juicy rumors and gossip to the point where their behavior affects a teacher's ability to deliver instruction. Perhaps one or more students are unable to pay attention in class because of the fallout from a distressing Web site created about them and fear for their own safety. Perhaps repeated verbal correction by teachers or administrative staff fails to quiet the uproar stemming from mean and inflammatory messages circulating on Facebook. Perhaps fights are breaking out between classes in the hallways because of hostile text messages being forwarded from one cell phone to another across the entire student body. All of these instances could be classified as a "substantial disruption" within the meaning of *Tinker,* thereby allowing the school to move swiftly and with certainty to quell the problem.

School districts need to demonstrate clearly that they are exercising reasonable care to address instances of cyberbullying so as to not appear deliberately indifferent. For example, districts should update their harassment and bullying policies to account for electronic forms of harassment. They should provide information to students and parents about bullying and cyberbullying and develop a mechanism for students to report all forms of harassment (more on this in Chapter 6). Even though these are the responsible things to do, many school districts are lagging behind. As a result, like Arkansas, many state legislatures are stepping in and drafting legislation that would require districts to update their policies to include cyberbullying. In the section that follows, we point out the most common elements of such legislation and discuss the essential features of an effective cyberbullying policy.

SCHOOL DISTRICT POLICY

One of the most important steps a district can take to help protect its students and protect itself from legal liability is to have a clear and comprehensive policy regarding bullying and harassment, technology, and their intersection: cyberbullying. The above discussion of prior judicial and legislative rulings should help district guide administrators in fashioning a thorough policy. Nevertheless, noted Internet lawyer Parry Aftab (2006) acknowledges the challenges that school districts face when trying to establish a harassment policy that prohibits cyberbullying:

> Put your pen to paper . . . and explain what you are now doing, what you will be doing and the rules. Once that is done, lay out the range of disciplinary actions that might be taken and the parameters. Use simple language that the students and non-techies can understand. When that's all done, run it by the lawyers to make sure you

haven't done anything wrong and haven't left anything out. *Then cross your fingers, hold your breath and wait* [emphasis added].

This quote highlights the difficulty in creating and implementing policies to curb or respond to cyberbullying. However, it should not be used as a justification to do nothing, because that can result in harm to students and potentially make the school district vulnerable to civil litigation.

Though progress has been slow, a number of states are moving forward with legislation that would direct districts to update harassment and bullying laws to include electronic forms (see Box 5.5). The primary problem that legislators face is how to craft a law that protects students but does not overly restrict student speech, thus violating the First Amendment's guarantee of free expression. Also at issue is whether school district personnel have the ability to intervene in electronic threats that do not involve school resources or that originate from off-campus sources. As discussed at length above, however, there are consistently clear areas where school personnel can, and must, intervene.

Box 5.5 States With Proposed or Passed Cyberbullying Laws (as of March 2008)

Arkansas	Missouri
Delaware	New Jersey
Idaho	New York
Illinois	Oregon
Iowa	Rhode Island
Kansas	South Carolina
Kentucky	Vermont
Maryland	Washington
Minnesota	

While each of the bills varies to some extent, they generally involve one (or more) of the following elements:

- Direct school districts to add cyberbullying to school antibullying policies.
- Criminalize or provide specific penalties for cyberbullying.
- Include new provisions to allow administrators to take action when off-campus actions have affected on-campus order.
- Require schools to develop new reporting and disciplinary procedures in cyberbullying cases.
- Mandate that school districts create and implement Internet safety, ethics, and etiquette training and curriculum.

Many states are currently working (in some capacity) to create and pass legislation requiring school districts to address cyberbullying. Therefore, interested individuals should contact their local representatives to find out what is being done in this area.

Since the status, wording, and significance of each state bill and policy varies depending on a number of factors, we thought it would be fruitless to simply list them. Rather, after carefully reviewing the language from many of the proposals and discussing this issue with policy makers, we have come up with the six primary elements of what would constitute an effective school policy. This approach moves beyond simply adding "electronic bullying" to existing district policies. Box 5.6 lists these six components, and we discuss each of them in more detail below.

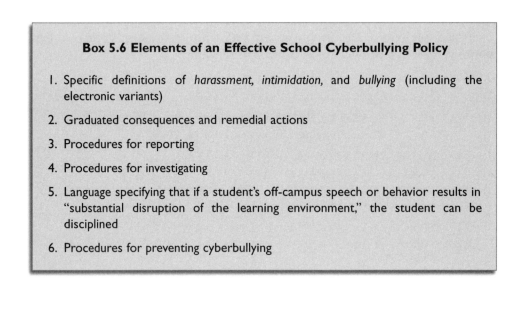

Box 5.6 Elements of an Effective School Cyberbullying Policy

1. Specific definitions of *harassment, intimidation,* and *bullying* (including the electronic variants)

2. Graduated consequences and remedial actions

3. Procedures for reporting

4. Procedures for investigating

5. Language specifying that if a student's off-campus speech or behavior results in "substantial disruption of the learning environment," the student can be disciplined

6. Procedures for preventing cyberbullying

Definition of Relevant Terms

It is important that the policy clearly defines the behaviors it seeks to proscribe. The more specific the policy is, the more likely it will withstand legal challenges. As William Shepherd, a statewide prosecutor in Florida's Office of the Attorney General, cautions, however,

> *the law or policy should be specific, but behavior changes over time, so you must have the ability to grow with the times.*

In Box 5.7, we provide several sample definitions that you should consider including in your policy. These definitions are based in part on

Box 5.7 Sample Policy Definitions

Bullying or harassment: Any intentionally insulting or humiliating written, verbal, or physical conduct or threat directed against a student or school employee that

    (a) places a student or school employee in reasonable fear of harm to his or her person or damage to his or her property; or

    (b) is sufficiently severe, persistent, or pervasive that it creates an intimidating, threatening, or abusive educational environment for a student or school employee; or

    (c) interferes with a student's educational performance or experience; or

    (d) substantially disrupts the orderly operation of the school.

Bullying or harassment also involves retaliation against a student or school employee by another student or school employee for asserting or alleging an act of bullying or harassment or the reporting of an act of bullying or harassment that is not made in good faith.

Box 5.8 Forms of Bullying

Bullying can occur by one individual or a group of individuals, can be direct or indirect, and can take the following forms:

    (a) *Physical bullying:* Demonstrations of aggression by pushing, kicking, hitting, gesturing, or otherwise invading the physical space of another person in an unwelcome manner or the unwanted tampering with or destruction of another person's property

    (b) *Verbal bullying:* Demonstrations of aggression through insults, teasing, cursing, threatening, or otherwise expressing unkind words toward another person

    (c) *Relational bullying:* Demonstrations of aggression through exclusion, rejection, and isolation to damage a person's position and relationship within a social group

    (d) *Cyberbullying:* Willful and repeated harm inflicted through the use of computers, cell phones, and other electronic devices. The following are examples of cyberbullying, when they are intentional, repeated, and result in harm to another:

- Sending text messages over the Internet or using a cell phone
- Posting text, images, audio, or video to a Web page
- Sending or posting text, images, audio, or video on or over the Internet or through a cell phone network
- Sending a picture or video via the Internet or using a cell phone

Cyberbullying can result in discipline whether it occurs on or off campus, irrespective of whether it involves an electronic device at school, at home, or at a third-party location, if it results in a substantial disruption of the school learning environment as defined in this policy.

an "ideal" law designed as a template by Bully Police USA (www.bully police.org), a watchdog organization that follows antibullying laws across America. In Box 5.8, we list several forms of bullying that should be clearly delineated in your policy. Generally speaking, any communication that has been perceived by a student as unwanted, vulgar, obscene, sexually explicit, demeaning, belittling, or defaming in nature or is otherwise disruptive to a student's ability to learn and a school's ability to educate its students in a safe environment, or that causes a reasonable person to suffer substantial emotional distress or fear of bodily injury, should be subject to discipline.

It is also important to remember that many districts already have policies in place that prohibit various forms of harassment, including harassment based on race or sex. Any behavior that constitutes sexual harassment, for example, should be handled under those provisions, irrespective of whether the behavior is also considered bullying or cyberbullying.

Graduated Consequences and Remedial Actions

Any student found to be participating in, contributing to, and/or encouraging acts of cyberbullying and/or harassment toward another student or staff member must be disciplined. Your policy must identify what specific actions will be taken. To determine the severity of the harassment or discrimination, the following may be considered: how the misconduct affected one or more students' education; the type, frequency, and duration of the misconduct; the number of persons involved; the subject(s) of harassment or discrimination; the situation in which the incident occurred; and other related incidents at the school. Any cyberbullying that has been perceived as a criminal act, such as a threat to one's personal or physical safety, should be subject to discipline and result in the notification of law enforcement.

Discipline can include a number of different actions (see Box 5.9). As we discuss in detail in Chapter 7, it is important to link specific behaviors with specific disciplinary outcomes so that students know exactly what may happen if they are caught engaging in cyberbullying behaviors. Don't be afraid to think creatively about alternative sanctions instead of relying on detention or suspension. For example, cyberbullies could be required (based on the grievance) to research and write an essay on the negative effects of cyberbullying. They could also be required to write a formal apology to the aggrieved party or parties. Disciplinary outcomes should be considered and carried out on a case-by-case basis.

Box 5.9 Disciplinary Options

- Parental contact
- Behavioral contracts
- Loss of privileges (either in-school or extracurricular)
- Conferences with students, parents, teachers, or administrative staff
- Interventions by school guidance personnel
- School service work or student work detail
- Removal of student from class
- Loss of bus privileges (parents are thus responsible for transportation)
- In-school alternative assignments or intervention programs
- Detentions (before, during, or after school or on Saturday)
- Restitution
- Assignment to alternative program in lieu of suspension days
- Suspension—Removal of student from school for up to ten days
- Assignment to an alternative educational facility
- Expulsion—Removal of student from school for remainder of year plus one additional year

Procedures for Reporting Cyberbullying

Every student should be encouraged to report instances or evidence of cyberbullying to a teacher or staff member. They must be made aware of the proper channels through which to report inappropriate behaviors of all varieties. As we discuss in Chapter 7, every school should designate one or more staff members to serve as "trustees" who are specifically trained to deal with cyberbullying incidents. Students should feel comfortable confiding in them when they experience or witness cyberbullying.

Also, an anonymous reporting system should be set up so that youth can inform adults of a problem without fear of repercussions (see Chapter 6 for a more detailed discussion). Retaliation or reprisal against any student who anonymously or publicly reports an act of cyberbullying must be expressly forbidden. Students who retaliate should, as a consequence, be subject to disciplinary and remedial action. Of course, intentionally false accusations of cyberbullying by a student against another must also be subject to discipline.

Procedures for Investigating Cyberbullying

We believe all forms of cyberbullying, no matter how minor, need to be investigated and documented. Even if you don't feel the school has the authority to discipline the student for the behavior, the incident should be investigated and put in the student's file for future reference. It is important to track the behavioral history of youth, even relatively minor incidents, as this history might be instructive in future considerations. A number of minor behaviors can add up to something more serious. Also, cyberbullying behaviors can signal that something more serious is going on with a particular student; therefore, they must be thoroughly investigated.

The appropriate authorities at each school should immediately investigate all reports of suspected, impending, and actual cyberbullying incidents. This may will involve collecting statements from the victim(s), the alleged target(s), and any witness(es) or bystander(s). This may also involve collecting and documenting electronic evidence from computer screens, computer hard drives, optical media, external or flash drives, computer server and network logs, Internet service providers or cellular service providers, cell phones, printouts, or related items. It is important to remember that in many cases, you may need a warrant to search personal property where a student has an expectation of privacy. While the Supreme Court has ruled that the probable cause requirement of the Fourth Amendment does not apply to students at school (*New Jersey v. T. L. O.,* 1985), a student search must nevertheless satisfy the "reasonableness requirement" (*Klump v. Nazareth Area School District,* 2006). We have included a comprehensive "Cyberbullying Incident Tracking Form" (Resource G) that you can use to record and document all instances of cyberbullying.

Substantial Disruption

Regardless of whether the behavior occurs on or off campus, if it can be demonstrated that the instance of cyberbullying resulted in a substantial disruption of the school learning environment or infringed upon the civil rights of other students or staff, the school district can restrict student speech or behavior and discipline those who were responsible. As pointed out earlier in Box 5.4, substantial disruption occurs when an incident forces the cessation of instructional activities, prevents students and/or staff from focusing on learning and accomplishing the educational goals of the institution, leads to severe or repetitive disciplinary measures to keep students on task or preempt further interpersonal conflict, or otherwise leads to conduct that detracts from the educational process and requires intervention to restore orderly operation. All of these factors should be spelled out in a comprehensive policy.

Procedures for Preventing Cyberbullying

It is important, and in some cases even required, that each school educates its students and staff on a regular basis regarding the nature and consequences of, and prohibitions and penalties associated with, all forms of bullying, including cyberbullying, so that constant and updated awareness of the problem is promoted. Education should occur through training workshops and seminars, as well as formalized continuing education initiatives for all members of the school community. Students should be exposed to cyberbullying prevention strategies through signage at school, assemblies with speakers, the dissemination of related documents and resources, and curricular enhancements that discuss unacceptable use of computers and communication devices. Internet safety modules should be devised and implemented in Grades K–12 with the intent of safeguarding youth from cyberbullying and other forms of online victimization. A joint task force that involves multiple school and community stakeholders should also meet regularly during the school year to review existing policies, procedures, and programming and make improvements. We return to the issue of prevention in Chapter 6.

SUMMARY

It is important to remember that legal issues with respect to technology use are continuously evolving (Shariff & Hoff, 2007). As such, while the information contained in this chapter was current as this book went to press, new developments in case law and statutory law are continually affecting the state of cyberbullying legal issues. For the most up-to-date information, the reader is encouraged to consult with an attorney who has expertise in school and/or Internet law. Similarly, the improper use of technology by students will continue to evolve with the advent of user-friendly advances in electronic devices and communications. Vigilance is important in continually modifying and improving the base of school district policies that address electronic harm.

After reading this chapter, you can see why so many educators are confused about what they can and cannot do with respect to intervening in incidents involving off-campus speech and behavior. We hope, however, that we have clarified these issues sufficiently to give you a general understanding of how to approach these situations. Simply put, you cannot formally discipline students for speech or behavior that occurs away from school with which you merely disagree (or are uncomfortable). You must demonstrate how such behavior or speech materially and substantially interferes with the learning environment at school.

That said, please don't use this principle as justification for not getting involved. As we will discuss in Chapter 7, you can utilize a number of strategies to respond to a variety of cyberbullying situations (those that occur on campus and off). Before we address responses to cyberbullying, the next chapter covers some practical solutions you can use to help prevent cyberbullying from happening in the first place.

QUESTIONS FOR REFLECTION

1. Should legislatures step up and pass laws that criminalize electronic harassment? If yes, what punishments should be provided?

2. Is the policy at your school effective at addressing cyberbullying? (If your answer is "I don't know," you have a lot of work to do!)

3. How would a student at your school go about reporting cyberbullying?

4. Should parents be punished for the cyberbullying behaviors of their children?

5. When can a school district discipline a student for cyberbullying?

Table 5.1   Notable Court Cases Relevant to Electronic Behaviors and Cyberbullying

Court Case	Ruling
Tinker v. Des Moines Independent Community School District (1969)	For school district personnel to restrict student expression of controversial or inflammatory opinions, they must demonstrate that such behaviors substantially interfere with school discipline or the rights of others.
Bethel School District No. 403 v. Fraser (1986)	Highly offensive speech on a school campus can be restricted if it infringes upon the rights of others or is inconsistent with the values being promoted at school.
Klein v. Smith (1986)	Schools cannot discipline students for off-campus behavior that does not negatively affect the school environment.
Hazelwood School District v. Kuhlmeier (1988)	Schools can exercise editorial control over speech or content that appears to be (or is) part of a school-sponsored expressive activity, if the activity is related to legitimate pedagogical goals.
Beussink v. Woodland R-IV School District (1998)	Schools cannot restrict a student's inflammatory online speech that occurs off campus simply because it expresses an unpleasant, unpopular, or upsetting viewpoint.
Gebser v. Lago Vista Independent School District (1998)	The school district is liable for demonstrating "deliberate indifference" in a case involving teacher-on-student sexual harassment.
Davis v. Monroe County Board of Education (1999)	The school district is liable for demonstrating "deliberate indifference" in a case involving student-on-student sexual harassment.

Court Case	Ruling
Emmett v. Kent School District No. 415 (2000)	Schools must provide evidence that seemingly threatening online speech is, in fact, threatening to others or disturbs school operations.
J.S. v. Bethlehem Area School District (2000)	Schools can restrict off-campus online speech that threatens the safety of another person when they can demonstrate harm to the victim.
Wisniewski v. Board of Education of Weedsport Central School District (2006)	Students who create online content that could reasonably cause a disruption at school can be sanctioned, particularly when it involves a threat.
Layshock v. Hermitage School District (2006)	Schools must diligently and comprehensively collect and provide evidence proving that a substantial and material disruption occurred within the school environment to support their position in a court case.
Klump v. Nazareth Area School District (2006)	School administrators cannot violate students' Fourth Amendment protection against unreasonable searches of their cell phones for voice-mails or text messages, unless they have clear, articulated, documentable, and reasonable suspicion that school policy has been violated.
Drews v. Joint School District No. 393 (2006)	School districts are not responsible in cyberbullying cases between students when the victim cannot show that any educational benefits were denied or that any rights were infringed.
Morse v. Frederick (2007)	Schools can restrict controversial expressions during school-sponsored events, especially if those expressions appear to endorse behavior that is contrary to their educational mission.
J.S. v. Blue Mountain School District (2007)	Schools will be supported in court when they can demonstrate that off-campus online speech by a student substantially disrupted school operations or interfered with the civil rights of others.
A.B. v. State of Indiana (2007)	Some off-campus online speech by a student may be protected, if it can be considered "political speech" that legitimately criticizes a school administrator.
Requa v. Kent School District No. 415 (2007)	Covert digital video recordings of teachers made by students and then posted to YouTube materially and substantially disrupt the work and discipline of the school, particularly when they involve demeaning, derogatory, and sexually suggestive behavior.

6

Preventing Cyberbullying

My child struggles with her weight. In whom she thought were two of her best friends she confided her weight during a sleep over and the next day it was posted on their Bebo site. How cruel can kids be? Anyhow, I see profanity and slams every day on the Internet while kids are so-called "chatting," as a parent my kids know that I am going to step in and read what is going on at any given minute. More should do so.

—Submitted anonymously

One of the questions we are asked most often when we speak with school professionals, parents, and the media is "How can cyberbullying be prevented?" Indeed, some of you have picked up this book solely to figure out the answer to that important question. We devote this chapter to identifying a number of practical approaches that we believe can decrease the frequency of online harassment among youth. While there is no magic bullet to deal with it, there are a number of informed steps that can minimize the likelihood of adolescent aggression in cyberspace. Moreover, the advice in this chapter should equip you not only to prevent cyberbullying but also to lay the groundwork for when you must respond to cyberbullying (see Chapter 7).

Some suggest that the only way to prevent cyberbullying and some of the other negatives associated with adolescent Internet use is to forbid kids from going online. To be sure, this is the least appropriate course of action. Think about it for a moment. Would you agree that visiting and touring Washington, D.C., would be a fantastic learning opportunity for students? Sure it is: The war memorials, presidential monuments, and governmental buildings are all great places for kids to see and come to appreciate.

Maybe you would like to take the students in your class or school to the nation's capital for a tour. Well, how would you go about it? You certainly wouldn't just drop them off at the steps of the White House and say, "Have fun!" You know that in addition to all of the wonderful educational opportunities in Washington, D.C., there are many things you wouldn't necessarily want your students to see: violence, prostitutes, homeless people, drunkards, gang members, and so forth. That urban environment holds a number of dangers; in fact, Washington, D.C., has one of the highest crime rates in the United States. Still, that doesn't mean we should prohibit our students from visiting the city and taking advantage of its historical, political, and cultural attractions.

The Internet should be approached in the same manner. It contains in its seedier corners many things we just don't want our kids to see: foul language, hateful and prejudiced speech, pornography, bomb-making instructions—and the list goes on. The Internet also has many potential dangers: sexual predators, kidnappers, and others with malicious or perverse intent who may want to bring harm to children. Just as we wouldn't leave our kids alone to explore Washington, D.C., we shouldn't leave them alone to explore the Internet without supervision, guidance, and explicit instruction. It is critical to provide them with a clear road map and framework for staying safe and being responsible online and to check in on them regularly to make sure they are following through.

Eventually, all children will be exposed to things in cyberspace that are problematic. What they do at that point depends on the instruction they have received and the habits they have developed. The time, energy, and effort you put in toward this end will pay great dividends in the lives of the youth in whom you invest. While it is not a lost cause to talk to adolescents about appropriate Internet use when they are 17 or 18 years old, so much should be done earlier. We encourage introducing this topic as early as possible—and definitely before they start exploring the Internet alone. We find that between fifth and seventh grade, students begin to use computers and the Internet more often and for more varied purposes, and we have spoken with elementary school children who are vastly more proficient than their teachers and parents. You may not have taught them how to use a computer and the Internet, but they seem to have learned it somewhere.

Kids will undoubtedly become well versed with technology at an increasingly younger age as we move forward in the 21st century. What is encouraging is that adults have a great deal of influence and can meaningfully shape behavior at these earlier ages. You may know from experience that this influence lessens as youth approach the teenage years, so it is vital to step in as soon as possible. This simply means *now,* if it hasn't happened already. We believe that they'll not only hear you speak but actually listen to what you are saying.

A comprehensive strategy to prevent cyberbullying, or any other form of adolescent aggression, requires the cooperation of a number of important stakeholders. Parents, teachers, law enforcement officers, other community leaders, and children themselves all have a role to play. None of these players will be able to do it by themselves. This chapter will detail the steps you can take to help prevent cyberbullying and other adolescent problems that arise with the utilization of technology. We first turn our attention to the role of the educator, whose responsibilities include formally assessing the current level of cyberbullying, educating students and staff, establishing clear rules, utilizing the expertise of students, maintaining a safe and respectful school culture, installing monitoring and filtering software, implementing and evaluating formal anticyberbullying programming, and educating parents.

THE EDUCATOR'S ROLE IN PREVENTING CYBERBULLYING

Assessment

The first proactive step you can take is to assess the level of cyberbullying occurring in your school and the impact it is having on the student body and educational environment. Determining the current state of online behaviors among your school population can best be accomplished through an anonymous survey of students and staff. In fact, this should be done on a regular basis so that trend data can be reviewed to determine whether certain problems are improving or worsening over time. There are a number of general concepts specific to cyberbullying that your assessment instrument should attempt to address (see Box 6.1).

Box 6.1 Sample Assessment Questions

- Does cyberbullying occur among students at this school?
- How big a problem is it?
- Have you ever been the victim of cyberbullying?
- Have you ever been afraid to come to school because of something somebody said to you online?
- Have you ever cyberbullied another student?
- If so, why did you do it?
- What should teachers do help prevent cyberbullying?

It is important that you clearly define what *cyberbullying* is to the students so they understand the kinds of behaviors that you are interested in. For example, in our surveys, we inform respondents that "Cyberbullying is when someone repeatedly makes fun of another person online or repeatedly picks on another person through e-mail or text message or when someone posts something online about another person that they don't like." Just asking them if they have been *cyberbullied*, without clearly describing what it is, can lead to confusion among students and make interpreting the results difficult.

If the assessment is coordinated districtwide, numbers can be broken down by school, demographic characteristics (e.g., age, gender, race), region, special populations, and any number of other variables and even compared and contrasted with districtwide data on the general makeup and distribution of students. This analysis can be very instructive in identifying exactly which schools or groups require the most support, education, and resources to deal with cyberbullying. To get you started, we have included a copy of the cyberbullying survey questions we constructed and used when collecting our data from middle schoolers in 2007 (Resource F). Of course, this instrument can be modified to suit your school population.

Additionally, your school may want to consider partnering with a local college or university to help with the collection, analysis, interpretation, and presentation of these data. University faculty generally have experience conducting assessments and can assist in all aspects of the project. In addition, other resources are available, both online and in print, that provide more specific guidance for administrators about how to conduct a thorough assessment. Barbara Trolley, Connie Hanel, and Linda Shields (2006), for example, provide a number of practical recommendations toward this end in their book *Demystifying and Deescalating Cyber Bullying in the Schools*.

Educate Students and Staff

It almost goes without saying that school districts must educate both students and staff about the harmful nature of online aggression. School administrators should take the time to learn about these issues and pass this important information along to teachers and counselors. As an example, the district could convene a staff meeting related to youth Internet safety and bring a specialist in to speak on the topic, provide actual case studies, and summarize the latest research findings.

After being so equipped, teachers and counselors need to pass this information on to students. Teachers should take time to discuss cyberbullying in their classrooms when they discuss broader issues of bullying and peer harassment. They should proactively engage students in conversations about a variety of negative online experiences and possible solutions. For instance, teachers can use vignettes or even real examples of cyberbullying to illustrate its harmful nature and point out that what is written or disseminated online is equally as damaging as face-to-face bullying (or worse). A few sample vignettes are presented in Box 6.2, and others are provided in Resource C of this book. We believe these aptly portray real-life cyberbullying situations and prompt productive, ongoing discussions as to what to do (and how to do it).

Box 6.2 Cyberbullying Scenarios

Scenario #1

A girl had her picture taken, which made her feel uncomfortable. Later that week, her friends tell her that the picture has been posted on another student's blog. What should the girl do? Should she fight back?

Scenario #2

A boy has written a poem for his crush and decided to e-mail it to her. The girl then e-mails it to all of her friends on her buddy list. The next day at school, all of the kids are making fun of him and his poem. What should the boy do? Is using e-mail always safe?

Scenario #3

A teacher notices that during computer lab, one student is not using the computer. The teacher approaches this girl and asks her why. The girl does not speak up right away and nervously looks around the room. Then she replies that she does not feel like using the computer today. However, the teacher notices that a few of the other students are looking over and laughing. What should the teacher do? Is the teacher to assume that the girl is being bullied online? If the teacher finds out that cyberbullying is taking place, what should she do next?

Scenario #4

A boy has brought his camera phone to school one day. He is using the phone to take pictures of other students in the class. The next day, the teacher sees that some of the students are threatening to beat up the little boy. The teacher then finds out that the boy posted pictures of students on the Web and was making fun of them. What punishment should the little boy get? Should the other students be punished as well for fighting? What should the school do to prevent this sort of thing from happening?

Scenario #5

Two boys at school are teasing each other during lunch time. They are calling each other names and laughing at one another. Both boys are punished, and the teacher thinks that the fighting has stopped. Rather than fight at school, however, the students have actually started an online fight. One boy created an entire Web page to make fun of the other. The boy who is on the Web site has told his parents. Now the parents have come to the teacher asking why and what is going on. What should the teacher recommend to the parents? What should the teacher do while the students are at school?

Moreover, we recommend that schools sponsor an assembly or presentation on a regular basis that provides information for the school community about safe and responsible Internet use and "netiquette" (network or online etiquette). To make these presentations more vivid and true-to-life, we recommend showing hard-hitting video clips related to cyberbullying that are freely available online. For example, the National Crime Prevention Council (www.ncpc.org/cyberbullying) has created public service announcement videos that powerfully portray the real-world harm that online aggression can inflict. The students to whom we have shown these videos are visibly moved as the message sinks in. Repeatedly piquing the consciences of youth about questionable or deviant behavior seems to make them more sensitive to the issues at hand and more apt to "think twice" before making an unwise decision. They should also be deterred to some extent after being reminded of the potential consequences that follow rule breaking and that virtually all forms of wrongdoing online leave a digital footprint that aids in identifying the perpetrator(s).

Several nonprofit organizations have also developed curricula that a school can utilize to educate staff and students about the nature and consequences of cyberbullying. For example, the Anti-Defamation League (ADL) recently launched a nationwide initiative, entitled "Cyberbullying: Understanding and Addressing Online Cruelty," which includes lesson plans for elementary, middle, and secondary school levels. The organization also offers interactive workshops for middle and high school staff. More information about the ADL's cyberbullying programming can be found at www.adl.org.

The Ophelia Project, a nonprofit organization that works with schools to create safer social climates to reduce aggression among students, also provides trainings and workshops for schools about cyberbullying. Their work focuses on combating relational and other nonphysical forms of aggression by promoting emotional well-being and helping youth develop healthy peer relationships. More information can be found at www.opheliaproject.org. Finally, i-SAFE (www.isafe.org) has created an extensive Internet safety curriculum for K–12 youth classrooms and also works to educate community members through comprehensive outreach programs. We encourage you to check out the available materials at these Web sites and see which best meet your goals.

Have Clear Rules Regarding the Use of Computers and Other Technological Devices

When we were in seventh-grade "shop" class, we remember spending several weeks at the beginning of the school year studying the safety practices and procedures associated with the power tools before being allowed to use them. Before being permitted to drive a car a couple of years later, we were required to take a comprehensive driver's education course and pass both a written exam and a road test. Society recognizes that power tools and automobiles can be dangerous if used inappropriately or irresponsibly, so we take the time to educate students about the inherent dangers in their operation.

The same approach should be taken before students are allowed to use computers and the Internet at school. Youth cannot be expected to exercise complete wisdom. They need to be taught how to use technology responsibly. Just as there are rules for using power equipment, there should also be clear rules about what is expected when using computers. As long as students know the rules, they cannot plead ignorance if and when they are caught violating them. They should also know the potential consequences for any wrongdoing. (This is discussed in more detail in the next chapter).

Every school district should have a comprehensive Acceptable Use Policy (AUP) governing the use of technology provided by or used in the schools. The Computer Crime and Intellectual Property Section of the U.S. Department of Justice provides a model AUP, which schools can adapt for their needs. The policy includes detailed information about the safe and responsible use of computers and the Internet and provides suggestions for discipline, supervision, and monitoring. Parents and students must read and sign the AUP (thereby indicating agreement with its terms) at the beginning of every school year. That way, all parties are aware of the policy and the potential consequences associated with any violations of its terms. Interested readers are encouraged to go to www.cybercrime.gov and search for "school acceptable use policy."

In addition to a broad policy, it is also beneficial to post specific principles to guide the behavioral choices of students on computers at school. In Box 6.3, we list several specific rules that educators might consider posting near the workstations in a computer lab or classroom. At the bottom of the list, we also recommend specifying certain Web sites and software applications that are forbidden at school (e.g., MySpace, AOL Instant Messenger, Google Talk, and Second Life).

In addition to classroom computer use, students need to know which (if any) portable electronic devices are allowed on campus, as we are seeing a surge in the number of youth who possess laptop computers, smartphones (e.g., iPhones, Blackberrys, Sidekicks), and other portable electronic devices that are Web enabled in some capacity. Coupled with the increasing number of cell phones that provide Internet access, the possibilities for cyberbullying incidents are exponentially rising.

Accordingly, schools must have a clearly defined policy regarding all portable electronic devices. Some schools have simply elected to ban all such devices from campus. These actions have lead to criticism by some parents, who say they need to be able to contact their kids in the case of an emergency. It can also be very difficult to enforce a complete ban without searching all students as they enter the school each day. A better approach would be to have clearly specified guidelines for when and where the devices are allowed and what will happen if a student is caught using a device at a prohibited time or place. Box 6.4 lists some rules you may want to consider.

Box 6.3 Rules for Classroom Computer Use

I understand that using the school computer is a privilege that is subject to the following rules:

1. I am allowed to use computers for approved, educational purposes only.

2. I will only play games authorized by my teacher.

3. I will not alter computer settings or damage computer equipment.

4. I agree never to write or post anything online that I would not want my teacher or parents to see.

5. I will not use the computer to bring harm to anyone else.

6. I will not type profanity or otherwise offensive language.

7. If I receive harassing messages or accidentally view any offensive or pornographic content, I will report it to my teacher immediately.

8. I will use the Internet to search only areas appropriate to the school curriculum.

9. I agree not to download install software, shareware, freeware, or other files without obtaining permission from my teacher.

10. I will only save material in my personal folder appropriate for educational use.

11. I will only alter my own files and documents.

12. I will not plagiarize from the Internet.

13. If I ever feel uncomfortable about an experience online, I will immediately tell my teacher. I understand that my teacher is willing to help me and will not punish me as long as these rules are followed.

14. I will not agree to meet with anyone I have met online without parental approval. If anyone wants to meet with me and makes me uncomfortable, I will bring it to the attention of an adult I trust.

15. I will not share any of my passwords (my school network account, my e-mail account, my social networking site account, etc.) with anyone else.

16. I will not use a proxy to attempt to access Web sites or other forms of Internet content and communications technology that have been blocked from my school network. I will also report any instances of other kids using a proxy.

17. I am prepared to be held accountable for my actions and for the loss of computer privileges if these policies are violated.

List of prohibited Web sites and software applications:

We would also like to emphasize here that when portable electronic devices are confiscated, schools should not overstep their bounds and search their contents, even when there is a clear violation of school policy.

This is best left either to parents or to law enforcement, who know when the circumstances call for such an intrusion of privacy. Schools should limit their actions to seizing but not searching these devices.

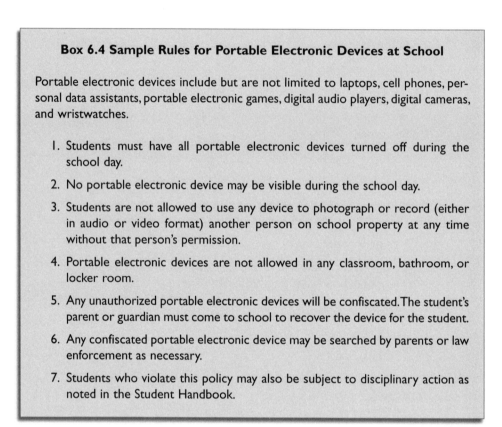

Box 6.4 Sample Rules for Portable Electronic Devices at School

Portable electronic devices include but are not limited to laptops, cell phones, personal data assistants, portable electronic games, digital audio players, digital cameras, and wristwatches.

1. Students must have all portable electronic devices turned off during the school day.
2. No portable electronic device may be visible during the school day.
3. Students are not allowed to use any device to photograph or record (either in audio or video format) another person on school property at any time without that person's permission.
4. Portable electronic devices are not allowed in any classroom, bathroom, or locker room.
5. Any unauthorized portable electronic devices will be confiscated. The student's parent or guardian must come to school to recover the device for the student.
6. Any confiscated portable electronic device may be searched by parents or law enforcement as necessary.
7. Students who violate this policy may also be subject to disciplinary action as noted in the Student Handbook.

All schools also have (or should have) policies on the books that prohibit bullying incidents and outline their disciplinary consequences. Administrators must take the time to review and revise them to ensure that they cover cyberbullying behaviors that negatively affect the school environment (see Chapter 5). This policy should be disseminated at the beginning of the school year so that parents and students understand what behaviors are within the disciplinary reach of the school. It may also be instructive to highlight particular situations that have resulted in disciplinary actions (examples from within the district or elsewhere). As Paul R. Getto, policy specialist for the Kansas Association of School Boards, says,

> *The schools need to promote a safe and friendly environment for all students, teachers and other staff, all of whom can be subjected to bullying in many forms, including cyberbullying. Simply passing policies which prohibit bullying is not, in our opinion, going to accomplish the desired results. Bullying in any form, regardless of the media used, is*

wrong, destructive, and potentially a problem for students and, in some cases, teachers, if they fear for their peace of mind or their safety while in school.

The importance of clear policies is illustrated in a recent example from Florida. In 2007, a middle school student recorded and subsequently uploaded to the Internet (www.youtube.com) video footage of one of her teachers in class and included a profanity-filled caption. Even though there was no substantial disruption of or interference with the school's educational mission, utilization of school-owned technology, or threat to other students, it was within the bounds of the administration to have her transferred to an alternative school, because the school policy expressly forbids the recording of teachers in the classroom.

The policy stated, in part, that "Any student who uses an article disruptive to school to inappropriately photograph, audiotape, videotape or otherwise record a person without his/her knowledge or consent will be subject to disciplinary action." We applaud this school for being progressive and forward-thinking enough to have formulated and included such a policy within its conduct manual. It is imperative that other schools and school districts do the same so that the simple and clear violation of a policy prohibiting certain behavior can serve as the basis for punitive sanctions (including changes of placement) by a school on a student.

Utilize the Expertise of Students Through Peer Mentoring

Parents and teachers can get up and preach, but if they hear it from another kid, they will remember it.

—Parent from California

The concept of peer mentoring generally involves older students advising and counseling younger students about issues affecting them. Since younger adolescents tend to look up to (and seek to emulate) older adolescents, this dynamic can be exploited to teach important lessons about the use of computers and communications technology. Peer mentoring has been fruitful in reducing traditional bullying and interpersonal conflict within schools (Miller, 2002) and, as such, should be considered in a comprehensive approach to preventing cyberbullying as well. Accordingly, newer cohorts of students can learn from the wisdom of adolescents who have already experienced online aggression and have figured out effective ways to deal with it. This wisdom may sink in more quickly and deeply since it comes from peers rather than adults, as kids have the tendency to tune out adults when being taught certain life lessons (can you relate to that?). On a larger scale, these efforts can significantly and positively affect the social climate within the school community, benefitting youth and their families, teachers and staff, and the community as a whole. As Mike Tully (2007), a noted school law attorney, points out: "Never overlook the possibility of using students themselves as agents of change" (p. 6).

The basic purpose of peer mentoring is to employ older students to change the way younger students think about the harassment or mistreatment of others in certain situations. Mentors can also be utilized to help younger students appreciate the responsibility and risks associated with the use of computers, cell phones, and the Internet. Overall, the goal is to encourage youth to take responsibility for the problem and to work together in coming up with a solution. It also seeks to foster respect and acceptance of others—no matter what—and to get kids to see how their actions affect others and how they can purposefully choose behaviors that promote positive peer relations.

> *I have started to talk to other children who have had a similar experience and try and help them because they are going through the same thing that I went through and it helps to talk to people who understand. I tell them to be brave and not to worry because everything will be OK.*
>
> —Student from England

Highly adaptable, depending on your needs, peer mentoring can be accomplished in a number of ways. For example, one-on-one sessions might take place where a high schooler is called in to meet with a middle school victim to offer support and help. Or high school students could regularly talk to groups of middle schoolers in the cafeteria during lunch. A few high school students could also organize a presentation for small classroom-sized (20+) middle school groups. Finally, skits can be presented in auditoriums or cafeterias by high schoolers for assemblies of younger students. All of these interactions can be comprised of one or more activities. Box 6.5 lists several messages that can be communicated to the school community using trained student mentors. Over time and as needed, additional formal and informal lessons—as well as continued interaction between the high school mentors and the middle school mentees—can occur.

A number of nonprofit organizations have also developed materials to help teach students to be ambassadors in Internet education. For example, i-SAFE, discussed earlier in this chapter, offers an i-MENTOR Training Network. This program consists of six online videos that educate older youth about Internet safety issues and how to talk to other students about the lessons. The program is designed for students in 5th through 12th grade who are interested in becoming Internet Safety Leaders in their school. The Ophelia Project, also discussed above, has a "Creating a Safe School" mentorship program that "empowers older students as trained

Box 6.5 Mentor Messages

Schools can utilize older students to convey a number of important messages of Internet safety and responsibility to younger students, including the following:

- Reiterating that they are not alone in experiencing victimization and the resultant pain, rejection, humiliation, and loneliness
- Encouraging them to speak up and not remain silent when confronted with cyberbullying
- Sharing one or more highly relatable vignettes or stories about cyberbullying
- Explaining the "language" of cyberbullying, including the relevant terms and technology
- Describing positive ways in which conflict between peers can be de-escalated or resolved
- Using role-playing examples to get students thinking about the various ways to address a cyberbullying situation
- Providing an opportunity to discuss and answer any questions, clarify any confusion, and reinforce how to deal with cyberbullying problems

mentors to their younger classmates and model positive social interaction and courageous intervention" (The Ophelia Project, 2006, ¶ 4). We encourage you to check out these programs to learn more about creating a safer school climate by utilizing student mentors.

Maintain a Safe and Respectful School Culture

School culture can be defined as the "sum of the values, cultures, safety practices, and organizational structures within a school that cause it to function and react in particular ways" (McBrien & Brandt, 1997, p. 89). Overall, it is critical for educators to develop and promote a safe and respectful school culture or climate. A positive on-campus environment will go a long way in reducing the frequency of many problematic behaviors at school, including bullying and harassment. In this setting, teachers must demonstrate emotional support, a warm and caring atmosphere, a strong focus on academics and learning, and a fostering of healthy self-esteem.

In our research, we found that students who experienced cyberbullying (both those who were victims and those who admitted to cyberbullying others) perceived a poorer climate or culture at their school than those who had not experienced cyberbullying. Youth were asked whether they "enjoy going to school," "feel safe at school," "feel that teachers at their school really try to help them succeed," and "feel that teachers at their school care about them." Those who admitted to cyberbullying others or who were the target of cyberbullying were less likely to agree with those statements. As you can see from Chart 6.1, the difference may not seem like much, but it is statistically meaningful. While we don't know whether a poor school climate *caused* cyberbullying behaviors (or was the result of them), we do know that the variables are related.

Chart 6.1   Cyberbullying and School Climate

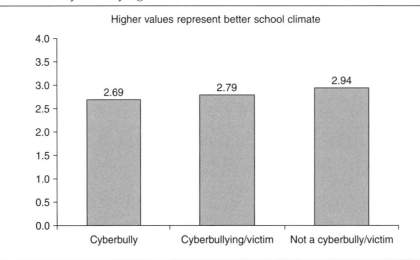

In addition, strategic efforts to promote bonding among students should be in place, as this is related to personal, emotional, behavioral, and scholastic success. Toward this end, we often champion what can be termed a "respect policy" or "honor code" when working with schools. For example, one with which we are familiar reads as follows (North High School, 2005):

> *Respect is the cornerstone of our relationships with each other. We are committed to respecting the dignity and worth of each individual at North High School and strive never to degrade or diminish any member of our school community by our conduct or attitudes. We benefit from each other. Our diversity makes us strong. (¶ 1)*

The goal of such a statement is to specify clearly to students and staff alike that all members of the school community are expected to respect each other and that such respect should govern all interpersonal interactions and attitudes among students, faculty, and staff on campus (and hopefully off campus as well). Respect policies serve as reference points against which every questionable thought, word, and deed can be measured and judged. Every instance of harm between individuals lacks a measure of respect for the victim, including those that occur through the use of electronic devices.

Apart from their inclusion in policy manuals, respect policies should be disseminated within school materials to both students and parents and posted visibly in hallways and classrooms. While one might wish that students would automatically and naturally treat each other (and the adults in their lives) with respect, we know that in reality this does not always happen. As such, the respect policy reminds them of a standard that has been set and will be enforced.

It is also crucial that the school seeks to create and promote an environment where certain behaviors or language simply is not tolerated—by students and staff alike. In a school with a positive culture, students know what is appropriate and what is not. In these schools, there are a number of behaviors that the community as a whole would agree are simply "not cool." It isn't cool to bring a weapon to school. It isn't cool get up in the middle of class and walk out of the classroom. It isn't cool to assault a teacher physically. It isn't cool to use racial slurs. Certain behaviors are simply not acceptable in the eyes of both adults and youth.

We hope that with education and effort, cyberbullying will someday be deemed "not cool." This ideal may be wishful thinking, but it is worth pursuing. All forms of bullying, no matter how minor, need to be condemned—with the responsible parties disciplined. If teachers deliberately ignore minor (or even serious) bullying because they just don't want to deal with it, what message does that send to the students? Students need to see that their teachers, counselors, and administrators take these behaviors seriously.

Install Monitoring and Filtering Software

The Children's Internet Protection Act (CIPA), passed in 2000, requires that public schools (and libraries) install filtering software on computers that have access to the Internet if they want to remain eligible for federal funding assistance. Filtering software blocks Internet content that is deemed inappropriate for children (e.g., violent or pornographic material). This is typically done in two ways: site blocking and content monitoring.

Site blocking filters typically prohibit computer users from accessing Web sites designated as inappropriate (those on a "black list"). Alternatively, some site blocking filters only allow users to access sites that have been preapproved (those on a "white list"). Both approaches usually do not block instant messaging, e-mail, peer-to-peer (P2P) applications, or other software that may pose problems or threats.

Content monitoring, on the other hand, generally uses a key word-blocking approach. Here, data are analyzed against a library of user-defined words and phrases deemed unfitting. The software then blocks that data regardless of the Internet application (or medium) through which it comes. In addition, most software programs allow users to block specific categories that identify certain types of Web sites. Box 6.6 lists some of the common Web site categories that one school district blocks so that students and staff cannot access these types of sites from school computer labs.

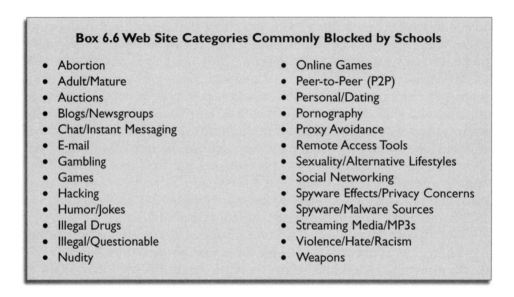

Box 6.6 Web Site Categories Commonly Blocked by Schools

- Abortion
- Adult/Mature
- Auctions
- Blogs/Newsgroups
- Chat/Instant Messaging
- E-mail
- Gambling
- Games
- Hacking
- Humor/Jokes
- Illegal Drugs
- Illegal/Questionable
- Nudity
- Online Games
- Peer-to-Peer (P2P)
- Personal/Dating
- Pornography
- Proxy Avoidance
- Remote Access Tools
- Sexuality/Alternative Lifestyles
- Social Networking
- Spyware Effects/Privacy Concerns
- Spyware/Malware Sources
- Streaming Media/MP3s
- Violence/Hate/Racism
- Weapons

Most school districts use hardware and software firewalls and filters to block access to social networking Web sites (e.g., MySpace and Facebook), third-party e-mail services (e.g., Hotmail and Yahoo), instant messaging software programs (e.g., AOL Instant Messenger and MSN Messenger), and P2P file sharing programs (e.g., KaZaA, LimeWire, eDonkey, and BitTorrent) from school computers. Nevertheless, it is still relatively easy to access these sites and programs from school if the student knows where to go and how to do it.

Specific Web sites—called "proxies"—are popping up every day that redirect individuals to sites that have been "blacklisted," or prohibited by hardware or software rules at school. Basically, an adolescent can access MySpace (for example) at school through his or her Web browser—even if it is blocked by the school network administrators—by first accessing another Web site (such as www.leafdrink.com), inputting "www.myspace .com" into a Web page form field, and then being rerouted to that site (thereby circumventing a direct connection to MySpace and bypassing the block or filter). The proxy serves as an intermediary site (that is not prohibited) from which a user can access a prohibited site, because the school network has allowed a connection to the proxy site. (It is virtually impossible to block all of these types of sites!) Finally, instant messaging software programs can be run off of a pocket USB drive (also known as a flash, thumb, or key drive) that a student brings to school and plugs into his or her computer. Those programs can also use a proxy site to reroute a connection to the proper instant messaging network, even if traditional access and use of such programs is restricted.

We all know that the Internet is a great instructional tool but that its content varies in quality and appropriateness. While schools are able to evaluate text books and library books carefully before approving them for school use, this remains a difficult task when dealing with material from the Internet. Filtering and blocking software is unfortunately limited in its utility and is primarily a reactive measure that serves more as a short-term solution to the problem of inappropriate Internet use among adolescents. A more proactive approach is required, involving the creation of a safe school culture, educational initiatives, formal assessment, and systemic programming affecting multiple stakeholders. In keeping with this philosophy, Nancy Willard (2003), the director of the Center for Safe and Responsible Internet Use, aptly points out: "By developing a comprehensive approach to address such concerns, schools can help young people develop effective filtering and blocking systems that will reside in the hardware that sits upon their shoulders" (p. 4).

Implement and Evaluate
Formal Anticyberbullying Programming

We also suggest that school officials actively work to develop and implement an antibullying curriculum that includes training modules on online aggression. Before implementation, it may once again be helpful to partner with researchers from a nearby university so that a scientific evaluation of the programming can occur to determine its worth. Very little is currently known about what works to educate youth about cyberbullying and online safety; even less is known about what works in responding to cyberbullying. At this early stage, it is important to try a variety of different approaches, starting with those with demonstrated success at preventing traditional bullying (for example, the Olweus Bullying Prevention Program [Olweus, Limber, & Mihalic, 1999b]). This curriculum can be supplemented with netiquette lessons covering the unique features of online communication and responsibility.

Whatever approach you decide to take, it is essential to conduct a formal and systematic evaluation of its merits so that others can learn from your experience. A thoughtful and well-designed evaluation is crucial for securing funding for more antibullying initiatives and for convincing others of the utility of the program—especially given the fiscal and organizational constraints currently facing most districts. Remember that a program is only as good as the quality of its evaluation.

Educate Parents

As educators, you have a unique platform from which to reach the parents of your students about these important issues. As such, it is important for you to pass along information to parents regarding adolescent use of electronic devices—thereby partnering with them in promoting positive online experiences among youth. For example, a letter can be sent to encourage them to do their part (see Box 6.7).

Box 6.7 Sample Letter From School to Parents

Dear Parents:

We wanted to send this brief letter home to let you know about some of the activities that students are involved in when using computers, cell phones, and other electronic devices. As you may have heard, many adolescents have reported experiencing "cyberbullying." Cyberbullying is when students use computers, cell phones, or other electronic devices to repeatedly harass or mistreat another person.

We have no reason to believe that this is a greater problem in our district than others, and we want to keep it that way. We are taking a number of important steps to help prevent cyberbullying, including educating the school community about its harmful nature. We have also recently updated our district policy and Student Handbook to reflect the changing nature of adolescent aggression. We have informed students and are now letting you know that we will discipline any cyberbullying that negatively affects the school environment or infringes upon the rights of others.

We encourage you to talk with your child about these issues. It is also important that you monitor their behavior to make sure they are responsibly using computers and cell phones. We are doing our part at school and trust that you will do your part at home so that we can jointly reduce the likelihood that cyberbullying will become a problem in our community.

Feel free to contact us if you have any questions or concerns.

Sincerely,

A newsletter can also be distributed to parents on a regular basis, updating them on new developments in the way kids are using and abusing technology. For example, the newsletter might make parents aware of new Web sites that teens are frequenting or innovative ways that youth are circumventing Internet safeguards on home computers. In addition, we recommend sponsoring regular community events to discuss issues related to Internet safety and cyberbullying. Through these initiatives, school personnel and parents can work together in addressing the inappropriate behaviors that will inevitably arise. After reading this book, you (yes, you!) should consider giving a presentation to parents after school or at a PTA meeting. You are now much better informed than the majority of adults out there, and you can do your part by working to educate those around you.

This school is an elementary school (K–5), so our prevention has been educating the parents about cyberbullying and encouraging them to be involved with their child's Web page access and content. We have also asked students to come forward if they experience cyberbullying that would have an impact on the school community.

—Principal from Florida

As a final point concerning the role of educators, an increasing amount of information is available across the Internet about cyberbullying. On our Web site, www.cyberbullying.us, we provide a large number of downloadable resources that you can distribute in electronic or hard-copy format to fellow administrators, staff, teachers, counselors, parents, and youth as needed. There are no restrictions on their dissemination, and we are frequently creating and uploading new resources as we continue to study the problem and work with those affected. For quick reference, some are included in Resource B of this book; however, they are cleanly formatted and suitable for distribution as PDF files on our Web site. In addition, we provide a multitude of Web links related to online aggression so that you can learn more from other professionals who are doing great work in this area.

THE PARENT'S ROLE IN PREVENTING CYBERBULLYING

It was an argument with my two best friends. I had fallen out with both of them for many reasons. Since we had been best mates, I put up with lots of rubbish. I was sick of it and wanted to get out of the pain and trouble I had been through. So once I had got out of it I thought I would be free. But no. They continued to harass me. Via e-mail, MSN, text messages. Made me feel very lonely and depressed. It was just before the summer holidays, so during them I was pretty much on my own all the time. Parents at work all day and since they were my best mates who I used to do every-thing with, I didn't really have anyone to see. They had turned everyone against me you see. So I got into depression and it was absolutely horrid. My parents were extremely supportive and helpful, I can't thank them enough. But no matter how great they can be, there is always the fact that you're on your own in the rest of the world—that is saddening.

—15-year-old girl from the United Kingdom

The anecdote above underscores the fact that parents cannot protect their children from everything wrong, bad, or evil in this world. However, there is much that they *can* do. They can engage their kids in a dialogue about the relevant issues, venture into cyberspace with them, and informally or formally monitor their electronic activities. Cumulatively, these efforts should demonstrate to youth that the adults in their life actively care about their online safety.

Communication Is Key

First and foremost, it is important for parents to develop an open dialogue with their children so they feel comfortable approaching them if confronted with an unpleasant online experience. It's often difficult to talk about these issues at first, but it is essential. As discussed earlier, our research suggests that only a minority of teens who experience cyberbullying tell their parents (or other adults). Much of this lack of openness relates to the youth's perception that they will be blamed or will lose their computer, cell phone, or Internet privileges. Conveying to them that you will patiently listen to their problem or situation and respond in a nonjudgmental and responsible manner is essential in cultivating and preserving an open line of communication.

> *Bullying boils down to communication. Teach your kids to communicate with you about the small stuff and they'll tell you about the big stuff too.*
>
> —Mother from Minnesota

If parents are unsure of how to bring up these issues with those under their care, we have provided some sample "scripts" to help get the conversation started (Resource C). These examples can demonstrate the ease with which the topic of cyberbullying can be discussed and the most productive, noncritical ways of doing so. Research has consistently identified the utility of ongoing discussions by parents, caregivers, or teachers with children about their online interactions and activities (Berson et al., 2002; Ybarra & Mitchell, 2004). Says Suzanne Stanford, CEO of My Internet Safety Coach (as cited in Writer, 2006),

> Often, kids are afraid to tell their parents for fear that their computer will be taken away or that their parents will make the situation worse. What they don't realize is that unless the bullying stops immediately, it can escalate and leave permanent psychological scars. (¶ 9)

Essentially, there must exist a crystal-clear understanding about what is appropriate and what is not with respect to online activities. Toward that end, we have created an "Internet Use Contract," which can be used as is or as a template to create your own custom contract (Resource D). Its purpose is to promote a trusting relationship between parents and children when it comes to the latter's use of computers and the Internet. Both parties agree to abide by certain mutually acceptable rules of engagement and indicate their acceptance and understanding of those rules with their signatures at the bottom of the form. To remind the child of this pledged commitment, we recommend that this contract be posted in a highly visible place (e.g., next to the computer). Just as in the "Rules for Classroom

Computer Use" detailed above, a parent should also specify which Web sites and software applications are prohibited.

In addition to implementing and enforcing rules for computer use, parents should consider corresponding rules for cell phones. Resource E provides a sample "Family Cell Phone Use Contract" that parents can adapt and utilize. The point to emphasize is that having a cell phone is a privilege (like computers) that can be revoked for misbehavior. That said, it is also important for parents to realize that they need to give their kids some space with respect to their communications with others. Parents should resist constantly hovering over their child when that child is text messaging friends and should not go through the phone's text message logs when it is unattended (unless there is a serious cause for concern). Instead, they should focus on developing a trusting relationship with their children and only invade privacy as a last resort.

Go Online

It is imperative that parents go online with their children. Many adults are intimidated by electronic devices and/or the Internet, which is completely understandable given that we have not grown up with computers like adolescents today have. Nonetheless, this should not prevent parents from exploring the mediums and venues through which youth communicate and interact in cyberspace. In fact, unfamiliar parents can enlist the assistance of their children in getting acclimated with Internet-based activities. Parents should ask their children to show them where they go online and why they like certain Web environments. Some youth will be immediately open to this, while others may resist. Parents should be patient and slowly work their way into the online lives of their children. It may take time, but it will pay dividends down the road.

Once online with their kids, parents can casually inquire further about the technologies and Web sites: Why are they so popular? What do you and your friends do on these sites or with this software? Can everyone see the messages you send or post? Do you really "know" everyone with whom you are communicating? Who are "BBallDude19" and "foxyFLgal"? What sort of pictures or video have you posted online? Parents must remember to keep an open mind and resist knee-jerk reactions of a condemning or criticizing nature. Once parents have a trusting relationship with their children, they will be able to influence their Internet behaviors accordingly.

Box 6.8 provides several additional questions to help get the proverbial ball rolling. Expressing interest in their cyberspace experiences without criticizing or condemning their activities online paves the way for a long-term positive relationship with the adolescents in your life. Responses to these questions should serve to bring about deeper discussion about issues related to cyberbullying and online harassment, and will open the door for parents to the online worlds in which their kids are living.

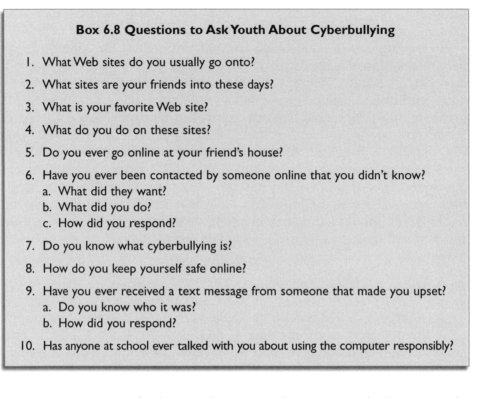

Box 6.8 Questions to Ask Youth About Cyberbullying

1. What Web sites do you usually go onto?

2. What sites are your friends into these days?

3. What is your favorite Web site?

4. What do you do on these sites?

5. Do you ever go online at your friend's house?

6. Have you ever been contacted by someone online that you didn't know?
    a. What did they want?
    b. What did you do?
    c. How did you respond?

7. Do you know what cyberbullying is?

8. How do you keep yourself safe online?

9. Have you ever received a text message from someone that made you upset?
    a. Do you know who it was?
    b. How did you respond?

10. Has anyone at school ever talked with you about using the computer responsibly?

At some point, further probing may be warranted. For example, parents might seek to determine the tendency of their child to rationalize cyberbullying given a specific circumstance or situation. Then, they can point out the faulty reasoning in those decision-making processes so that the youth's behavioral choices are not swayed by emotion or opportunity. To be sure, it is impossible for parents to protect and watch over their children at all hours of the day and night. Still, it is possible through a combination of these efforts to instill in them safe Internet practices that will guide their online (and consequently even offline) activities.

The Earlier the Better

Developing safe Internet practices very early on in the lives of children is essential to ensure that they internalize those habits as their computer and Internet proficiency grows. Kids these days become technologically adept at a very early age (see the tech-savvy youngster in Figure 6.1), and parental guidance is of the utmost importance in teaching them to use electronic devices in responsible ways. Moreover, it will be much easier for parents to insist upon going online with their children at 8 or 9 years of age than when they are 15 or 16. Positive habits instilled at an early age will pay dividends in their decision-making processes later in life. To be sure, developing appropriate belief systems and behavioral choices is a much more valuable and enduring approach than simply threatening them with punishments for particular rule violations.

Figure 6.1   Educate Youth From an Early Age

SOURCE: Photo courtesy of Christine Sellers.

Monitor Their Activities

We also feel that it is key for parents to monitor their children closely when they are on the computer. Most parents and guardians realize this; recent data show that 73 percent keep the home computer in an open family area—either purposefully or inadvertently providing at least casual surveillance of the online activities of youth at home (Lenhart, Madden, & Hitlin, 2005). Relatedly, we believe it is a bad idea to put an Internet-enabled computer in the privacy of your child's bedroom (though a computer unconnected to the Internet is not expected to be a problem).

> *I would never bully online because it hurts. Also, if the kids had half a brain they would consider that a parent is monitoring it like mine do.*
>
> —13-year-old girl from Massachusetts

Another solution to be considered is the installation and use of monitoring software programs. Since parents cannot watch over their child's online activities all of the time, they may want to consider employing specialized software to do the job. A number of commercial software programs are on the market that can help in this regard. Some allow adults to block access to certain Web sites, while others only allow the computer user to access specified sites (as discussed above). Still others track all the places computer users go when connected to the Internet.

We certainly support using these programs as a part of a comprehensive approach to online safety and responsibility, but it is naive to think that these software programs alone will keep kids safe or prevent them from bullying others or accessing inappropriate content. Indeed, some research has shown that filtering software and the specification of Internet usage rules is not significantly related to a decreased chance of Internet harassment victimization (Ybarra & Mitchell, 2004).

Other research has determined that 54 percent of parents use some type of Internet filter, 62 percent check up on the Web sites their children visit, and 64 percent have specified rules for the time their children spend online (Lenhart et al., 2005). Even with filters, proactive inquiries, and rule setting, motivated youth can easily find a way to visit objectionable Web sites or participate in inappropriate online behavior. They may go to a friend's house, the library, or a local coffeehouse with free wireless Internet access. They may even learn to subvert the hardware and software filters that responsible adults have implemented, as previously discussed. This is why software alone is often insufficient.

> *Many parents use parental controls at home, which is a great first step. But relying solely on parental controls can provide a false sense of security since many children access the Internet from various locations. It is crucial that children, parents and educators are informed and well-versed as to potential risks our children may face online.*
>
> —Jace Galloway, Internet
> Safety Coordinator from Illinois

Use Discretion When Spying

If parents choose to use filters and tracking software, we encourage them to tell their children about it. Not only will this act as a deterrent, but parents can then explain *why* they have chosen to incorporate such controls on the computer. It is important for parents to communicate to their children that there are people in cyberspace intent on causing harm and that the software will help to keep them protected.

Some parents with whom we speak are adamant that it is perfectly acceptable—if not demanded—that they covertly and surreptitiously spy on their children's Internet activities. Of course, parents ultimately decide what they think is appropriate in monitoring the online behaviors of the youth in their household. However, if parents do this without informing their children, there is a significant risk of damaging any positive relationship that exists between them. At that point, children may no longer trust their parents at all, which means they will not confide in them about problems they are having—online or offline. We strongly believe that parents should be honest and upfront with their children at all times.

THE STUDENT'S ROLE IN PREVENTING CYBERBULLYING

Responsibility for youth safety online should largely be shared among the adults that serve this population, because it appears that the problem of cyberbullying would quickly grow out of hand if kids were left to their own devices. That said, adolescents can take a number of steps to help protect themselves from victimization. Safeguarding personally identifiable information (rather than heedlessly posting it in public spheres) and being careful with the passwords to their online accounts are the two most vital practices for avoiding victimization at the hands of bullies on the Internet.

Protecting Personal Information

While it seems like common sense, adolescents often need to be reminded that they should never give out their personal information anywhere on the Internet—especially to people they don't know in real life. They may think that the person on the other side of the computer is a friend, but how can they ever know for sure? Even if that person is a friend, there is no way of knowing if someone else in the room is looking over that person's shoulder. Youth should know that anything they reveal about themselves online can (and likely will) be used against them. Cyberbullies can use the personal information to cause a significant amount of emotional harm.

> *I was talking to my friend about something that was bothering me on an e-mail, I sent it to her then the next day another friend of mine had hacked onto my e-mail and took it, and she was the friend that was bothering me, saw it and printed it out, she took it to school with her the next day and showed every one, and it had personal stuff on it, it wasn't just about the person, that was only about 1 line of it. Everyone saw the personal information and teased me for a few days.*
>
> —12-year-old girl from an undisclosed location outside the United States

Along these same lines, youth should be careful in posting anything to a Web site that they wouldn't want the entire world to see. We discussed this initially in Chapter 4 when we considered social networking Web sites. Many kids today enjoy posting pictures or videos on sites like Flickr, Photobucket, YouTube, or MySpace for their friends or family members to check out. They need to understand fully that individuals with malicious motives may also access this content and do with it what they will. For instance, pictures can be downloaded and then manipulated to make it look as though something inappropriate is occurring. Similarly, there have been numerous stories in the news detailing how predators and pedophiles have been able to contact minors based on personal data and digital photos posted on publicly accessible Web sites or social networking profile pages. Cyberbullies are also easily able to use such content to inflict serious emotional and psychological harm on those who unwittingly, naively, or carelessly post it.

Finally, adolescents must remember that photos, videos, and text cannot be easily deleted from the Internet because of the ease and speed with which digital content is reproduced and archived. Search engines or Web sites like www.archive.org regularly index (i.e., add to their databases) the contents of Web pages across the Internet, including a student's personal Web or profile page. After being indexed, the content is retrievable and viewable by others who look for it—*even after it is removed from the original site.* Moreover, people you know (and people you don't know) may have saved the pictures, videos, and text on their own computer hard drives and can repost the material online or send it around to others at any time. Suffice it to say that the permanence factor of anything on the Internet can have significant and long-lasting repercussions for youth who have not been careful or discrete with what they've decided to share with others in cyberspace.

Password Protection

Passwords are necessary to access personal accounts on a computer network. They serve as "authentication" devices and uniquely identify someone as being who they claim to be. Of course, correct authentication prevents others from accessing or altering your personal data. In our current Information Age, passwords are a part of everyday life. However, some users inadvertently make themselves vulnerable to cyberbullying by exposing or carelessly distributing their password.

> *A guy from school changed my MSN e-mail password, I still can't get into my account. He also threatens to beat me up if don't break up with my girl friend.*
>
> —16-year-old boy from Kentucky

Many youth simply don't see the risk in telling others their password. In our school assemblies to students, we ask how many of them know their best friend's computer password, and (perhaps not surprisingly) a majority of the hands are raised. To be honest, this is very alarming to us. Even if youth are responsible enough not to distribute their passwords deliberately, they might inadvertently expose them to others. Many users leave their passwords on a sticky note next to their computers (in case they forget it!). Someone who visits may see it and remember it for later use.

Why is it important to keep passwords secret? An example will help to illustrate the potential problems. A teenage boy might select a MySpace password that is very difficult to guess, but because it is so difficult, might write it down on a small slip of paper taped underneath his keyboard. When his best friend comes over for a visit, the keyboard might accidentally be dropped—revealing the taped paper and, consequently, the password. If that friendship goes sour, the password could be used by the (ex-) best friend to access the account and then upload humiliating content for everyone to read or see.

As a guidance counselor in my present setting, I have experienced students telling me of problems mentioned over AOL Instant Messenger. Students get on other students' accounts due to the sharing of passwords and then say mean or horrible things as a joke or as intimidation. This can leave a student feeling highly scared to come to school, or even more distraught than normal as a teenager with his or her peer relationships.

—School counselor from Florida

Even if adolescents are extremely careful in never writing down their passwords or disclosing them to others, a password might still be discovered through other means. For example, some Internet content providers have "password hint questions," which allow users to retrieve forgotten passwords to online accounts by responding correctly to the questions presented. If the response is successful, an e-mail is sent to the address associated with the account. Within this e-mail, the current password or a new password is given. One of these password hint questions might be "What is my pet's name?" If someone knows your pet's name and you've used it as a password hint, an e-mail with password information would be sent to the relevant e-mail account. If a person knows how to access *that* e-mail account, access to *other* Internet accounts may be possible. Through this procedure, a person can change the passwords of all of your other online accounts simply by having access to your e-mail and knowing a few facts about you.

Finally, some people use the same password for multiple purposes—school and personal e-mail, MySpace, eBay, PayPal, and many other accounts online. As such, finding out the password to one account can lead to simple access to other accounts. While we are considering cyberbullying in this text, there are obvious risks associated with identity theft when someone commandeers another person's password. Box 6.9 lists some recommendations that everyone—children and adults alike—should follow when creating passwords to Web- and software-based accounts.

Box 6.9 Recommendations for Creating a Unique Password

- Use passwords with at least seven characters.
- Use a mixture of upper- and lower-case letters, numbers, and nonalphabetic characters.
- Use first letters of an uncommon sentence, song, poem, quote, etc.
- Use word fragments not found in the dictionary (mihtaupyn).
- Use short words separated by characters (dog%door, candy$trip).
- Use transliteration as seen on vanity license plates (e.g., "Elite One" becomes "E1te0nE").
- Use lines from a childhood verse or popular song ("It's 3am, I must be lonely" becomes I3amimbL).
- Use phrases from movies ("May the Force be with you" becomes MtFBwu).
- Use expressions inspired by the name of a city ("Rice-a-Roni, the San Francisco Treat" becomes RaRtSFT).
- Interweave characters in two words ("Play Date" becomes PateDlay).

LAW ENFORCEMENT'S ROLE IN PREVENTING CYBERBULLYING

Law enforcement will undoubtedly need to become involved in responding to serious forms of online aggression (e.g., threats to someone's personal safety or in other situations where a law has been violated), but we also feel they have a role to play in a comprehensive prevention plan. First, educators should invite law enforcement officers or utilize school resource officers in their classroom discussions and schoolwide assemblies about responsible Internet use. Students need to realize that inappropriate online conduct may result in serious legal consequences offline. Second, officers should also discuss the ways in which online deviance is investigated, so students recognize that just about everything is traceable when sent or posted electronically. Using specific examples of cases will also reinforce the seriousness of these situations to many youth.

> *I have found that students use the Internet to bully and harass each other. These students particularly use the site MySpace.com. Cyberbullying has become the way kids threaten each other and intimidate each other. Kids feel that they can't be tracked or get in trouble for acts that they're not caught doing so they use the Internet to hide behind, and bully and intimidate other kids.*

> —School Resource Officer from Florida

WARNING SIGNS: WHAT TO LOOK FOR

It is often difficult to determine whether behavioral or attitudinal changes in youth are signals of distress or simply the usual "adolescent angst" commonly associated with this often-tumultuous transitional period in their lives. Nevertheless, it is important for educators, parents, and other adults to learn to read the behavior of their students and children so that real problems can be detected, diagnosed, and promptly handled. A number of signals may suggest that a child is experiencing some type of distressing event while online (see Box 6.10). Identifying these indicators may help to minimize the negative emotional and psychological effects of Internet-based harm.

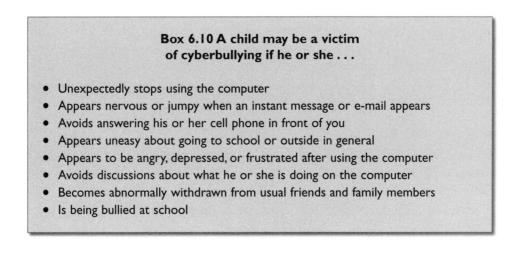

**Box 6.10 A child may be a victim
of cyberbullying if he or she . . .**

- Unexpectedly stops using the computer
- Appears nervous or jumpy when an instant message or e-mail appears
- Avoids answering his or her cell phone in front of you
- Appears uneasy about going to school or outside in general
- Appears to be angry, depressed, or frustrated after using the computer
- Avoids discussions about what he or she is doing on the computer
- Becomes abnormally withdrawn from usual friends and family members
- Is being bullied at school

The most obvious sign that something is going on involves a marked change in the adolescent's computer habits. Students may suddenly stop using the computer or overtly refuse when asked to do something online. If a child has been known to go on the computer every day at school but then unexpectedly goes several days without logging on, this change of behavior may signal an underlying problem. In addition, if a student appears nervous when a new e-mail or instant message arrives or is constantly looking over his or her shoulder when at the computer, this behavior may indicate that something is amiss. If a student seems extraordinarily angry, upset, or depressed, especially when using the computer, those emotions may signal a cyberbullying incident. And if youth try to avoid discussions about what they are doing on the computer or put up emotional walls when questioned about harassment or bullying, a serious problem may be at hand.

Relatedly, adults know that many youth try to avoid having to go to school for a variety of reasons. However, if a teenager adamantly refuses to go and will not discuss why, further probing is essential. From our discussions with victims, we know how difficult it can be to face cyber-bullies at school—as well as face the rest of the student body who may know about the electronic harassment. Consider Vada's story from Chapter 1; she likely would be mortified to return to school the next day knowing that everyone had seen the printouts of the Web page that Ali had created.

There are also a number of red flags that may indicate that a child is mistreating others in cyberspace (see Box 6.11). If a youth quickly switches or closes screens or programs when you walk by, he or she is probably trying to hide something. In these situations, it may be important for you to restress the rules and let the student know that if he or she gives you reason to be concerned about online activities, you will install tracking software (if you haven't already done so) or restrict Internet access to times when you will be able to supervise and monitor online behavior.

**Box 6.11 A Child May Be Cyberbullying
Others if He or She . . .**

- Quickly switches screens or closes programs when you walk by
- Uses the computer at all hours of the night
- Gets unusually upset if he or she cannot use the computer
- Is using multiple online accounts or an account that is not his or her own
- Laughs excessively while using the computer
- Avoids discussions about what he or she is doing on the computer or becomes defensive

---

Furthermore, parents should be advised that if their children are using the computer during all hours of the night, they may be using it for inap-propriate activities. They should put reasonable restrictions on computer use and determine exactly what their children are doing online all night. If the children appear to get unusually upset when their usage is limited, they are likely using it too much. Again, be reasonable. Parents should lis-ten to their children when they tell them what they are doing on the com-puter and rationally assess whether further restrictions are necessary. Give them the benefit of the doubt but check up on them to make sure they are keeping their end of the bargain.

As another point, parents should be encouraged to learn their children's e-mail addresses and social networking profile names and make clear that the children are not allowed to create multiple online profiles or accounts. They should inquire further if they see that a youth is logged onto what seems to be a different e-mail address or MySpace account. Many youth we speak to admit to that they have a "parent-friendly" MySpace page that they don't regularly use and a completely separate one that they constantly use when interacting with their friends. Obviously, a level of trust must exist so that such outright deception does not occur. Not only does it make it difficult for parents to prevent their child's victimization and assist if something does happen, it also subverts any efforts to create the open line of communication indispensable for a healthy, functional parent-child relationship.

If a young person is laughing excessively while using the computer, or if a group of students is gathered around the computer laughing or giggling, they may be cyberbullying others. If they appear jumpy, nervous, or unwilling to share the humor with you, they are probably doing something they shouldn't be doing. However, there are many appropriate humorous pieces of content on the Internet, so don't jump to conclusions. We all appreciate a hilarious comic or funny video; just ask them to show you what is so funny. In general, avoiding discussions or becoming defensive about what they are doing online is a clear sign that they are engaging in activities that likely don't align with your standards of appropriate behavior, thus meriting further inquiry.

SUMMARY

Educators, parents, students, and law enforcement are all important pieces of the cyberbullying prevention puzzle, as shown in Figure 6.2. Individually, it is difficult for any one person to stop cyberbullying from occurring; together, however, adults can present a formidable force against online cruelty. As this chapter has discussed, teachers must supervise students who are using computers in their classrooms and educate the school community about responsible Internet use and netiquette. School administrators must take online aggression seriously and ensure that policies are in place that allow the school to take action against cyberbullies when their actions substantially and materially affect the learning environment or infringe upon the rights of others (as discussed in Chapter 5).

It is also clear that parents must be educated and encouraged to participate in their child's online experiences—which also involves disciplining unacceptable online behaviors when necessary. Youth need to exercise care when it comes to the personal information they post online and should carefully protect their passwords. Law enforcement officers should

Figure 6.2   Pieces of the Cyberbullying Prevention Puzzle

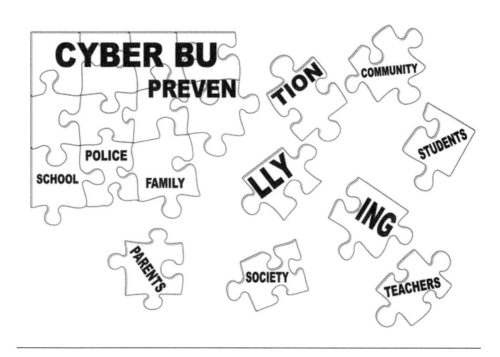

collaborate with school officials to provide education about Internet safety in a way that conveys to students both that threats using electronic devices will be punished and that help is available if they are afraid for their safety. With all of this said, though, prevention efforts can only do so much. Unfortunately, even the best prevention strategies are not 100 percent effective. The following chapter provides guidance and direction on when and how to respond to cyberbullying incidents when they do occur.

QUESTIONS FOR REFLECTION

1. Do you think it is possible to prevent all forms of cyberbullying completely? If yes, how? If not, why not?

2. Whose responsibility is it to prevent cyberbullying?

3. How can students be used to help prevent cyberbullying?

4. At what age do you think it is appropriate for a youth to have a computer in his or her bedroom?

5. How do you know when someone is being cyberbullied? How do you know when someone is cyberbullying others?

7

Responding to Cyberbullying

My daughter was the target of cyberbullying. Although it occurred only once on the computer, I still consider it bullying. A group of girls down-loaded her MySpace pictures and wrote hateful and obscene comments about her. They then sent it out to all of their friends. People began call-ing our home and telling us about the site. As soon as I called one of the parents, the Web page began deleting—but not before a friend printed a copy of the first page of it. I didn't get all of it, but I got enough. These same girls continue to make references to my daughter on line, without actually saying her name, but we know they are talking about her. The worst part is that none of the parents will hold their daughters account-able because only one actually did the typing. We are left angry, hurt, and paranoid about what these girls will do next. These people were sup-posed to be friends, but one got mad at my daughter and then a group of these girls just thought it would be funny to make this Web page. What recourse is there? That's what I'd like to know.

—Submitted anonymously

Throughout this book we have covered quite a range of topics, from an introduction to cyberbullying to findings from relevant research and the legal issues inherent in cases of online aggression by students. What we have not yet covered—and what perhaps is one of the primary reasons why you've picked up this book—is how to respond to cyber-bullying incidents when they take place. Many adults have come to the realization that electronic bullying can be just as detrimental to the development of adolescents as traditional schoolyard bullying but still struggle to identify suitable courses of action.

In this chapter, we explore appropriate responses from several different perspectives. Obviously, *educators* play a critical role in responding to cyberbullying incidents that negatively affect the school environment and infringe upon the rights of others. *Parents* who are made aware of cyber-bullying activities must discipline their children. *Bystanders* need to step up and do something about peers being victimized instead of tacitly condoning it through inaction. *Students* must be equipped with strategies they can employ if they experience cyberbullying. And *law enforcement* should become involved in those cases when cyberbullying involves threats to someone's physical safety or when a criminal law violation may have occurred.

In many ways, we feel it is the educator who serves to link all of these stakeholders together in a comprehensive response strategy. We believe that educators have the power to influence positively the thought processes and behaviors of youth (and the parents of youth) and can appreciably reduce the occurrence of cyberbullying. Before we delve into a discussion of practical responses for all parties involved, we'd first like to begin with an oft-invoked solution that, to be honest, drives us crazy. It may be well intentioned, but as we will point out, it is completely off-base.

JUST TURN OFF THE COMPUTER!

We have spoken to many parents, teachers, and youth about cyberbullying over the last several years. Those who do not completely understand the phenomenon often wonder, "What's the big deal? Why don't kids just turn off their computers?" In fact, here is an illustrative example from a visitor to the online safety Web site BlogSafety (www.blogsafety.com):

> *HOW DO YOU GET BULLIED ONLINE?!?!?!?!?! It's called the "exit" button. People are so incredibly stupid. "Now I've got to go, because I'm going to cyber steal someone's lunch money and then cyber call somebody names (even though they can just click the exit button, morons) before cyber beating someone up and giving him a cyber-wedgie." This is about the dumbest thing I've ever heard of.*
>
> —Posted by: son of liberty on August 2, 2006 at 8:15am

We feel this comment (and those expressing similar sentiments) is flippant, dismissive, and naive, to say the least. There are a number of reasons why "clicking the exit button" or "turning off the computer" simply aren't viable options for those being cyberbullied.

First, why should a victim be required to interrupt an online experience because of someone else's maliciousness? Since when is it appropriate to blame the victim for another's aggressive actions? In fact, this is one of the main reasons many youth don't tell adults about their negative online experiences: They don't want to be blamed and, as a consequence, lose their Internet privileges or otherwise be forced to miss out on all of the benefits of the Internet. A 13-year-old girl from Virginia expressed this, stating, "I wanted to tell my parents but I was afraid that they would never let me chat again, and I know that's how a lot of other kids feel."

Another reason "turning off the computer" is not practical is that cyberbullying can continue irrespective of whether the target is online. For example, a bully could set up a defamatory Web page or spread rumors via e-mail among his or her classmates. A bully could also circulate information through a social networking Web site or even create a fictitious online profile for the victim. In these examples, the mistreatment continues and the victimization still occurs (as others see the hurtful content), even when the victim is offline.

Finally, if we counsel youth just to "turn off the computer," we are sending the wrong message. What do you tell them if they are being bullied at school? We doubt that you would tell them, "Just don't go to school!" While schools are among the safest places for kids to be, many harmful, uncomfortable, and at times violent behaviors do happen there. We know that victimization actually can happen anywhere, but that potential should not (and cannot) cause children to miss out on all of the educational and social benefits that accompany going to school.

Therefore, if we still want to encourage computer and Internet use, what should be done when youth are harassed or mistreated in cyberspace? We begin with practical advice for educators, which revolves around determining an appropriate informal or formal punitive response, using creative methods to discipline the inappropriate use of technology and teach about its acceptable use, becoming someone whom students can approach and trust, being sensitive to the concerns of cyberbullying victims, creating an anonymous reporting system, recognizing special circumstances of an incident that warrant enhanced penalties, and contacting relevant Internet and cell phone service providers as necessary.

SCHOOL'S RESPONSE TO CYBERBULLYING

As discussed in Chapter 5, liability concerns arise when technology provided at school (or brought to school) is used to cause harm. If a student reports being cyberbullied, the school is obligated to intervene. Harassment and discrimination in general is a violation of the Civil Rights

Act of 1964 and other state and federal legislation. School district personnel who fail to respond to it when it is brought to their attention can be held legally responsible. While it is not expected that teachers and other school employees actively police the Internet to make sure youth are not involved in inappropriate electronic behaviors, they must move to action when they become aware of a cyberbullying situation that affects students under their care (see Box 7.1).

**Box 7.1 What Schools Should Do
When Made Aware of a Cyberbullying Incident**

- Assess the immediate threat.
- Ensure the safety of the target.
- Demonstrate compassion and empathy to the target.
- Restrain the bully if necessary (separate from target; closely monitor).
- Investigate and gather evidence.
- Contact parents.
- Contact the Internet service provider.
- Contact the police when physical threats are involved.
- Enforce disciplinary policy.
- Contact legal counsel if considering serious disciplinary action.

To review briefly what was covered in Chapter 5, the common theme woven throughout the decisions of courts is that school officials can place educationally based restrictions on student speech and behavior necessary to maintain an appropriate school climate. This can involve content created and disseminated through the school district's Internet system or through cell phone text messaging that occurs at school. It also involves incidents where students bring in printouts of cyberbullying or encourage others to visit specific online environments (e.g., Web sites or social networking profile pages) where cyberbullying is occurring or when these sites are accessed through Internet connectivity at school. Finally, we have stressed that restrictions on student speech can be made on content created and disseminated away from school when it results in a substantial and material disruption on campus or infringes upon the rights of others to work and learn in a safe and nonthreatening atmosphere.

Intervening does not necessarily mandate student suspension or expulsion or some other formal sanction. Indeed, zero-tolerance policies are often problematic, because they are inflexible when dealing with situations that may require discretion on the part of the educator. Many cyberbullying incidents can readily be addressed using a variety of informal mechanisms (see below). Simply approaching the student and having a quick talk about the issue may be enough. In fact, teachers engage in this kind of activity on a day-to-day basis. If this doesn't work and the behavior continues, perhaps the student's parents need to be called and/or the principal needs to conference with them. Parents often wield immense power in dictating the behaviors of their children and are usually quick to take action when informed of wrongdoing.

Along these lines, educators should defer to parental authority when possible. Hopefully the parents of the offending student are willing to work with you to resolve the situation. Addressing cyberbullying informally and working closely with parents keeps the school district reasonably safe from any accusations of inappropriate discipline. Indeed, attorney Mike Tully of the West Regional Equity Network in the University of Arizona's College of Education—an expert on school law— argues that the wisest course of action for educators is to limit or forego formal discipline (Tully, 2007). Not only does this approach preempt litigation, but it avoids subsequent negative fallout to the district and community. This latter fact is underappreciated but tremendously vital, as you cannot put a price on the value of positive morale and a peaceable environment among school staff, students, and parents.

It also deserves comment that school districts may be inclined to make emotionally laden punitive decisions when one of their administrators, teachers, or students is victimized. The district is presented with an affront to the sanctity of the school environment, sees digital content that is offending, and immediately becomes defensive and exacts a severe sanction. Sometimes this is clearly warranted. Other times, it is disproportionate, done in haste, and oversteps the bounds of acceptable corrective action against a student. Overstepping disciplinary bounds is an open invitation for lawsuits because of the First and Fourth Amendment rights of students (Tully, 2007). The attendant factors in many cyberbullying incidents are obviously complex and multifaceted, which makes a proper response even more challenging.

Overall, school district policy should clearly spell out a range of penalties based on the severity of the incident. The type of response should be proportionate to the weight of the offense and convey the extent of its gravity and severity (and go no further). Feel free to use our basic model as a starting point to develop your own comprehensive continuum of strategies for responding to cyberbullying (Table 7.1). The measure of an effective response is that the offender comes away knowing that the behavior is clearly inappropriate and will not be tolerated and that subsequent refusal to follow the rules will result in future disciplinary action.

Since they can foster a hostile school climate and escalate into more serious behaviors if left unchecked, even minor forms of harassment should not be ignored. We believe that *every* cyberbullying incident should be investigated and documented (see Resource G, the sample "Cyberbullying Incident Tracking Form"). Many times, bullying behaviors intensify because nothing is done to stop them, and perhaps cyberbullying is attractive to students because it is often overlooked by adults.

Table 7.1   Continuum of Cyberbullying Behaviors and Appropriate Responses

<------------------Behaviors------------------>		
Minor	*Moderate*	*Serious*
Teasing Ignoring Name calling Taunting Flaming	Identity theft Spreading rumors Posting pictures online without permission Creating video of bullying	True physical threats Stalking Intimidation Death threats
<------------------Responses------------------>		
Minor	*Moderate*	*Serious*
Meeting with parents Meeting with counselor Creative sanction (e.g., anticyberbullying posters)	Meeting with principal Behavior plan Civility education Extracurricular consequences Detention	Legal/criminal punishment Civil punishment Suspension Expulsion

Generally speaking, cyberbullying incidents should be addressed using many of the same strategies that the school uses to deal with traditional bullying. We are pleased to see an increasing number of school districts crafting formal policies that specifically mention harassment and aggression through electronic means. The examples reviewed in Chapter 5 can serve as templates in new districtwide implementations designed to counter the problem proactively, which should then be followed when cyberbullying affects your school.

Be Creative in Your Response

Educators should be encouraged to be creative in addressing cyberbullying situations when they arise. This can occur in a number of ways. For example, many like to capitalize on "teachable moments" that present themselves throughout the school year, and an instance of cyberbullying could serve to promote quality dialogue and discussion about the topic.

As another suggestion, cyberbullies (or all students) might be required to write a research paper on the effects of harassment from the perspective of the victim—perhaps even in "the old-fashioned way"—using the library and a pen (no Internet or computer). Through this, they will learn what it feels like not to be able to use technology, which should promote a greater respect for those valuable tools. We have previously covered how victims of cyberbullying may not feel comfortable using the computer and, therefore, may miss out on all of the advantages it affords. Cyberbullies need to understand the effect their harmful behavior can have, and hopefully this assignment will make that point.

As a third suggestion, online aggressors might also be required to create informative posters to be displayed throughout school hallways or classrooms about the nature of electronic bullying. Fourth, they might work with their school's digital media teacher to create public service announcements (PSAs) in the form of digital videos to educate the school or broader community on the subject. Jace Galloway, an Internet Safety Coordinator from Illinois, points out that "making posters or creating videos has a greater impact on the participants and educates others."

Overall, there are a number of innovative ways to teach and reinforce positive behavioral choices, and adolescents themselves are very capable of tackling a novel, instructive approach. Their efforts may even be more fruitful than those enacted by school administration in modifying peer conceptions about the proper use of electronic devices.

Be a Trustee

Schools should designate one or more staff members to serve as "trustees." Trustees can be teachers, guidance counselors, or other staff members who work directly with students. They must be specifically trained to deal with online aggression and be staff members whom students feel comfortable approaching for help. We recommend that a trustee post a sign on his or her door (such as the sample provided in Resource K) indicating to youth that this staff member has been specially trained and designated a cyberbullying trustee and is capable of helping with any problems related to online aggression. That way, students know who really understands the phenomenon on their campus and where they can turn for assistance.

You (yes, you!) can and should become a trustee. Ask yourself: "If I were in their shoes, would I feel comfortable coming and talking to a person like me?" Better yet, specifically ask your students if they have experienced cyberbullying and whether they would be comfortable talking about it with you (or another adult). Do what it takes so that they know you are available for them and that you will work with them to improve the situation. Become someone they can trust with these types of problems.

Be Sensitive to the Concerns of Victims

Why is there so little sympathy towards people who are bullied? It's like, it's gotten to the point online where you either take it, or get offline. Why did it ever get to this point, and what can I do that I haven't already done?

—Submitted anonymously

When cyberbullied, many youth will try to avoid conversations about their experiences, be dismissive about the extent of their impact, or shun offers for assistance in responding to the problem. Well, we can tell you that they do want help but don't think adults can really do anything to improve the situation. In fact, they fear the opposite—that any action taken by teachers or parents will only make the situation worse. They may be afraid of being publicly singled out for special attention, protection, nurturing, or care at school. They may be afraid that seeking help will incite further victimization. They may be afraid that requesting assistance means they are completely unfit and unable to deal with typical teenage life.

If a student comes to you to talk about an experience with cyberbullying, you must take certain steps to address the situation. In fact, a swift and appropriate response is important so that the victim knows that the school is doing something to alleviate the problem. If it is not taken seriously, schools risk alienating students who might then continue to suffer from victimization or attempt to take matters into their own hands through misguided retaliation or revenge.

Educators can start by asking the student what he or she would like to see happen—what would make things better. If the student doesn't know what to do, one reactive measure might be as basic as discretely separating the bully from the victim at school (to the extent possible). Along these same lines, all staff (including cafeteria workers, bus drivers, coaches, and other support staff) should be briefed on any harassment incidents so that they can quickly identify and respond to any situations that may flare up.

> *It seems like I can't ever get anyone to take me seriously. I know how important it is to report cyberbullies, but peer-pressure says "it's the Internet, take it, get over it, stop being a you know what" kind of thing. I WANT to do something but I'm told not to, I'm told I will be marked for direct attacks if I do.*
>
> —16-year-old boy from unknown location

Recently, we spoke with a school counselor at a local middle school who described the ways that she deals with relatively minor forms of harassment when they come to her attention. After speaking with the victim, she calls the accused party into her office to discuss the allegations. The very first thing she tells the student is: "Right now, you are not in trouble. But I've been made aware that you are engaging in bullying, and if this behavior continues, or you discuss our meeting with anyone other than your parents, you will be in trouble." She then reminds the student about the school's conduct policy and refers to the section in that policy that defines harassment. Next, she points out the listed consequences for violations of the policy. She then warns the student that disciplinary action *will* be taken if the behavior continues. Finally, she reiterates the importance of not talking to other students about their office meeting. In many cases, the counselor doesn't even tell the accused bully who reported the behavior. This also makes retaliation less likely.

We believe this last point is particularly important. As mentioned, many targets of harassment fail to tell adults about their experiences because they are concerned about retribution. The counselor with whom we spoke preemptively alleviated this concern by conveying separately to the target and the bully that discussion of the incident(s) will not occur outside of her office. In most cases, the inappropriate behavior has been identified and addressed, which will hopefully be the end of the problem. If not, all parties clearly understand the progression of steps that will follow.

Create an Anonymous Reporting System

As mentioned earlier in this book, students are often reluctant to discuss their cyberbullying experiences with adults for a number of reasons. Moreover, victims or others who witness bullying may be disinclined to report their experiences for fear of fallout. Every school should therefore have a system in place that allows students who experience or witness cyberbullying (or any inappropriate behavior) to report it anonymously. Being able to broach the subject without being forced to reveal one's identity may prove advantageous in alerting faculty and staff to harmful student experiences and thereby promote an informed response to bring positive change.

The reporting system could be as simple as a box located near the office labeled "Report Inappropriate Behavior Here." The challenge is placing the box in a location that is visible and easily accessible but where students can discreetly submit information. Alternatively, the school might set up an e-mail reporting system where students can anonymously send their concerns through a Web form on the school or district Web site (see Figure 7.1). That way, concerned students can contact the school from the privacy of their own homes without the anxiety associated with another student seeing them dropping something in the reporting box. Of course, if you provide such a resource, every complaint should be taken seriously and thoroughly investigated.

Aggravating Circumstances

As described above, cyberbullying incidents vary in seriousness from relatively minor teasing and name calling to very serious threats to a person's physical safety. While we argue that educators have the ability and responsibility to intervene (at least informally) in all cases, administrative sanctions should escalate in accordance with the severity of cyberbullying behaviors—or if there are aggravating circumstances surrounding the incident. Below we discuss several factors that may warrant increased or more serious repercussions to the offender.

Figure 7.1   Example of an Anonymous Web-Based Reporting System

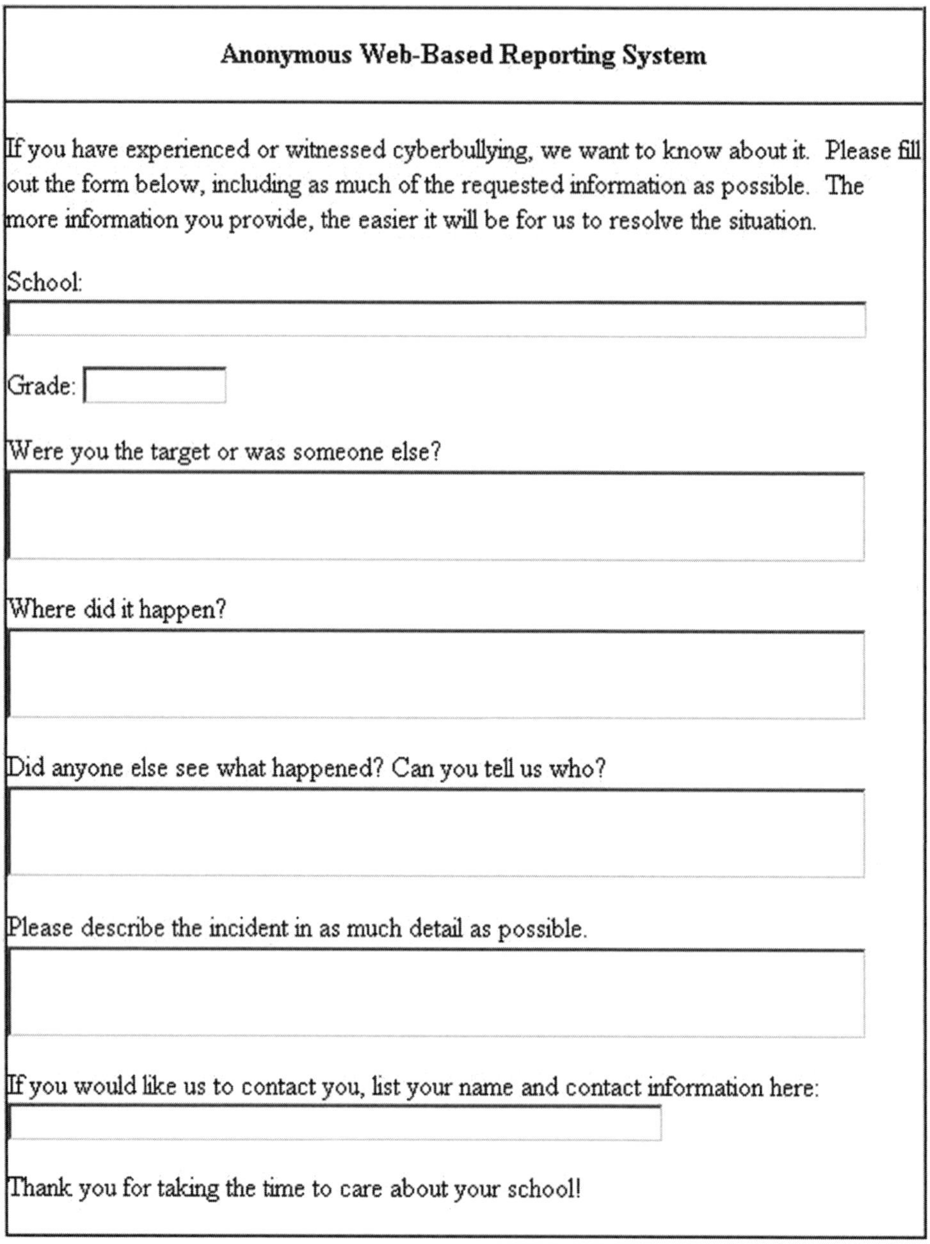

Anonymous Web-Based Reporting System

If you have experienced or witnessed cyberbullying, we want to know about it. Please fill out the form below, including as much of the requested information as possible. The more information you provide, the easier it will be for us to resolve the situation.

School:

Grade:

Were you the target or was someone else?

Where did it happen?

Did anyone else see what happened? Can you tell us who?

Please describe the incident in as much detail as possible.

If you would like us to contact you, list your name and contact information here:

Thank you for taking the time to care about your school!

Substantial Disruption of the Learning Environment

As we discussed at length in Chapter 5, educators have the ability to discipline students for behavior or speech that results in a substantial disruption of the learning environment. While most cyberbullying incidents will not have this effect (at least if they are dealt with quickly before they have a chance to intensify), those that do warrant firm penalties. While a difficult task, it is critical to articulate and document the "substantial disruption" so that if a student challenges a disciplinary action, it will hold up in court.

If school administrators are forced to spend inordinate amounts of time dealing with the incident, it has clearly disrupted the order and workings of the school. If the school district computer system needs to be shut down for a meaningful period of time because students are accessing and disseminating hurtful content, that will notably hinder the delivery of some curriculum and the provision of electronic resources to all. Finally, if it becomes the "topic of conversation" during the school day and forces teachers to rein in the attention of students repeatedly, it has negatively affected their ability to promote learning through instruction.

Cyberbullying Based on Race, Class, Gender, Sexual Orientation, or Any Other Protected Status

Any cyberbullying incident that appears to be motivated by race, class, gender, or sexual orientation must be taken more seriously than those that are not. While it may be directed solely at one person, it reflects malice and bias toward an entire group of people who share the same distinguishing demographic feature. This has the potential to inflame the emotions of multiple individuals and to incite further violence due to its extremely sensitive nature. What is more, such behavior is completely intolerable and often invokes the criminal law in the vast majority of jurisdictions. The school has an absolute responsibility to take strong action any time staff witness or are made aware of electronic harassment that discriminates against a particular group of people.

Digital Video Recordings

We are seeing more and more situations where students are making video recordings of bullying or cyberbullying incidents and uploading them to YouTube or another video-sharing Web site (see "Happy Slapping" in Chapter 2). We've covered the repetitive aspect of victimization in these situations, as the content is viewed by hundreds, thousands, and even millions of people and continually shared, discussed, and mocked among them. Students need to be made aware that any bullying that is digitally recorded will be dealt with more seriously than other forms and that *everyone* who is involved will be disciplined. This includes the student behind the recording device, any others who are filmed participating in the mistreatment, those who upload it to the Internet, and those who disseminate it through Web page hyperlinks, mass e-mails, instant messages, or social networking Web site posts (see the discussion of *Requa v. Kent School District* [2007] in Chapter 5 for a real-life example). Criminal law may also be implicated in these situations, as some states require consent of both parties whenever an audio recording is made of a telephone conversation. Courts in these states appear likely to extend this rule of law when evaluating cases involving covert digital video because, of course, the audio component is also recorded without both parties' consent.

Repeated Cyberbullying Following Intervention

Ideally, students who engage in cyberbullying behaviors will stop after an initial disciplinary response. Some, however, may continue to harass others as if this behavior were perfectly acceptable. In these cases, it is imperative that educators step up and intervene once more—but with enhanced severity. In your initial meeting with the perpetrator, you hopefully outlined what would happen if the online mistreatment continued. Now, you must follow through. It is also critical that you establish a new set of repercussions if the behavior still continues.

Informing Service Providers

Another response option exists that doesn't involve informal resolution with parents or formal resolution through a disciplinary measure. In many cases, it can be quite useful in ending the problem by cutting it off at the source. It may also deter the offender from committing similar misbehavior in the future for fear of the same result. Educators can very simply place a call to an Internet service provider, content host, or cell phone service provider, inform the company of the cyberbullying, request it to check for itself (or provide the company with electronic evidence in the form of screenshots or logs), and consequently to close the account. These providers each have formal agreements that a user agrees to abide by when signing up.

For example, the MySpace "Terms of Service" (2008) states the following conditions. We have only included those that are directly or indirectly related to cyberbullying.

Content/Activity Prohibited. The following are examples of the kind of Content that is illegal or prohibited to post on or through the MySpace Services. Prohibited Content includes, but is not limited to Content that, in the sole discretion of MySpace:

8.1 is patently offensive and promotes racism, bigotry, hatred or physical harm of any kind against any group or individual;

8.2 harasses or advocates harassment of another person;

8.3 exploits people in a sexual or violent manner;

8.5 solicits personal information from anyone under 18;

8.6 publicly posts information that poses or creates a privacy or security risk to any person;

8.7 constitutes or promotes information that you know is false or misleading or promotes illegal activities or conduct that is abusive, threatening, obscene, defamatory or libelous;

8.14 includes a photograph or video of another person that you have posted without that person's consent;

8.16 violates the privacy rights, publicity rights, copyrights, trademark rights, contract rights or any other rights of any person; or

8.25 [involves] impersonating or attempting to impersonate another Member, person or entity;

8.29 [involves] using any information obtained from the MySpace Services in order to harass, abuse, or harm another person or entity, or attempting to do the same;

8.31 [involves] using the MySpace Services in a manner inconsistent with any and all applicable laws and regulations.

The "Terms of Service" also state that MySpace may terminate an account at any time, without warning. As another example, Sprint (2005) posts the following within its "Acceptable Use Policy and Visitor Agreement":

You are responsible for any transmission you send, receive, post, access, or store via our Network, including the content of any communication. ("Illegal or Harmful Use")

Sprint (2005) also prohibits the following activity, among many others:

Disseminating or posting material that is unlawful, libelous, defamatory, obscene, indecent, lewd, harassing, threatening, harmful, invasive of privacy or publicity rights, abusive, inflammatory or otherwise objectionable. ("Illegal or Harmful Use")

Accounts that violate these policies through cyberbullying can be terminated. As a final note, many service providers have set up specific phone numbers and e-mail addresses to facilitate easier contact with them to deal with inappropriate behaviors through their networks. For example, as we pointed out in Chapter 4, educators can contact MySpace at (310) 969–7398 (phone), (310) 969–7394 (fax), or schoolcare@myspace.com. MySpace also has customized Web forms on its site to allow quick reporting of instances of cyberbullying (see Figure 7.2).

Figure 7.2   Contacting MySpace

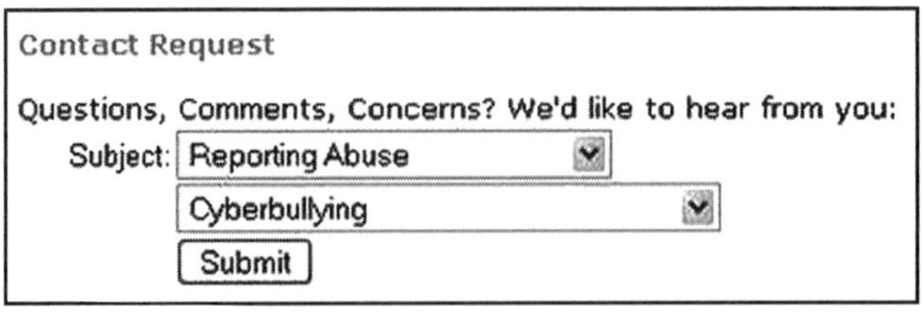

RECOMMENDATIONS FOR PARENTS

We now shift gears to focus on parents, as we have received numerous inquiries from them over the past several years asking us for advice on dealing with cyberbullying. They often feel helpless when they are confronted with a cyberbullying situation in their family, and this is compounded by the fact that nobody was willing to help them (or they wouldn't have needed to contact us). Parents typically encounter apathy, resistance, and disregard from uninformed or ill-equipped educators and law enforcement. They are then left to their own wisdom as to what appropriate response to make.

Just as school personnel should work hard to develop trust among their students, they should also work to gain the trust of the parents of their students and offer themselves as a resource in these situations. Ask the parents what they would like to see happen. Calmly explain your role as an educator and as a representative of the school district. If both parties are students in your district, offer to mediate a meeting among the students and parents of all involved. Point to district policy forbidding interpersonal harassment and discuss the various response options moving forward.

**Box 7.2 What Parents Should
Do if Their Child Is Cyberbullied**

- Make sure their child is, and remains, safe.
- Collect evidence.
- Contact the school.
- Contact the parents of the offender.
- Contact the service provider or content provider.
- Contact the police when physical threats are involved.

Many parents respond to their child's victimization by immediately banning access to instant messaging, e-mail, social networking Web sites, or the Internet in general. This may be the easiest short-term solution, but it obviously does not address the underlying problem of interpersonal conflict. Moreover, it fails to eliminate current or future instances of cyberbullying victimization. Knee-jerk, defensive reactions to difficult experiences their child has bravely shared with them will likely close off a candid line of communication, which must be maintained. Such a response may also promote overt rebellion, as youth so inclined will find a way to use the technologies at different times and in different places. As we have discussed throughout this book, they are indispensable components of 21st-century adolescence.

The best tack parents can take when their child is cyberbullied is to convey unconditional support (see Box 7.2). They should do this at a time when their children seem really open to them (parents know how teenagers are: one minute they are your best friend, the next they "hate" you). Parents should solicit the child's perspective as to what might be done to improve the situation. If necessary, they should explain the importance of scheduling a meeting with school administrators (or a teacher they trust) to discuss the matter. Overall, parents must demonstrate to their children through words and actions that they both desire the same end result: that the cyberbullying stop and that life does not become even *more* difficult. This can be accomplished by working together to arrive at a mutually agreeable course of action.

> *I need to remember that they might not always be the victim but the perpetrator. That is the true test of parenting. Defending your child because you want to believe everything they tell you when there could be little bits and pieces left out to avoid the wrath of Mom or Dad.*

> —Mother from Minnesota

Parents also need to be prepared that if their child is the perpetrator, they have an obligation to do something about it (see Box 7.3). This ties into the groundwork laid in Chapter 6; part of a preventive strategy is informing parents that cyberbullying is a violation of school policy and is subject to discipline. Parents of the aggressor sometimes need to be contacted and briefed on the facts of the case in as nonthreatening a manner as possible. It is important here to explain calmly to parents that such misbehavior interferes with the mission and mandate of the school and that parents and educators must work side by side when these situations arise. Ideally, they will respond quickly and effectively because of the authority they have over their child and because that authority was respected and treated with deference.

**Box 7.3 What Parents Should
Do if Their Child Is the Cyberbully**

- Talk about the hurtful nature of bullying.
- Apply reasonable consequences.
- Set firm limits and stick to them.
- Consider installing tracking software.
- Closely monitor computer/cell phone usage.
- Convey firmer consequences if the behavior continues.

Parents can start by discussing how cyberbullying (and bullying in general) affects others. Depending on the level of seriousness of the incident, and whether it seems that the child has realized the inappropriate nature of his or her behavior, consequences should be applied. If parents were proactive and had their child sign the "Internet Use Contract" discussed in Chapter 6 (example in Resource D), this process is going to be much easier. The child knew the rules and knew that there would be repercussions for violations of the contract. Parents may revoke their child's Internet or cell phone use for a period of time or temporarily revoke other privileges (remember to be reasonable). If the behavior was particularly serious, parents may want to consider installing tracking or filtering software as a consequence as well. Moving forward, it is essential that parents pay even greater attention to the Internet and cell phone activities of their children to make sure that they have internalized the lesson and are acting in appropriate and responsible ways.

WHAT TO DO IF YOU
WITNESS CYBERBULLYING

Bystanders—those who witness cyberbullying and its fallout among their classmates—are admittedly in a tough position. They generally do not want to get involved because of the hassle and problems they fear it might bring upon them, yet they often recognize that what they are seeing is not right and should stop. We've said it before and we say it again: By doing *nothing*, bystanders are doing *something*. As members of a peer group and of society, we have a responsibility to look out for the best interests of each other. Humans are relational beings, and relationships continue and thrive because of this willingness to dismiss the cost to oneself temporarily and come to the aid of those who are in distress. In fact, we argue that bystanders can make a huge difference in improving the situation for cyberbullying victims, who often feel helpless and hopeless and need someone to come to the rescue.

It is true that many instances of cyberbullying occur outside of the watch of third parties—such as through e-mail and instant messages. However, those who observe cyberbullying in a chat room, on an online discussion board, or within a social networking site should be moved to action (see Box 7.4). That action might simply be anonymously reporting the incident to an adult or to the owners/administrators/moderators of a particular Internet-based environment. More bold and assertive steps would include communicating with the victim and encouraging him or her to talk to someone who can help. Bystanders must feel empowered to do something about injustices they witness and must believe that positive outcomes will result from their efforts—or they will simply be discouraged and much more hesitant to step up in the future. Along these lines, educators must convey to students that if they see or receive electronic content that mistreats or makes fun of another person, they should immediately contact an adult. As we've discussed in the previous chapter, they should be able to remain anonymous in their reporting.

**Box 7.4 What Youth Should
Do if They Witness Cyberbullying**

- Document what they see and when.
- Don't encourage the behavior.
- Don't forward hurtful messages.
- Don't laugh at inappropriate jokes.
- Don't condone the act just to fit in.
- Don't silently allow it to continue.
- Stand up for the victim.
- Tell an adult they trust.

RECOMMENDATIONS FOR YOUTH
WHO EXPERIENCE CYBERBULLYING

Don't let yourself just be a victim thinking nobody can do anything because it's online, don't do nothing in hopes it will go away. Don't give them the satisfaction of getting upset and yelling at them. Solve the problem in the real world. Don't give them the satisfaction by responding to what they say.

—17-year-old boy from Canada

Adolescents who are cyberbullied are often overwhelmed by the resultant emotional and psychological pain, and so responding to the problem in a healthy and productive way is usually not their first inclination. In fact, level-headed youth who do confide in a parent or teacher sometimes react with concern and panic when that adult suggests certain steps be taken to reduce or stop the problem. Their anxiety revolves around the desire to avoid being labeled a tattletale, not being strong enough to handle the harassment on their own (e.g., capably defend themselves against the cyberbully or simply ignore the cyberbullying), the impact the response might have on how their peers perceive or treat them, the actual utility that such steps will have in stopping the problem and preventing future victimization, and the possibility that the aggressor (and perhaps others) might increase the intensity and frequency of harm to "get back" at the victim for telling an adult and trying to get the cyberbully in trouble.

Victimized youth first need to realize that they are not to blame for the way they have been treated. They need to be reminded that no one deserves to be harassed in any environment (on the Internet or in the real world). Then, they need strategies to help them fend off cyberbullies (see Box 7.5). For example, the most effective response to minor forms of cyberbullying is simply no response at all (don't give the bully the satisfaction of knowing you've been provoked to respond!). Similarly, we also recommend that youth don't read (and wallow in) e-mails and instant messages they know (or expect) to be of a harassing or upsetting nature and to exit online environments in which they are continually being cyberbullied. This step should cause the cyberbullying behavior to stop (at least in the short term), as the bullies realize the target is choosing to ignore or refusing to accept the mean statements they send or post, thus removing some of the satisfaction they receive when seeing that their behavior is negatively affecting someone.

If the behaviors continue or escalate in seriousness, however, swift action must be taken. If adolescents are threatened with physical harm, please remember that such threats are criminal offenses and they have every right (and every obligation!) to tell an adult, who should strongly consider calling the police. As we've repeatedly mentioned, such statements from cyberbullies cannot be taken lightly or casually dismissed as frivolous. All threats to another's well-being must be thoroughly investigated.

Then, youth must learn to exercise due diligence in reducing their vulnerability to online aggression. For example, targets of cyberbullying may also consider installing filters on their e-mail, instant messaging, and chat programs to block or regulate the content they receive. Automatic logging and archiving can be set on these programs so that every computer-based communication with others is tracked and stored on the computer's hard drive. Most social networking Web sites also have tools to moderate and delete questionable or objectionable content that is posted or sent. It does take time to read "Help Files" and "Frequently Asked Questions" documents within the software or on the associated Web site to learn how to apply the proper settings to delete, block, filter, and log certain messages. However, we believe it is well worth the time spent.

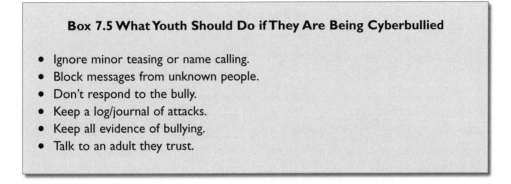

Box 7.5 What Youth Should Do if They Are Being Cyberbullied

- Ignore minor teasing or name calling.
- Block messages from unknown people.
- Don't respond to the bully.
- Keep a log/journal of attacks.
- Keep all evidence of bullying.
- Talk to an adult they trust.

As a general rule, we strongly encourage youth to approach an adult they trust regardless of whether they think it will improve the situation. This can be extremely difficult for kids, as discussed above. As an adult, you should begin very early in laying the groundwork for youth to feel comfortable approaching you to discuss these and other issues they are confronting. Adolescence is a painfully difficult journey on hazardous terrain that should not be traveled alone. Technology has increased the number of land mines youth can stumble upon, and they need trustees in their lives to help them avoid those pitfalls and pick them up when one takes its toll.

Though we do not want adolescents to be steeped in their cyberbullying experiences, it remains important to document those instances so they can be used as evidence against the aggressor. Victims must be encouraged to *save all evidence* without internalizing or becoming otherwise consumed by the mistreatment. Along these same lines, youth who are harassed online should be encouraged to keep a log or journal of their experiences. They should note specific incidents with as much detail as possible, including who was involved, where and when it happened, how they responded, who witnessed the incident, and what was done to prevent its reoccurrence. This will become powerful evidence if disciplinary action is to be taken against the bully. Moreover, writing the experiences down may help youth reconcile and then expel the experiences from their mind, much like sitting down with a close friend and sharing a difficult time.

People choose to use the Internet for this because they're too cowardly to say it in front of you so they do it anonymously. If someone's going out of their way to do this, it's because something about you or something you have that they don't is making them so angry that they can't stand to see you happy, they're just compensating for something they don't have by trying to destroy it. E-mail addresses can be changed. Web site administrators can track IP addresses which can be used to locate the computer used to post that message. Keep log files of their offenses as evidence, report it to someone (parent, teacher, police), nobody will just stand by and allow this to happen and these people can be found and will be dealt with seriously.

—17-year-old boy from Canada

We certainly do not want to trivialize any instance of cyberbullying and would encourage teens to seek help in addressing those they perceive as serious. However, it bears repeating that they should do all they can to keep from internalizing hurtful words they know are false and only said to promote controversy, conflict, and drama. This is an acquired skill, to be sure, and even as adults we do not always perceive of, and respond to, interpersonal conflict in the most productive way. Cultivating *resiliency* is vital to relational success in adulthood, and perhaps youth (with the help of involved teachers and parents) can use the more minor instances of cyberbullying as life lessons in that regard.

CIVIL RESPONSES

When school-based responses handed down by administration leave victims without a sense of equity or justice, U.S. civil law can be applied as a remedy to interpersonal wrongdoing between private citizens. These remedies exist in cyberbullying cases where the victim (whether student or staff) can seek monetary damages from the offender and offender's parents or a formal injunction against the harmful behavior. What is interesting is that often the simple initiation of legal action against an aggressor is enough to quell the malicious behavior immediately and permanently. Of course, continuing on to trial can be a significant financial burden to the defendant—so most individuals would seek to avoid such an outcome. The major actions that meet the standard for an intentional tort (or wrongdoing) are defamation, invasion of privacy, intentional infliction of emotional distress, and negligence. While a detailed examination of these torts is well beyond the scope of this book, they are briefly summarized below. Those so inclined should obtain legal counsel for more information as it relates to their own situation.

Defamation

Defamation involves "an intentional false communication, either published or publicly spoken, that injures another's reputation or good name"

(Black, 1990, p. 417). Defamation originates in the torts of slander (spoken defamation) and libel (written defamation). Online communications would be considered libelous since they are not fleeting and have a measure of permanence associated with them.

> I started getting flamed and harassed, and I became afraid to go outside . . . I told my mother and showed her the page. We couldn't do anything. We tried about everything. I got sick from all the stress and ended up in the hospital, but I became a bit better now that the harassing has let down a bit. My friends in my neighborhood found the page on that site, and thought those lies were all true so I have lost about all of my friends under their false words. And I have changed my e-mail address multiple times, and I am being flamed again for that page with false, imprudent and horrible words.
>
> —Submitted anonymously

Invasion of Privacy

Invasion of privacy involves "the unwarranted appropriation or exploitation of one's personality, publicizing one's private affairs with which public has no legitimate concern, or wrongful intrusion into one's private activities, in such a manner as to cause mental suffering, shame or humiliation to person of ordinary sensibilities" (Black, 1990, p. 824).

> Just want to say that I've had a bad experience with death threats from a crazy person that I met through ebay. I bought an item that she was selling on ebay about 1 month ago, and on ebay when you buy something that seller gets access to your address and name. It's a long story, but to make a long story short she became attached to me and my family and after a week of her contacting me when I demanded for her to leave us alone she became very angry and told me she was going to kill me and my family, then she said she was going to kill my family and let me live so I can live the rest of my life in pain. She also said she sent people over to my house. As I said she has our address, our names, and phone number.
>
> —Submitted anonymously

Intentional Infliction of Emotional Distress

Intentional infliction of emotional distress involves intentionally or recklessly causing "severe emotional distress to another" by "extreme and outrageous conduct" (American Law Institute, 1965, p. 71). It is not necessary that the act be meant to cause distress; reckless disregard for the potential of distress occurring is enough. Furthermore, the conduct must be beyond a certain established standard of decency or civility.

> *Its one thing for freedom of speech, but it's another when you're actually harming the person where they can't even eat anymore without feeling horrible all the time.*

> —Submitted anonymously

Negligence

Negligence involves "the omission to do something which a reasonable man, guided by those ordinary considerations which ordinarily regulate human affairs, would do, or the doing of something which a reasonable and prudent man would not do" (Black, 1990, p. 1032). A claim of negligence can also be brought against a school, seeking to make the institution liable for harm. In these cases, the plaintiff must prove that the school had a duty of reasonable care to prevent harm in a situation, that the harm was foreseeable, that harm occurred, and that the breach of duty led to the harm. To be sure, this is not limited to physical harm but also covers emotional, psychological, or mental forms, which are amply present in most cyberbullying situations.

RECOMMENDATIONS FOR WORKING WITH LAW ENFORCEMENT

While it would be nice to live in a society where law enforcement never had reason to be at school, preserving the safety and security of students often requires their presence. It is necessary that school districts develop official relationships with the local police so they have a point of contact in the event of a serious cyberbullying incident (or any other incident requiring their assistance). To be sure, most districts (and even many schools) have school resource or liaison officers assigned to them. These officers are either stationed at a specific school or are dispatched to schools when the need presents itself. In areas where this is not the case, an administrator at each school should interface with the local police department to provide for continual discourse concerning safety issues, threats and vulnerabilities, and formal response plans.

In some (rare) situations, cyberbullying rises to the level of criminal behavior. As explained earlier, the primary factor in these cases is a threat to the physical safety or personal property of oneself or one's family. Threats are often made by youth involved in interpersonal squabbles and adolescent melodramas, and most have limited potential to escalate into real-world violence. Still, some merit deeper inquiry and demand a formal response. Discerning which threats are viable is difficult, to say the least.

The matter is complicated when considering Internet-based content, as it is largely devoid of socioemotional cues (such as tone of voice or body language) that can indicate the seriousness of ostensibly threatening words.

The criminal law may also be implicated when the behavior involves stalking, can be characterized as a hate or bias crime (against protected populations), or involves sexually explicit images or the sexual exploitation of youth. In situations where a student is threatening another student or a staff member and an attempt at informal resolution does not immediately end the problem, law enforcement should (and must) get involved. In our post-Columbine era, no threat—regardless of how trivial or humorous it might seem—should be taken lightly or rationalized away. That said, we don't advocate that educators frivolously devote significant resources toward each threat unless there is an articulable and verifiable cause for concern. We do, however, recommend that they always inform law enforcement and let *them* investigate the matter.

SUMMARY

As an educator you will eventually—if you haven't yet already—face a cyberbullying incident that affects a student, staff member, or your entire school. It is crucial to have a solid idea of possible courses of action to pursue after evaluating the circumstances of every unique situation. Clearly, victims and witnesses of cyberbullying need to be supported and empowered, while cyberbullies need to be disciplined and impelled to demonstrate positive choices and behaviors in the future. We have sought to provide you with a variety of ways in which these goals can be accomplished; it is up to you to determine which to implement when the time comes.

To determine where your school stands in terms of meaningful efforts to address cyberbullying, we've created a "Cyberbullying Report Card for Schools" (Resource H). This should be useful in determining the areas in which you are prepared and those that require more attention. We hope that you are able to answer yes to each of the statements; if not, create a plan to correct the deficiencies. By now you've understood the severity of the problem, and it's time to be part of the solution. When you have conscientiously engaged in all of the proactive steps listed, you should be in great shape to deal with any instances of online aggression that arise.

QUESTIONS FOR REFLECTION

1. Why is the suggestion to "turn off the computer" not an appropriate response to cyberbullying?

2. What are some creative punishments for students who engage in cyberbullying?

3. How can a cyberbullying incident be used to educate and prevent further cyberbullying at school?

4. Why is cyberbullying based on gender, race, or sexual orientation more serious than other forms of cyberbullying?

5. What should you do if you witness cyberbullying?

CONCLUDING THOUGHTS

This book has attempted to serve as a comprehensive guide describing how to identify, prevent, and respond to cyberbullying. As we've described in detail throughout this book (and especially in Chapter 2), cyberbullying involves sending harassing or threatening messages (via text message or e-mail), posting derogatory comments about someone on a Web site or social networking site (such as MySpace or Facebook), or physically threatening or intimidating someone in a variety of online settings. Minor forms include being ignored, disrespected, picked on, or otherwise hassled. The more debasing forms involve the spreading of rumors about, stalking, or physically threatening another person. Since some types are clearly more harmful than others, they can result in a variety of effects for the target. It is important to evaluate the seriousness of the incident with consideration for all of the contextual circumstances that surround it. That is, receiving harassing e-mails by itself may not be that significant of a problem. This type of cyberbullying coupled with other malicious behaviors online or offline, however, can create a very hostile and frustrating environment for the victim, especially if threats are made about what might happen to the youth at a particular physical location.

We are very concerned that if ignored, cyberbullying among youth will lead to the same harm and long-term consequences as traditional bullying. As such, we believe it requires—and even demands—us to be responsible in educating ourselves and others to understand and address it. There exists a great disconnect between what youth are doing in cyberspace and what adults know about what youth are doing in cyberspace. Both parties, to be sure, share some responsibility. As noted throughout this book, youth are hesitant to talk to most adults for fear of judgmental and overly harsh responses, and adults are hesitant to discuss these issues with youth because of unfamiliarity, busyness, or indifference. This book has been an attempt to get you "up to speed" with respect to the ways many teens are using and misusing computers and communications technology.

If you have made it this far, you are clearly very committed to helping your students and children avoid the land mines on the landscape of high technology. You now have a solid foundation from which to operate and a wealth of resources at your disposal to assist you along the way. Start with our Web site (www.cyberbullying.us), to which we have regularly referred throughout this book. There you will find the latest research and an ever-expanding list of resources. You will also find links to other excellent cyberbullying-related Web sites. Next, spread the word about cyberbullying. With your help, we hope to make great headway in educating the general public and enlisting their active support. Finally, keep us informed (hinduja@cyberbullying.us or patchin@cyberbullying.us) with regard to your struggles and successes on the front lines of this issue. Recognizing that bullying has moved beyond the schoolyard, we will help in any way we can.

Resource A

Glossary

Acceptable Use Policy (AUP): A policy that organizations create to define the responsibilities and appropriate behaviors of computer and network users.

Anonymizer: An intermediary Web site that hides or disguises the IP address associated with the Internet user. Generally, these sites allow a person to engage in various Internet activities without leaving an easily traceable digital footprint.

Bash Board: An online bulletin board on which individuals can post anything they want. Generally, posts are malicious and hateful statements directed against another person.

Blocking: The denial of access to particular parts of the Internet. Usually a message will be shown on screen to say that access has been denied. For example, instant message users can block other screen names from sending them messages.

Blog: Interactive Web journal or diary, the contents of which are posted online where they are viewable by some or all individuals. The act of updating a blog is called "blogging." A person who keeps a blog is referred to as a "blogger." The term was created by combining *web* and *log*.

Buddy List: A collection of names or handles (also known as screen names) that represent friends or "buddies" within an instant messaging or chat program. They are useful in informing a user when that person's friends are online and available to chat.

Bullying: Repeated and deliberate harassment directed by one in a position of power toward one or more. Can involve physical threats or behaviors, including assault, or indirect and subtle forms of aggression, including rumor spreading. The term *bullying* is usually reserved for young people and most often refers to these behaviors as they occur at or near school.

Cell Phone: A wireless handheld device that allows for telephone communications.

Chat: An online conversation, typically carried out by people who use nicknames instead of their real names. A person can continually read messages from others in the chat room and then type and send a message reply.

Chat Room: A virtual online room where groups of people send and receive messages on one screen. Popular chat rooms can have hundreds of people all communicating at the same time. What you type appears instantly as a real-time conversation. All of the people in the room are listed on the side of the screen with their screen names.

Computer: An electronic device that stores and processes information and facilitates electronic communication when connected to a network.

Cookie: A file on a computer that records user information when visiting a Web site. Cookies are often used to identify the Web sites that the computer has visited, save login information and customization preferences, and enable the presentation of more personalized information or content.

Cyberbullicide: Suicide stemming directly or indirectly from cyberbullying victimization.

Cyberbullying: Intentional and repeated harm inflicted through the use of computers, cell phones, and other electronic devices.

Cyberspace: The electronic "universe" created by computer networks in which individuals interact.

Cyberstalking: Repeated harassment that includes threats of harm or that is highly intimidating and intrusive upon one's personal privacy.

Cyberthreats: Electronic material that either generally or specifically raises concerns that the creator may intend to inflict harm or violence to himself- or herself or others.

Digital Footprint: Evidence of a person's use of the Internet. This includes anything that can be linked to his or her existence, presence, or identity.

Digital Immigrant: A person who has not grown up with digital technology, such as computers, cell phones, and the Internet, but has adopted it later. Many adults are referred to as digital immigrants, because they have known a time when the Internet and cell phones didn't exist.

Digital Native: A person who has grown up with digital technology, such as computers, cell phones, and the Internet. Many adolescents or young adults would be classified as digital natives, because they have not known a time without the Internet or cell phones.

E-mail: Electronic mail. Allows Internet users to send and receive electronic text to and from other Internet users.

Facebook: The second-most popular social networking Web site with over 70 million active users. Users create personal "profiles" to represent themselves, listing interests and posting photos and communicating with others through private or public messages.

Filtering: The act of restricting access to certain Web sites (usually using software programs). For example, a filter might check the text on a Web page with a list of forbidden words. If a match is found, that Web page may be blocked or reported through a monitoring process. Generally speaking, a filter lets data pass or not pass based on previously specified rules.

Firewall: Hardware or software that restricts and regulates incoming and outgoing data to or from computer systems. Firewalls allow or disallow using certain Web sites or certain Web-based software programs.

Flaming: Sending angry, rude, or obscene messages directed at a person or persons privately or an online group. A "flamewar" erupts when "flames" are sent back and forth between individuals repeatedly.

Friending: The act of requesting another person to be your friend (and thereby formally connect with you) on a social networking Web site (like MySpace or Facebook).

Gaming: Participation in online games, which often involve individuals adopting roles of fictional characters, thereby directing the outcome of the game.

Happy Slapping: An extreme form of bullying where physical assaults are recorded on mobile phones or digital cameras and distributed to others.

Harassment: Unsolicited words or actions intended to annoy, alarm, or abuse another individual.

Harm: Physical or emotional injury to someone.

Resource A
Glossary

Instant Messaging: The act of real-time communication between two or more people over a network such as the Internet. This can occur through software such as AOL Instant Messenger, Microsoft Instant Messenger, or Google Talk. This can also occur while logged into social networking Web sites or via cellular phone.

Internet: A worldwide network of computers communicating with each other via phone lines, satellite links, wireless networks, and cable systems.

IP Address: "Internet Protocol" address. A unique address assigned to a computing device that allows it to send and receive data with other computing devices that have their own unique addresses.

IRC: "Internet Relay Chat." A network over which real-time conversations take place among two or more people in a "channel" devoted to a specific area of interest. *See also* chat or chat room.

ISP: "Internet Service Provider." The company that provides an Internet connection to individuals or companies. ISPs can help with identifying an individual who posts or sends harassing or threatening words.

MMORPG: "Massively multiplayer online role-playing game." A game in which large numbers of individuals from disparate locations connect and interact with each other in a virtual world over the Internet.

Monitoring: The recording and reporting of online activity, usually through software, which may record a history of all Internet use or just of inappropriate use. A person can also serve this function.

MySpace: The most popular social networking Web site with over 230 million accounts created. It allows individuals to create an online representation or "profile" of themselves to include biographical information, personal diary entries, affiliations, likes and dislikes, interests, and multimedia artifacts (pictures, video, and audio). Blogging, messaging, commenting, and "friending" are the primary methods of interacting with others.

Netiquette: "Network etiquette." The unofficial rules of accepted, proper online social conduct.

Network: Two or more computers connected so that they can communicate with each other.

Newbie: Someone who is new to, and inexperienced with, an Internet activity or technology. Also referred to as a newb, n00b, nob, noob, and nub.

Offender: The one who instigates online social cruelty. Also known as the "aggressor."

Profile: When considered in the context of online social networking, this is a user-created Web page—the design of which can be customized—where a person's background, interests, and friends are listed to reflect who that person is or how that person would like to be seen. Streaming music, video, and digital pictures are often included as well.

Proxy: Software or a Web site that allows one's Internet connection to be routed or tunneled through a different connection or site. If a user's computer is blocked from accessing certain Web sites or programs, the user could employ a proxy to redirect the connection to that site or program. For example, if a software filter prohibits a user from visiting MySpace, a proxy Web site could be used to circumvent the filter and provide access.

Shoulder Surfing: Peering over the shoulder of someone to see the contents on that person's computer or cell phone screen.

SMS: "Short message service." A communications protocol that allows short (160 characters or less) text messages over cell phone.

Social Networking Web Sites: Online services that bring together people by organizing them around a common interest and providing an interactive environment of photos, blogs, user profiles, and messaging systems. Examples include Facebook and MySpace.

Spam: Unsolicited electronic mail sent from someone unknown to the recipient.

Texting: Sending short messages via cell phone.

Threat: Making a statement of taking an action that indicates harm to another.

Trolling: Deliberately and disingenuously posting information to entice genuinely helpful people to respond (often emotionally). Often done to inflame or provoke others.

Victim: The person who is on the receiving end of online social cruelty. Also known as the "target."

VoIP: "Voice over Internet Protocol." The transmission of voice over an Internet connection.

Web: Short for "World Wide Web" or pages linked together via the Internet.

Wireless: Communications in which electromagnetic waves carry a signal through space rather than along a wire.

Wireless Device: Cell phones, personal digital assistants, handheld PCs, and computers that can access the Internet without being physically attached by a cable or data line.

Resource A
Glossary

Resource B

Recommendations for Further Information

WEB SITES

Cyberbullying.us (www.cyberbullying.us)
This is our public service research Web site, which shares findings from our scientific studies and has a vast array of resources to help youth, adults, educators, counselors, and law enforcement in their responses to cyberbullying.

Be Web Aware (www.bewebaware.ca)
"A national, bilingual public education program on Internet safety. The objective of everyone involved in this project is to ensure young Canadians benefit from the Internet, while being safe and responsible in their online activities."

Connect for Kids and Child Advocacy 360 (www.connectforkids.org)
Information and tools needed to learn about issues affecting children, families, and communities and to take action to improve policies and programs and, ultimately, the fabric of our nation as a whole.

Connect With Kids (www.connectwithkids.com)
An organization focused on improving the lives of children and, along the way, helping parents to become better parents. It works with hundreds of communities, school districts, and schools nationwide and has produced award-winning documentaries dealing with kids' issues.

Cyber Bully 411 (www.cyberbully411.com)
Produced by Internet Solutions for Kids. Includes resources for preventing and dealing with cyberbullying and online harassment.

Cyber Bully Help (www.cyberbullyhelp.com)
Based on the book *Cyber Bullying: Bullying in the Digital Age* (Kowalski et al., 2007), this Web site offers kids and parents guidance toward preventing and dealing with cyberbullying. Also includes links to additional help sites and defines common terminology used on the Internet.

Cyberbully.org (www.cyberbully.org)
Run by the Center for Safe and Responsible Internet Use, provides specific downloadable guides for educators, parents, and youth who are dealing with cyberbullying incidents.

Cyberbullying.org (www.cyberbullying.org or www.cyberbullying.ca)
A comprehensive site created by Bill Belsey. Useful facts and prevention strategies are detailed throughout. A large list of relevant external links is also provided.

i Keep Safe (www.ikeepsafe.org)
"To give parents, educators, and policy makers the information and tools that empower them to teach children the safe and healthy use of technology and the Internet."

i-Safe.org (www.isafe.org)
"The worldwide leader in the Internet safety education. Founded in 1998 and endorsed by the U.S. Congress, i-SAFE is a non-profit foundation dedicated to protecting the online experiences of youth everywhere. i-SAFE incorporates classroom curriculum with dynamic community outreach to empower students, teachers, parents, law enforcement, and concerned adults to make the Internet a safer place."

Internet Super Heroes (www.internetsuperheroes.org)
Produced by WiredKids.org, Safety.org, and Marvel.com. Delivers smart, safe, and responsible surfing messages to children, teens, schools, and parents, online and offline.

Make a Difference for Kids Inc. (www.makeadifferenceforkids.org)
"A Non-profit organization dedicated to the awareness and prevention of cyberbullying and suicide. The organization was created in memory of Rachael Neblett and Kristin Settles, two Mt. Washington, Kentucky teens who died as the result of suicide."

Megan Meier Foundation (www.meganmeierfoundation.org)
Their mission is "to bring awareness, education, and promote positive change to children, parents and educators, in response to the ongoing bullying and cyber-bullying in our children's daily environments."

MindOH! (www.mindoh.com)

"A company that creates character-based, interactive computer modules that teach students problem-solving techniques and communication skills, reinforcing universally held virtues such as respect and responsibility."

National Crime Prevention Council (www.ncpc.org/cyberbullying)

Represented by McGruff the Crime Dog, this organization works to be "the nation's leader in helping people keep themselves, their families, and their communities safe from crime." They have created an extensive radio, television, and Web-based public advertising campaign to spread the word about the harms associated with cyberbullying.

Netsmartz.org (www.netsmartz.org)

Created by the National Center for Missing & Exploited Children (NCMEC) and Boys & Girls Clubs of America (BGCA). It provides an "interactive, educational safety workshop for children aged 5 to 17, parents, guardians, educators, and law enforcement that uses age-appropriate, 3-D activities to teach children how to stay safer on the Internet."

NSteens (www.nsteens.org)

Developed by the National Center for Missing and Exploited Children and Boys and Girls Clubs of America. "Meant to teach children and teens how to be safer when using the Internet. The NetSmartzWorkshop provides children with original, animated characters and age-appropriate, interactive activities that use the latest 3-D and web technologies to entertain while they educate."

Online Bully (www.online-bully.com)

This Web site offers information for parents and kids to help put an end to cyberbullying. A toll-free phone number is also made available.

Ryan Patrick Halligan (www.ryanpatrickhalligan.org)

Created by John P. Halligan, this Web site is dedicated to a young boy who commited suicide over online harassment. His parents provide information regarding cyberbullying and suicide, including where and how to stop it.

StopCyberbullying.org (www.stopcyberbullying.org)

Produced by Parry Aftab and Wired Kids Inc., this site provides a broad overview of the phenomenon. It also provides prevention tips and proactive measures that can be taken.

Students for Safer Schools (www.jeffreyjohnston.org)

This site contains information related to Debbie Johnston's crusade to improve Florida's antibullying and anticyberbullying laws.

BOOKS

Bast, D. (2007). *Teens and computers . . . What's a parent to do? A basic guide to social networking, instant messaging, chat, email, computer set-up and more.* Charleston, SC: BookSurge.

"The indispensable guide for parents of teens and tweens as they navigate the rapidly evolving world of My Space, Facebook, Instant Messaging, text messaging, Wikipedia, e-mail, and the internet."

—Amazon.com

Breguet, T. (2007). *Frequently asked questions about cyberbullying.* New York: Rosen.

Provides answers to common questions about what cyberbullying is and how it occurs.

Bocij, P. (2004). *Cyberstalking: Harassment in the Internet Age and how to protect your family.* Westport, CT: Praeger.

"Cyberstalking shows how new technologies can all too easily lend to harassment and what can be done to prevent technological harassment routines."

—MBR Internet Bookwatch as cited at Amazon.com

Farley-Gillispie, J., & Gackenbach, J. (2007). *Cyber rules: What you really need to know about the Internet.* New York: W. W. Norton.

"Filled with stories, self-assessment features and quizzes, and practical advice, this user-friendly guide will aid the Internet wary and experienced alike as they strive to make the best decisions for their children and clients."

—Amazon.com

Goodstein, A. (2007). *Totally wired: What teens and tweens are really doing online.* New York: St. Martin's Griffin.

"*Totally Wired* is the first inside guide that explores what teens are doing on the Internet and with technology. Speaking with a cross-section of industry professionals and teenagers, Anastasia Goodstein gets to the bottom of how teens use technology as well as the benefits and drawbacks of this use."

—Amazon.com

Kelsey, C. M. (2007). *Generation MySpace: Helping your teen survive online adolescence.* New York: Marlowe.

"Drawing on personal interviews with hundreds of teens, [the author] helps parents assess what they should—and shouldn't—be worried about when it comes to technology."

—Amazon.com

Kowalski, R. M., Limber, S. P., & Agaston, P. W. (2007). *Cyber bullying: Bullying in the digital age.* Malden, MA: Blackwell.

"Examining the latest research and methods for studying this issue, the authors have utilized vital studies involving over 3500 middle-school students, online research projects on cyber bullying on blogs, and data from focus groups of victims and perpetrators and their parents."

—Cyberbullyhelp.com

Leavitt, J., & Linford, S. (2006). *Faux paw meets the first lady: How to handle cyber-bullying* (ed. w/CD-ROM). Indianapolis, IN: John Wiley & Sons.

"If children learn early to safeguard their personal information and to keep far away from Internet strangers, they will not become victims."

—First Lady Laura Bush, from the
Foreword, as cited at Amazon.com

Magid, L., & Collier, A. (2006). *MySpace unraveled: A parent's guide to teen social networking.* Berkeley, CA: Peachpit Press.

"Discusses the booming MySpace social-networking phenomenon and shows you exactly what you need know about MySpace and how to create a safe online experience for your kids. This short and extremely useful guide discusses what children are doing on social-networking Web sites and why they have become so popular. While other books on this subject discuss how to use social networking sites, this is the first guide to address the topics important to parents."

—Amazon.com

Rosen, Larry D. (2007). *Me, MySpace, and I: Parenting the Net generation.* New York: Palgrave Macmillan.

"Offers a full overview of the various issues young people may experience in their online worlds (cyberbullying, addiction, sexuality, virtual friendships, and more) while at the same time challenging commonly held beliefs that these communities are damaging. Instead of using scare tactics, the book shows parents how to be proactive and anticipate potential problems. With his extensive background in both child development and the impact of technology, Dr. Rosen uses down-to-earth explanations of sound psychological theory, incorporates groundbreaking research, and shows parents and educators how social networking sites like MySpace and Facebook can improve adolescent socialization skills."

—Amazon.com

Shariff, S. (2008). *Confronting cyber-bullying: What schools need to know to control misconduct and avoid legal consequences.* New York: Cambridge University Press.

"This book is directed to academics, educators, and government policy-makers who are concerned about addressing emerging cyber-bullying and anti-authority student expressions through the use of cell phone and Internet technologies."

—Amazon.com

Also by Shaheen Shariff:

Shariff, S. (2008). *Cyber-bullying: Issues and solutions for the school, the classroom and the home.* Abington, Oxfordshire, UK: Routledge.

Trolley, B., Hanel, C., & Shields, L. (2006). *Demystifying and deescalating cyber bullying in the schools: A resource guide for counselors, educators and parents.* Bangor, ME: Booklocker.com.

"This resource guide provides school counselors, educators, administrators and parents with: Cyber bullying terminology; Policies and procedures information; Assessment tools; Psychological, educational, social therapeutic interventions; 'Hands on,' reproducible forms; and Easy to access text material and resource information."

—Amazon.com

Willard, N. (2007). *Cyberbullying and cyberthreats: Responding to the challenge of online social aggression, threats, and distress* (2nd ed.). Champaign, IL: Research Press.

"The book provides counselors, psychologists, teachers, and school administrators with cutting-edge information on how to prevent and respond to the increasingly common problem on cyberbullying and cyberthreats."

—Amazon.com

Willard, N. (2007). *Cyber-safe kids, cyber-savvy teens: Helping young people learn to use the Internet safely and responsibly.* San Francisco: John Wiley and Sons.

"Need-to-know information about online dangers and practical parenting strategies necessary to help children and teens learn to use the internet safely and responsibly."

—Amazon.com

VIDEOS

ABC Primetime (Producer). (2006, September 14). *ABC Frontline: Cyber-Bullying—Cruel intentions* [Television documentary available on DVD]. New York: ABC News
"Diane Sawyer reports on how cell phones, digital cameras and personal websites combine in new ways that seems to encourage and amplify the meanness of teenage behavior. From invading privacy and spreading gossip to humiliating one another, some teens have reached new heights of ruthlessness."

Adelson, O. (Executive Producer), & McLoughlin, T. (Director). (2005). *Odd girl out* [Motion picture available on DVD]. United States: Lion's Gate.
In this film based on *Odd Girl Out: The Hidden Culture of Aggression in Girls* by Rachel Simmons, "a mother and her daughter confront the intimidation of teen peer pressure and the emotionally brutalizing social rituals of high school. A well-adjusted teenager becomes depressed when she's ostracized by her friends at school. Her mother must help her daughter regain her confidence."

Dretzin, R. (Producer), & Maggio, J. (Director). (2008, January 22). *Frontline: Growing up online* [Television documentary available on DVD]. Boston: WGBH.
"*Growing Up Online* peers inside the world of this cyber-savvy generation through the eyes of teens and their parents, who often find themselves on opposite sides of a new digital divide. *Frontline* investigates the risks, realities, and misconceptions of teenage self-expression on the World Wide Web."

Heimowitz, D. (Director/Producer), & Azicri, J. (Director/Writer). (2007, October). *Adina's Deck: Solving cyber bully mysteries* [Informational DVD]. Stanford, CA: Adina's Deck.
A 30-minute film, Web site (www.adinasdeck.com), and parent/teachers guide to educate 9- to 15-year-olds about cyberbullying, including harassment via the Internet, digital technologies, and mobile phones.

Resource C

Cyberbullying Scenarios for Discussion

SCENARIO 1

> James is frustrated and saddened by the comments his high school peers are making about his sexuality. Furthermore, it appears a group of male students is creating fake e-mail accounts at Yahoo.com and sending love notes to other male students as if they came from James—who is mortified at the thought of what is happening.

If you were a school guidance counselor or administrator within the school, what would you do if James approached you with the problem? What about if you were James's mom or dad? What can James do to deal with the embarrassment? What would be some incorrect and unacceptable ways that James might try to deal with this problem?

SCENARIO 2

> Two female sixth graders, Katie and Sarah, are exchanging malicious instant messages back and forth because of a misunderstanding involving a boy named Jacob. The statements escalate in viciousness from trivial name-calling to very vicious and inflammatory statements, including death threats.

Should the police be contacted? Are both girls wrong? What should the kids do in this instance? What would you do as a parent if you discovered this problem? What might a school counselor do?

SCENARIO 3

A mother is walking by her son Jonathan while he is on the computer and notices that he keeps hiding the screen when she walks by. Upon further observation, the mother sees that Jonathan is making fun of someone else via instant messaging.

What should the mother do first? Does the mother need to contact the parents of the other child? Should Jonathan be allowed to use the computer?

SCENARIO 4

Lindsay has just moved to town from Oregon and enrolls in the local middle school. Very pretty, outgoing, and funny, she quickly wins the attention of a number of the school's football players—much to the chagrin of the school's cheerleaders. Bonnie, the head cheerleader, is concerned about Lindsay stealing away her boyfriend Johnny, who plays quarterback. With the help of her cheerleader friends, Bonnie decides to create a "We Hate Lindsay" Web site, where girls can post reasons why they hate Lindsay and why they think she should move back to Oregon. Soon, the entire school becomes aware of the site's Web address, and many others begin to post hurtful sentiments about Lindsay. Desperately wanting to make friends in a new town, Lindsay is crushed and begins to suffer from depression and a lack of desire to do anything aside from crying in bed.

If you were her mom or dad, what would you do? What might the school do to help Lindsay? If you were Lindsay's teacher, what would you do? If you were her best friend, what might you say or do to help?

SCENARIO 5

Chester, a tall, skinny teenager who excels in math and science classes, feels embarrassed when he has to change into gym clothes in the boy's locker room at school because he lacks muscularity and size. Other, more athletic, and well-built teens notice Chester's shyness and decide to exploit it. With their camera-enabled cellular phones, they covertly take pictures of Chester without his shirt on and in his boxer shorts. These pictures are then circulated among the rest of the student body via cellular phone. Soon enough, boys and girls are pointing, snickering, and laughing at Chester as he walks down the school hallways. He overhears comments such as "There goes Bird-Chested Chester" and "Wussy-Boy" and "Chicken-Legs Chester" and "Stick Boy." These words cut him deeply, and the perception that his classmates have of him begins to affect his math and science grades.

If you were his teacher, what would you do? If you were his parent, what would you do? What can Chester do to deal with the harassment—now and in the future? How can his harassing classmates really understand how much pain they are causing with their words and actions? What would you do if you were a bystander?

SCENARIO 6

Heather is a fourth grader who is extremely proficient at using the Internet. On Monday, she receives an e-mail from someone named "stalker@hotmail.com." The subject and body of the e-mail state: "I'm watching you. Be afraid." Heather immediately deletes it and thinks nothing of it. On Tuesday, she receives another e-mail from stalker@hotmail.com, and this time, the subject and body of the e-mail state: "I am getting closer, and I see you on the computer right now as you read this." Heather starts to get worried but doesn't want to tell her parents because she is concerned they will take away her Internet privileges. On Wednesday, she awakens to a new e-mail from stalker@hotmail.com that states: "Be very afraid. Today may be your last." Definitely frightened and concerned now, she makes up her mind to tell her parents about the e-mails when she returns from school that day. She is unable to concentrate in any of her classes because of intense fear as to what the e-mail meant when it said: "Today may be your last." She rushes home after school, bent on bringing it up to her mom and dad as soon as she sees them. To her dismay, she finds a note on the table stating that her mom went grocery shopping and that her dad will be home late. Her palms begin to sweat and her heart begins to race. She goes to her bedroom, throws her backpack on her bed, and checks her e-mail. Twenty-five new e-mails pop up. Each one is from the same sender: stalker@hotmail.com. They all say the same thing: "I am in your house. I am on a wireless Internet connection. You don't know where I am, but I know where you are!" Heather grabs her house key, rushes out of the front door, locks it, runs to her friend's house, and tells her friend's mom about her situation.

What would you do if you were her friend's mom? What can Heather do to ensure her safety now and in the future? To whom else should she turn for help?

SCENARIO 7

Stan is an eighth grader who is physically abused by his alcoholic uncle when he visits him on weekends. Additionally, Stan is being pushed around by some of his peers in middle school because he wears black all the time and is basically a loner. Recently, Stan has realized that on the Internet—in chat rooms and via instant messaging—he can freely become a person who seems much more attractive and fun and lighthearted than he is in real life. By taking on a different persona, he is finding social interaction with others much easier and more rewarding. Nonetheless, he still harbors much anger and bitterness within due to how his uncle and some of his classmates treat him. He decides to get back at his uncle and some of his classmates by posting personal information about them—along with some true stories about his negative experiences with them—on a very popular teen-oriented message board. This information includes their cell phone numbers, their home phone numbers, and their home addresses. Because Stan has made many friends on this teen-oriented message board, they rally around him in support and decide to exact some vigilante justice on their own to help Stan get revenge. A large number of his online friends use the phone numbers and addresses to make repeated prank calls, to order hundreds of pizzas to the victims' doors, and to sign them up for many, many pornographic magazines and Sears catalogs. Stan is extremely pleased at the harassment that his uncle and mean classmates are now experiencing.

What would you do if you were a parent or school administrator and the police alerted you, themselves contacted by Stan's Internet service provider after an online complaint was filed by Stan's uncle about these incidents? How might Stan learn that such vengeful behavior is inappropriate? How might Stan get help for the abuse he suffers and the way he feels?

SCENARIO 8

> Karen is a very devout teenager who leads a prayer meeting every morning by the high school flag pole. Many boys and girls are simply drawn to Karen as a friend because of her sweet nature and hopeful innocence. Other girls in her school, however, feel threatened by Karen's piety and commitment to holy living, and they begin to drum up ideas to expose her as a fraud. Specifically, they begin to spread rumors via the High School's social network on MySpace.com that Karen is sleeping around with the boy's track team. Karen is alerted to the online rumors by a close friend and is heartbroken. She tells her teachers and pastor, who then contact the school administration.

What would you do if you were the principal in this situation? What would you do if you were Karen? What would you do if you were Karen's close friend and really wanted to help? How could those who spread the rumors understand how hurtful their actions were?

SCENARIO 9

> Casey loves playing video games on his computer, especially those that allow you to link up to and compete with other players across the world through the Internet. He recently met one teenager in Russia named Boris while playing video games online, and they became fast friends because both enjoyed and excelled at one particular game. Together, they became almost unbeatable whenever they competed as a team against other teams online. At some point, though, Casey told Boris he had found a better gaming partner and didn't want to play with Boris anymore. Boris was outraged that he was being "dumped" as a gaming partner for someone else, and he began to tell other people on the gaming network that Casey "sucked" at all video games and that no one should ever be his partner unless they wanted to lose really badly. Soon after these statements started circulating,

Casey's new gaming partner dumped him, and everyone else on the network treated him like a pariah. Since the video game he loved so much could only be played with a partner, Casey was no longer able to play and felt totally rejected on the Internet (which had heretofore been a safe haven for him). When coupled with recollections of other instances of rejection in his life, this experience began to make Casey feel completely hopeless. He then started to express suicidal intentions to his sister.

If you were his sister, what would you say and do? Can this example really be characterized as cyberbullying?

SCENARIO 10

Trevor is 16 and into drag racing. He and his friends often go down to the local drag strip and race other 16- and 17-year-olds in their souped-up cars. Because drag racing is a testosterone-heavy event, egos get involved quickly. Speed is often equated to masculinity and strength, and physical fights sometimes break out when winners gloat too much over losers of drag races. Local police have had to report to the drag strip often in recent weeks and have threatened to shut down the strip completely if any more fights occur. Therefore, the aggression has been transferred from the real world to cyberspace, and winners are gloating over, and making fun of, losers online through e-mails and public forum posts at the local drag racing Web site. Trevor is undefeated in his racing exploits, and this has given him a very inflated self-conception. His success has gotten to his head, and he has been getting his kicks by berating and humiliating online those who lose against him. Some guys he has defeated are sick of how he's acting and are organizing a group to go over to his house, trash and mangle his hot rod with shovels and sledgehammers, and beat him up. Trevor gets tipped off about this plan the day before it is supposed to happen.

What should he do? Whom should he tell, and what should they do?

Resource D

Internet Use Contract

Internet Use Contract

Child Expectations

I understand that using the family computer is a privilege that is subject to the following rules:

1. I will respect the privacy of others who use this computer. I will not open, move, or delete files that are not in my personal directory.

2. I understand that Mom and Dad may access and look at my files at any time.

3. I will not download anything or install programs without first asking Mom or Dad.

4. I will never give out private information while online. At no time will I ever give out my last name, phone number, address, or school name—even if I know the person with whom I am communicating. My screen name will be:_____.

5. I understand that I can use the computer for approved purposes only.

6. I will never write or post anything online that I would not want Mom or Dad to see. I will not use profanity or otherwise offensive language. If I receive messages or view content with offensive language, I will report it to Mom and Dad immediately.

7. I will never agree to meet an online friend in person without first asking Mom or Dad. Dangerous people may try to trick me into meeting up with them.

8. If I ever feel uncomfortable about an experience online, I will immediately tell mom or dad. I understand that Mom and Dad are willing to help me and will not punish me as long as these rules are followed.

Parent Expectations

I understand that it is my responsibility to protect my family and to help them receive the best of what the Internet has to offer. In that spirit, I agree to the following:

1. I will listen calmly. If my child comes to me with a problem related to online experiences, I promise not to get angry but to do my best to help my child resolve the situation.

2. I will be reasonable. I will set reasonable rules and expectations for Internet usage. I will establish reasonable consequences for lapses in judgment on the part of my child.

3. I will treat my child with dignity. I will respect the friendships that my child may make online as I would offline friends.

4. I will not unnecessarily invade my child's privacy. I promise not to go further than necessary to ensure my child's safety. I will not read diaries or journals, nor will I inspect e-mails or computer files unless there is a serious concern.

5. I will not take drastic measures. No matter what happens, I understand that the Internet is an important tool that is essential to my child's success in school or business, and I promise not to ban it entirely.

6. I will be involved. I will spend time with my child and be a positive part of my child's online activities and relationships—just as I am offline.

List of prohibited Web sites and software applications:

Signed:

Resource E

Family Cell Phone Use Contract

Family Cell Phone Use Contract

Child Expectations

1. I acknowledge that using a cell phone is a privilege and, therefore, will not take it for granted.

2. I will not give out my cell phone number to anyone unless I first clear it with my parents.

3. I will always answer calls from my parents. If I miss a call from them, I will call them back immediately.

4. I will not bring my cell phone to school if it is prohibited. If allowed to bring it to school, I will keep it in my backpack or locker and turned off between the first and last bell.

5. I will not use my cell phone for any purpose after _____AM/PM on a school night or after _____AM/PM on a nonschool night, unless approved by my parents.

6. I will not send hurtful, harassing, or threatening text messages.

7. I will not say anything to anyone using the cell phone that I wouldn't say to them in person with my parents listening.

8. I will pay for any charges above and beyond the usual monthly fee.

9. I will not download anything from the Internet or call toll numbers without first asking my parents.

10. I will not enable or disable any setting on my phone without my parent's permission.

11. I will not take a picture or video of anyone without that person's permission.

12. I will not send or post pictures or videos of anyone online without that person's permission.

13. I will not send or post any pictures or videos to anyone without first showing them to my parents.

14. I will not be disruptive in my cell phone use. If my parents ask me to end a call or stop text messaging, I will.

Parent Expectations

1. I will respect the privacy of my child when my child is talking on a cell phone.

2. I will not unnecessarily invade my child's privacy by reading text messages or looking through call logs without telling my child first. If I have a concern, I will express it to my child, and we will look through this material together.

3. I will pay the standard monthly fee for the cell phone contract.

4. I will be reasonable with consequences for violations of this contract. Consequences will start at loss of cell phone privileges for 24 hours and progress according to the seriousness of the violation.

Signed:

Resource F

Cyberbullying Assessment Instrument

How often *in the last 30 days* have you experienced the following?

In the last 30 days, have you been made fun of in a chat room?
a. never   b. once or twice   c. a few times   d. many times   e. every day

In the last 30 days, have you received an e-mail from someone you know that made you really mad?
a. never   b. once or twice   c. a few times   d. many times   e. every day

In the last 30 days, have you received an email from someone you didn't know that made you really mad? This does not include "spam" mail.
a. never   b. once or twice   c. a few times   d. many times   e. every day

In the last 30 days, has someone posted something on your MySpace page that made you upset or uncomfortable?
a. never   b. once or twice   c. a few times   d. many times   e. every day

In the last 30 days, has someone posted something on another Web page that made you upset or uncomfortable?
a. never   b. once or twice   c. a few times   d. many times   e. every day

In the last 30 days, have you received an instant message that made you upset or uncomfortable?
a. never   b. once or twice   c. a few times   d. many times   e. every day

In the last 30 days, have your parents talked to you about being safe on the computer?
a. never   b. once or twice   c. a few times   d. many times   e. every day

In the last 30 days, has a teacher talked to you about being safe on the computer?
a. never   b. once or twice   c. a few times   d. many times   e. every day

In the last 30 days, have you been bullied or picked on by another person while online?
a. never   b. once or twice   c. a few times   d. many times   e. every day

In the last 30 days, have you been afraid to go on the computer?
a. never   b. once or twice   c. a few times   d. many times   e. every day

In the last 30 days, has anyone posted anything about you online that you didn't want others to see?
a. never   b. once or twice   c. a few times   d. many times   e. every day

In the last 30 days, has anyone e-mailed or text messaged you and asked questions about sex that made you uncomfortable?
a. never   b. once or twice   c. a few times   d. many times   e. every day

How often *in the last 30 days* have you done the following?

In the last 30 days, have you lied about your age while online?
a. never   b. once or twice   c. a few times   d. many times   e. every day

In the last 30 days, have you posted something online about someone else to make others laugh?
a. never   b. once or twice   c. a few times   d. many times   e. every day

In the last 30 days, have you sent someone a computer text message to make that person angry or to make fun of that person?
a. never   b. once or twice   c. a few times   d. many times   e. every day

In the last 30 days, have you sent someone an e-mail to make that person angry or to make fun of that person?
a. never   b. once or twice   c. a few times   d. many times   e. every day

In the last 30 days, have you posted something on someone's MySpace, Xanga, or Friendster page to make that person angry or to make fun of that person?
a. never   b. once or twice   c. a few times   d. many times   e. every day

In the last 30 days, have you taken a picture of someone and posted it online without that person's permission?
a. never   b. once or twice   c. a few times   d. many times   e. every day

Cyberbullying is when someone *repeatedly* makes fun of another person online or repeatedly picks on another person through e-mail or text message or when someone posts something online about another person that the person doesn't like.

In my entire life, I have cyberbullied others:
a. never   b. seldom   c. sometimes   d. fairly often   e. often   f. very often

In the last 30 days, I have cyberbullied others:
a. never   b. once or twice   c. a few times   d. many times   e. every day

If so, what was the most important reason for cyberbullying that person?
a. to get revenge   b. they deserved it
c. because others were doing it   d. for fun
e. because they picked on me at school   f. to vent my anger
g. to demonstrate power   h. I hate them
i. other reasons   j. I have not cyberbullied another
                                              person in the last 30 days.

In my entire life, I have been cyberbullied:
a. never   b. seldom   c. sometimes   d. fairly often   e. often   f. very often

In the last 30 days, I have been cyberbullied:
a. never   b. once or twice   c. a few times   d. many times   e. every day

If you have ever been cyberbullied, tell us about the most recent experience.

Did you know who it was who did it to you?
a. friend   b. someone else from school
c. ex-friend   d. ex-boyfriend or girlfriend
e. someone I knew from a chat room   f. stranger
g. many people   h. other
i. No one has ever cyberbullied me.

Was the bully someone you have met in real life?
a. yes   b. no   c. don't know   d. No one has ever cyberbullied me.

Were you ever cyberbullied by another student at your school?
a. never   b. once   c. sometimes   d. often   e. many times

Are threats made online carried out at school?
a. never   b. once   c. sometimes   d. often   e. many times

Did you tell someone about the cyberbullying experience?
a. never   b. once   c. sometimes   d. often   e. many times

Did you tell your parents about the cyberbullying experience?
a. never   b. once   c. sometimes   d. often   e. many times

Did you tell a friend about the cyberbullying experience?
a. never   b. once   c. sometimes   d. often   e. many times

Did you tell a teacher about the cyberbullying experience?
a. never   b. once   c. sometimes   d. often   e. many times

How did you respond to the cyberbullying experience?
a. logged off computer   b. blocked bully
c. changed screen name or e-mail   d. left site
e. called the police   f. did nothing
g. did something else   h. No one has ever cyberbullied me.

How did you feel about this cyberbullying experience?

NOTE: If you have not been cyberbullied, choose *f. N/A,* which means "not applicable."

Were you sad?
a. never   b. once   c. sometimes   d. often   e. many times   f. N/A

Were you scared?
a. never   b. once   c. sometimes   d. often   e. many times   f. N/A

Were you frustrated?
a. never   b. once   c. sometimes   d. often   e. many times   f. N/A

Were you embarrassed?
a. never   b. once   c. sometimes   d. often   e. many times   f. N/A

Were you angry?
a. never   b. once   c. sometimes   d. often   e. many times   f. N/A

Were you not bothered by it?
a. never   b. once   c. sometimes   d. often   e. many times   f. N/A

Reliability

Cyberbullying Victimization Scale (Cronbach's alpha = 0.736)

Been made fun of in a chat room at least once in the last 30 days

Received upsetting e-mail from someone you know at least once in the last 30 days

Received upsetting e-mail from someone you didn't know at least once in the last 30 days

Had something posted on your MySpace page that made you upset at least once in the last 30 days

Had something posted about you on another Web page that made you upset at least once in the last 30 days

Received an instant message that made you upset at least once in the last 30 days

Been picked on or bullied online at least once in the last 30 days

Been afraid to go on the computer at least once in the last 30 days

Something has been posted about you online that you didn't want others to see at least once in the last 30 days.

Cyberbullying Offending Scale (Cronbach's alpha = 0.761)

I posted something online about another person to make others laugh at least once in the last 30 days.

I sent someone a computer text message to make that person angry or to make fun of that person at least once in the last 30 days.

I sent someone an e-mail to make that person angry or to make fun of that person at least once in the last 30 days.

I posted something on MySpace or a similar site to make someone angry or to make fun of that person at least once in the last 30 days.

I have taken a picture of someone and posted it online without that person's permission at least once in the last 30 days.

Resource F
Cyberbullying Assessment Instrument

Resource G

Cyberbullying Incident Tracking Form

Report taken by: _____ **Date of report:**_____

Complainant Information

Name:	Student Staff
	(circle one)
Age: Sex:	School:	Grade:

Target Information

Name:	Student Staff
	(circle one)
Age: Sex:	School:	Grade:

Offender 1 Information

Name:	Student Staff
	(circle one)
Age: Sex:	School:	Grade:

211

Offender 2 Information

Name:		Student Staff (circle one)
Age: Sex:	School:	Grade:

Offender 3 Information

Name:		Student Staff (circle one)
Age: Sex:	School:	Grade:

Other Party Information (witness, bystander, other)

Name:		Student Staff (circle one)
Age: Sex:	School:	Grade:

Other Party Information (witness, bystander, other)

Name:		Student Staff (circle one)
Age: Sex:	School:	Grade:

Other Party Information (witness, bystander, other)

Name:		Student Staff (circle one)
Age: Sex:	School:	Grade:

Resource G
Cyberbullying Incident Tracking Form

Cyberbullying Incident Tracking Form

(page 3 of 4)

Location of Incident: _____

Description of Incident (use additional sheets if necessary)**:**

Did the incident involve any of the following features?

	Yes
Threat to someone's physical safety	
Sexual harassment	
Discrimination based on race, class, gender, sexual orientation, or other protected status	
Repeated cyberbullying after previous intervention	
Image or video- or audiorecording of harassment	
Other notable feature (please list)	

Did the incident result in a substantial disruption of the school environment or infringe on the rights of other students or staff?   Yes   No
(if yes, please describe in as much detail as possible)

Attach printouts of all evidence and additional sheets with statements by individuals listed on page 1.

Cyberbullying Incident Tracking Form

(page 4 of 4)

Description of Action Plan:
What sanctions are being applied and what steps are being taken to ensure behavior does not continue? What additional consequences will be applied if offender fails to comply with action plan?

Comments by principal or other administrator:

Other comments:

I have been made aware of this incident and will discuss this issue further with my child.

Parent's signature:_____ **Date:**_____

Case closed date:_____ **Reason for closure:**_____

Resource G
Cyberbullying Incident Tracking Form

Resource H

Cyberbullying Report Card for Schools

Cyberbullying Report Card

Is your school adequately addressing or prepared for cyberbullying concerns? Fill out this Report Card to find out.

If you answer yes to all of these statements, you are prepared. If you answer no or don't know the answer, you have work to do!

General Assessment	?	no	yes
We know how many students at our school have been victims of cyberbullying.			
We know how many students at our school have cyberbullied others.			
Cyberbullying is a not a significant problem in our school.			

School Climate/Culture	?	no	yes
Students who witness cyberbullying are empowered to step up and inform a trusted adult rather than remain silent bystanders.			
Teachers regularly remind students to approach them for help if they are dealing with an issue related to cyberbullying or online safety.			
It is clear to students that the inappropriate use of technology will not be tolerated by school administration.			
We work to create a school climate in which cyberbullying is not considered "cool" among the student population.			

Curriculum and Education	?	no	yes
Students are taught about acceptable computer and Internet use during the school year through presentations and assemblies.			
Students are taught about safe password practices and the protection of personal information.			
Students are taught about how to recognize cyberbullying and threats to their online safety.			
Students are taught about how to respond to cyberbullying in an appropriate manner.			
Teachers know how to recognize cyberbullying issues and how to intervene in an appropriate manner.			
We distribute materials to students and parents to educate them about cyberbullying.			
We hold afterschool meetings and events during the school year for parents and community members about online safety among youth.			
We use older students to educate younger students about identification and prevention of cyberbullying and how to respond to it.			
We are (and stay) familiar with the relevant major court decisions related to student speech using computers and the Internet.			
We are familiar with the ways in which the school district might be civilly liable for negligently preventing or improperly responding to cyberbullying incidents, and we work to avoid them.			

Resource H
Cyberbullying Report Card for Schools

Cyberbullying Response	?	no	yes
We take suspected and actual incidents of cyberbullying seriously at our school.			
We have developed and made known a continuum of disciplinary consequences for cyberbullying incidents.			
We know when we can intervene in cyberbullying incidents that originated off-campus.			
We have developed a formal procedure for investigating incidents of cyberbullying.			
We have an anonymous reporting system to allow students and teachers to report instances of cyberbullying without fear of reprisal.			
We have a formal relationship with a local law enforcement department capable of conducting computer and network forensic examinations should the need arise.			

Policies	?	no	yes
Our school has a clear cyberbullying policy.			
Our cyberbullying policy includes language about off-campus behaviors being subject to discipline.			
Our school has a clear policy regarding cell phones and other portable electronic devices.			
Students know our policy regarding technology.			
Parents know our policy regarding technology.			
Signage about acceptable computer and Internet use is posted in school computer labs.			

Technology	?	no	yes
We have Web site-blocking and content-monitoring software/hardware installed on our network to ensure age-appropriate Web browsing and communications.			
We avoid putting student information on the district Web site.			

Other Areas	?	no	yes

Resource I

Cyberbullying Crossword Puzzle

(page 1 of 4)

Cyberbullying Crossword Puzzle

(page 2 of 4)

DOWN

1. Short for "World Wide Web" or pages linked together via the Internet.

2. Unsolicited electronic mail sent from someone you do not know.

3. Interactive Web journal or diary, the contents of which are posted online and then viewable by some or all individuals.

4. An intermediary Web site that hides or disguises the IP address associated with the Internet user.

5. An electronic device that stores and processes information and facilitates electronic communication when connected to a network.

6. Two or more computers connected so that they can communicate with each other.

9. The most popular social networking Web site.

10. An extreme form of bullying where physical assaults are recorded on mobile phones or digital cameras and the recordings are distributed to others.

11. A file on a computer that records user information when visiting a Web site.

12. Intentional and repeated harm inflicted through the use of computers, cell phones, and other electronic devices.

13. A wireless handheld device that allows for telephone communications.

14. A user-created Web page on a social networking Web site.

16. The denial of access to particular parts of the Internet.

17. The act of restricting access to certain Web sites (usually using software programs).

18. Sending short messages via cell phone.

21. Making a statement or taking an action that indicates harm to another.

24. Allows Internet users to send and receive electronic text to and from other Internet users.

ACROSS

7. Repeated and deliberate harassment directed by one in a position of power toward one or more.

8. Physical or emotional injury to someone.

15. Suicide stemming directly or indirectly from cyberbullying victimization.

17. The second-most popular social networking Web site.

19. Acronym for the company that provides an Internet connection to individuals or companies.

20. Unsolicited words or actions intended to annoy, alarm, or abuse another individual.

22. A worldwide network of computers communicating with each other via phone lines, satellite links, wireless networks, and cable systems.

23. The act of requesting another person to enter your social network.

25. Sending angry, rude, or obscene messages directed at a person or persons privately or via an online group.

Cyberbullying Crossword Puzzle

(page 4 of 4)

OPTIONAL WORD BANK

ANONYMIZER   EMAIL   ISP
BLOCKING   FACEBOOK   MYSPACE
BLOG   FILTERING   NETWORK
BULLYING   FLAMING   PROFILE
CELLPHONE   FRIENDING   SPAM
COMPUTER   HAPPYSLAPPING   TEXTING
COOKIE   HARASSMENT   THREAT
CYBERBULLICIDE   HARM   WEB
CYBERBULLYING   INTERNET

ANSWERS

DOWN

1. WEB
2. SPAM
3. BLOG
4. ANONYMIZER
5. COMPUTER
6. NETWORK
9. MYSPACE
10. HAPPYSLAPPING
11. COOKIE
12. CYBERBULLYING
13. CELLPHONE
14. PROFILE
16. BLOCKING
17. FILTERING
18. TEXTING
21. THREAT
24. EMAIL

ACROSS

7. BULLYING
8. HARM
15. CYBERBULLICIDE
17. FACEBOOK
19. ISP
20. HARASSMENT
22. INTERNET
23. FRIENDING
25. FLAMING

Resource J

Cyberbullying Word Find

Cyberbullying Word Find

```
I  H  G  R  G  R  X  N  R  E  Z  I  M  Y  N  O  N  A  N  E  F  B  E  N  O
G  N  A  N  E  M  E  X  W  E  Z  S  V  I  G  Q  U  E  N  L  A  H  L  T  F
H  N  T  P  I  T  T  V  S  N  Y  K  Y  Z  T  B  T  O  B  U  C  R  U  O  S
Y  Z  I  E  P  R  U  Z  E  F  K  A  V  E  Z  W  H  U  K  N  E  H  A  L  G
C  O  K  T  R  Y  E  P  Z  N  W  I  D  Y  O  P  L  X  D  L  B  Y  M  P  X
B  T  D  K  X  N  S  T  M  L  G  I  G  R  L  L  T  O  I  E  O  U  M  P  R
P  D  I  P  R  E  E  L  L  O  C  E  K  L  Y  O  O  O  G  A  O  B  V  D  S
Z  C  G  U  X  E  T  T  A  I  C  S  E  I  M  R  V  F  I  T  K  V  Q  D  C
L  T  C  Q  B  L  C  O  L  P  F  C  N  R  Z  R  I  J  T  J  N  E  R  Z  Z
U  Z  Z  T  T  I  H  L  B  M  P  G  D  T  S  F  V  B  A  W  A  X  V  W  D
M  I  S  U  S  D  U  X  W  Z  W  I  D  D  P  Y  C  V  L  Z  Q  W  I  I  G
G  S  U  P  N  B  E  M  A  I  L  X  N  M  Y  S  P  A  C  E  R  L  G  E  L
W  U  S  C  R  D  K  Q  K  N  T  M  G  G  W  J  U  C  I  H  P  O  N  Q  N
Q  D  V  E  G  U  G  I  Q  T  J  L  Y  K  I  Z  M  M  Z  O  L  V  I  O  I
W  O  B  R  F  P  K  G  N  J  U  I  N  H  X  M  J  H  C  R  W  S  M  I  H
N  Y  T  Z  Z  R  I  A  J  W  D  Y  R  A  L  B  K  T  A  C  S  E  A  H  A
C  I  S  Z  Y  D  T  A  Y  S  M  R  K  R  I  S  A  G  Q  H  U  D  L  P  R
D  Y  W  Y  X  S  O  P  J  T  G  E  B  M  F  I  G  I  M  J  O  V  F  E  A
F  R  I  E  W  D  I  W  G  A  I  Y  T  R  K  R  F  P  I  A  M  V  U  Z  S
N  F  H  I  V  E  D  I  M  E  U  C  Y  B  E  R  B  U  L  L  Y  I  N  G  S
V  Q  I  C  I  V  I  S  B  R  V  P  C  S  H  A  P  O  W  Z  N  F  Q  Y  M
G  N  I  K  C  O  L  B  W  H  J  B  S  E  L  I  F  O  R  P  O  B  E  W  E
R  D  O  I  A  G  D  Q  M  T  C  I  E  V  Y  R  W  W  A  D  N  L  J  C  N
N  O  T  K  D  Y  D  P  W  H  O  T  A  D  A  Y  Q  H  L  H  A  Q  C  S  T
C  W  J  B  S  G  D  F  I  N  N  D  Y  B  U  I  N  Z  F  O  N  E  F  X  S
```

AGGRESSION	DIGITAL	ISP
ANONYMIZER	EMAIL	MYSPACE
ANONYMOUS	FACEBOOK	NETWORK
BLOCKING	FILTERING	PROFILE
BLOG	FLAMING	REVENGE
BULLYING	FRIENDING	TEXTING
CELLPHONE	HAPPYSLAPPING	THREAT
COMPUTER	HARASSMENT	WEB
COOKIE	HARM	
CYBERBULLICIDE	INSTANT	
CYBERBULLYING	INTERNET	

Resource K

Cyberbullying Trustee Designation

DESIGNATED CYBERBULLYING TRUSTEE

**Talk to me if you or someone you know
is being electronically harassed or threatened!
I care about your online experience and can help!**

Resource L

Supplemental Staff Development Questions

Chapter 1

1. How is cyberbullying defined in the text?

2. Do you believe this definition effectively describes what cyberbullying is among the youth you care for? If not, how would you modify it?

3. How is cyberbullying similar to other forms of bullying?

4. What makes cyberbullying different from traditional bullying?

5. Aside from personal computers, what other electronic tools might be used to perpetrate cyberbullying?

6. Why might some adults fail to take cyberbullying seriously? How might this affect the identification and prevention of cyberbullying incidents?

7. What types of harm may victims experience as a result of cyberbullying? In what ways are these similar to other forms of bullying?

8. Why are educators so important with respect to identifying and responding to cyberbullying?

9. Do you expect cyberbullying to be an ever-increasing problem among youth? Why or why not?

10. How do teens and adults differ in their use of the Internet?

11. How could teens' use of the Internet make them more vulnerable to cyberbullying?

12. How might teens use cell phones to cyberbully peers while at school?

13. In what ways can online interaction be beneficial to youth?

14. How could experiences with cyberbullying prevent victims from utilizing the Internet as a learning tool?

15. How could keeping pace with new Internet-based technologies help educators address cyberbullying?

16. What are some of the emotional and psychological consequences for victims of traditional bullying? How could these be potentially life-threatening? Do you think victims of cyberbullying are at-risk for experiencing the same consequences as victims of traditional bullying? Why or why not?

17. What are some of the behavioral problems associated with bullying victimization? Could these problems ultimately lead to physical violence at school? How?

18. Which age groups are thought to be most susceptible to cyberbullying? Why is this so? What does this mean for teachers and parents?

Chapter 2

1. What distinction is usually made between harassment and bullying?

2. Give two examples of how technology could allow bullies to extend their reach of aggression beyond settings normally associated with traditional bullying. Are there any limits to this reach?

3. In what ways might cyberbullying cause recurring harm to the victim?

4. How might cyberbullies obtain a "position of power" over their victims in an online setting? How might this position of power change? How is this different than traditional bullying?

5. What are some examples of tools used by cyberbullies to inflict harm on their targets?

6. Aside from text messaging capabilities, what other components present in many PDAs and cell phones can be used for cyberbullying purposes?

7. Why might many adolescents choose to cyberbully their victims as opposed to bullying them in person?

8. How might cyberbullies use the Internet to shield their true identities from their victims? Why does the ability to remain anonymous seem to encourage cyberbullying?

9. Are cyberbullies ever completely anonymous while online? Why or why not?

10. If bullies seem to have the ability to hide their identities from their targets, how can they ever be identified?

11. What is the name for the unique identifier assigned to every device connected to the Internet?

12. Which is easier to investigate—cyberbullying or traditional bullying? What are the differences?

13. In what ways might the Internet remove inhibition for the bully? How could this lead to additional harm for the victim?

14. Why are parents often left trying to deal with their child's cyberbullying participation after it has already occurred? How might this be prevented or reduced?

15. With regard to cyberbullying, what is meant by the term "viral"?

16. Why might cyberbullying seem to cause unending suffering for those targeted?

17. Why would attacks by multiple aggressors be easier to coordinate through the use of cyberbullying techniques?

18. Why might many adolescents fail to make distinctions between their lives offline and their lives in cyberspace?

19. Why are some adults unable to understand how much the Internet has become a part of the social lives of adolescents?

20. What are some of the mediums through which cyberbullying often occurs?

21. Why are the e-mail addresses used in many school networks susceptible to exploitation by cyberbullies?

22. What are a few of the reasons teens are now avoiding some online chat rooms? What are many teens now using in place of chat rooms for online communication?

23. What do teens often use to mask their online conversations from eavesdropping parents? What do "PAW" and "POS" stand for?

24. What are some of the popular voting Web sites on the Internet? How might an individual use such a site to bully others? Why might adolescent victims be sensitive to this type of bullying?

25. What feature(s) inherent in some blogging sites may invite cyberbullying by the reader?

26. Which technology could adolescents use to cyberbully peers while playing online role-playing games or Internet-enabled video game consoles?

27. What are some of the popular instant messaging programs used by both adolescents and adults? Why have cyberbullies embraced this technology?

28. How are cyberbullies using cell phones to target individuals who have cell phones but lack free text messaging plans? How are cyberbullies currently using cell phones to invade their victims' privacy?

29. How are some individuals being bullied through the use of online services originally intended to help communicate with the hearing-impaired? Why are these cyberbullying tactics especially alarming?

30. What is "photoshopping"? How do some adolescents use this to cyberbully others?

31. Why do computers and cell phones make attractive tools for those desiring to spread rumors about others?

32. What does the term "flaming" mean?

33. How might cyberbullies use the hijacked accounts of their victims on social networking sites?

34. What is involved with the act of "happy-slapping"?

Chapter 3

1. Why do girls seem to be equally as likely to participate in cyberbullying as boys? Is this different than traditional bullying?

2. How are females likely to express their aggression online toward their victims?

3. How do females tend to feel after becoming a victim of cyberbullying? How is this different than feelings experienced by male victims? What might explain these differences?

4. When does cyberbullying activity tend to peak for adolescents? How does this compare to traditional forms of bullying?

5. According to recent research, which grade seems to signify an important shift for students with regard to cyberbullying activity?

6. What does recent research tell us about the relationship between cyberbullies and their victims? Do victims usually believe they know the identity of their aggressors?

7. Why do we believe there is a connection between cyberbullying and traditional bullying?

8. Are victims of cyberbullying likely to experience other forms of bullying as well? What does research tell us about cyberbullies and

their involvement in more traditional forms of bullying? What do these findings mean for educators seeking to counsel students believed to be involved with one particular type of bullying or victimization?

9. Why do you think cyberbullying victims are unlikely to tell an adult about their experiences?

10. With whom are female victims likely to share information about cyberbullying experiences? Does this differ from male victims of cyberbullying?

11. How do victims tend to deal with minor forms of cyberbullying? Are these techniques effective in dealing with aggressors? Why are these techniques simply short-term solutions?

12. What are some of the emotional consequences of cyberbullying victimization? Are these consequences similar to those experienced by victims of schoolyard bullying? Do you believe the emotional responses of cyberbullying victims are cause for concern? Why or why not?

13. Give two examples of the behavioral consequences associated with cyberbullying perpetration.

14. Give two examples of the behavioral consequences associated with cyberbullying victimization.

15. Why do you think adolescent victims of cyberbullying have an elevated risk of suicidal thoughts?

16. What explanation do youth often give for their acts of cyberbullying?

17. How might some victims of traditional bullying seek retribution? Why is this strategy attractive to those individuals?

18. Why are cyberbullies able to easily rationalize their attacks on others?

19. How could educators help students understand the seriousness of cyberbullying?

Chapter 4

1. What are some of the popular social networking Web sites in use today?

2. Which social networking Web site seems to be most popular among youth?

3. Give two examples of the methods used by individuals to communicate with others on social networking Web sites.

4. How might some youth measure their social success on these Web sites? Do you think youth equate this to social success outside the realm of cyberspace?

5. Regarding social networking Web sites, what is meant by the term "friend"?

6. What is a "profile page"?

7. Give some examples of items often found on users' profile pages.

8. Which portion of the profile page can be considered similar to one's diary? How might the information contained in this section facilitate acts of cyberbullying?

9. How do youth often make their pages stand out from those of others? What might an adolescent do or use to accomplish this?

10. Why do you think many youth are willing to divulge their personal information online?

11. Why might youth lie about their age when signing up for social networking Web sites?

12. Why has MySpace received so much negative media attention?

13. Which safety measures have been developed by MySpace to protect its users?

14. How has Bebo sought to promote safe and responsible use of social networking sites?

15. What are some of the safety features available to users of Xanga?

16. Do you think young people should avoid social networking Web sites altogether? Should parents forbid their children to use social networking sites? Why or why not?

17. What are some of the potential benefits of online interaction?

18. How are some schools currently using social networking Web sites as instructional tools?

19. How might an individual use a fictitious account to bully others online?

20. Why are social networking Web sites often ideal environments for cyberbullying?

21. Why might an adolescent decide to post personal information on their profile page, but not make this same information available to others in real life?

22. How do cyberbullies steal their targets' identities on social networking Web sites?

23. What are the Five Strategies for Safer Social Networking?

24. What simple step can students take to control who views the content of their profile pages?

Chapter 5

1. When do educators have the authority to discipline student behavior and restrict student speech on campus? According to the *Tinker* ruling, what must educators be able to do in order for this to be justified?

2. When are students' expressed views on campus not protected by the First Amendment? Does this mean individuals lose their constitutional rights regarding freedom of speech after stepping on school property? How has the Court made this distinction?

3. If the expressed views of students can be restricted on campus by school administrators, can students be disciplined for these same views when they express them off of school grounds? If so, when is such action appropriate? Can you think of any specific scenarios or situations?

4. With respect to *Morse v. Frederick,* what did the Court mean by "school speech"? What do you believe the ruling might have been if this incident had occurred outside the scope of a school-sponsored event?

5. What requirement has the Court set forth regarding the discipline of off-campus student speech? Do you believe off-campus acts of cyberbullying could warrant discipline by school administrators? Do you think disciplining students for cyberbullying would be supported by the courts? Why or why not?

6. What was the major difference between the two student-created Web pages cited in the *Emmett* and *J. S.* cases?

7. Aside from the important need to protect students, what might happen if educators fail to address harassment based on sex or race?

8. When can school districts legally intervene in incidents involving student off-campus speech or electronic communication?

9. How would you define "substantial disruption"?

10. Why would a formal school policy on cyberbullying help protect students, teachers, and school administrators?

11. What are some of the essential elements of an effective policy on cyberbullying? Can you think of any additional elements you believe should be added to the list found in the text?

12. Why is it important for administrators to properly define the terms contained in their policy?

13. Do you think it is necessary to investigate all known incidents of cyberbullying involving your students? Why or why not?

14. Would you encourage teachers to deal with acts of cyberbullying on their own? If not, who would you suggest they notify? What if the cyberbullying incident is thought to be relatively minor?

15. When students are involved in cyberbullying, do they have an expectation of privacy with respect to their personal property? What has the Court cited as a prerequisite to student searches? In your opinion, how might this be different than "probable cause"?

16. How can school districts help discourage acts of cyberbullying? What else can educators do to help protect students?

Chapter 6

1. Why do we believe forbidding youth from accessing the Internet is an inappropriate method of cyberbullying prevention?

2. When should teachers begin the process of educating students about safe Internet use? Who should be involved in this endeavor?

3. As an educator, what do you believe are your responsibilities regarding cyberbullying prevention?

4. How might educators make an assessment of online behavior at their school? What should be addressed during this assessment period?

5. If you were to develop an Acceptable Use Policy (AUP) governing the use of technology in your classroom, what rules would you include?

6. Do you think cell phones should be completely banned at school? What rules should be included in an AUP concerning cell phones?

7. If the seizure of an electronic device is acceptable by law or school policy, why would a search of its contents by educators be unacceptable? Who should be left to search these items?

8. Why is peer mentoring considered an effective method of reducing cyberbullying?

9. How could you use peer mentoring in your efforts to reduce cyberbullying?

10. What steps do you believe educators should take to help promote a safe and respectful school environment?

11. What is the underlying goal of developing an "honor code"?

12. How should an "honor code" be expressed?

13. How does "content monitoring" work?

14. With respect to the Internet, what is a "proxy"? How could a student use a proxy to access prohibited social networking Web sites?

15. What can parents do to help prevent cyberbullying?

16. How would you help parents become more proactive in preventing their child's involvement with cyberbullying?

17. What questions would you suggest parents ask their children regarding their child's online experiences?

18. What is an "Internet Use Contract"?

19. What methods can parents use to monitor their child's online activities?

20. Why do we consider monitoring software to be insufficient by itself?

21. What steps would you tell your students to take to help protect them while online?

22. What are some of the signs of cyberbullying victimization? What might lead you to believe your student could be involved in cyberbullying others?

Chapter 7

1. Why would "turning off the computer" be an impractical means of dealing with cyberbullying?

2. What connection does cyberbullying have with civil rights legislation? What does this mean for educators and school officials?

3. What steps should schools take immediately following the discovery of a cyberbullying incident?

4. Why are "zero-tolerance" policies not the best option for dealing with cyberbullying?

5. Which informal mechanisms might you use to respond to cyberbullying among your students? How could these help protect your school district?

6. Why do you think it is important to respond to varying levels of cyberbullying with varying levels of disciplinary action?

7. Why should schools designate cyberbullying "trustees"?

8. What is the importance of an anonymous reporting system? Why would this system be beneficial for students?

9. Why is it important to document the disruption caused by cyberbullying incidents?

10. Why should incidents centered on "protected statuses" be taken very seriously?

11. Why are incidents involving digital video especially harmful for those victimized?

12. Can educators contact Internet service providers and cellular service providers when investigating acts of cyberbullying? Why or why not?

13. What would you tell parents to do if they suspect their child has been cyberbullied? What would you discourage them from doing? Why?

14. What should parents do if they suspect their child is cyberbullying others?

15. What are some of the steps children should take if they believe they are being cyberbullied?

16. When can we consider cyberbullying as a *civil* matter?

17. When can we consider cyberbullying as a *criminal* matter?

18. When should law enforcement become involved in cyberbullying incidents?

Resource L
Supplemental Staff Development Questions

References

Aftab, P. (2006). *Parry Aftab's guide for schools on cyberbullying.* Retrieved December 10, 2007, from http://www.stopcyberbullying.org/educators/guide_for_schools.html

Akers, R. L. (1985). *Deviant behavior: A social learning approach* (3rd ed.). Belmont, CA: Wadsworth.

Alexa.com. (2008). *MySpace.com.* Retrieved March 24, 2008, from http://www.alexa.com/data/details/traffic_details/myspace.com

American Law Institute. (1965). *Restatement of the law, second, torts, § 46.* Washington, DC: American Law Institute.

An act to define bullying; to include cyberbullying in public school district antibullying policies; and for other purposes, Ark. House Bill 1072 (2007). Retrieved January 19, 2007, from http://www.arkleg.state.ar.us/ftproot/bills/2007/public/HB1072.pdf

Andreou, E. (2001). Bully/victim problems and their association with coping behavior in conflictual peer interactions among school-age children. *Educational Psychology, 21,* 59–66.

Angwin, J. (2007). *MySpace moves to give parents more information.* Retrieved January 18, 2007, from http://online.wsj.com/public/article/SB116900733587978625–52s20_rbQ79Mof75n5ZzVOGhN0U_20070216.html

Angwin, J., & Steinberg, B. (2006). *News Corp. goal: Make MySpace safer for teens.* Retrieved February 17, 2006, http://www.commonsensemedia.org/resources/news.php?id=66

Apollo, A. M. (2007). *Cyberbullying: Taking the fight online.* Retrieved May 31, 2008, from http://saferschools.blogspot.com/2007/02/october-9–2005-bonita-banner.html

Appel, J. (2007). Report identifies ed-tech trends to watch: Emerging forms of publication, massively multiplayer educational gaming among trends on the horizon expected to have a huge impact on schools. Retrieved February 15, 2007, from http://www.eschoolnews.com/news/showStoryts.cfm?ArticleID=6870

Aseltine, R. H., Gore, S., & Gordon, J. (2000). Life stress, anger and anxiety, and delinquency: An empirical test of general strain theory. *Journal of Health and Social Behavior, 41*(3), 256–275.

Bandura, A. (1969). *Principles of behavior modification.* New York: Holt, Rinehart, Winston.

Bandura, A. (1973). *Aggression: A social learning analysis.* Englewood Cliffs, NJ: Prentice-Hall.

Bandura, A. (1977). *Social learning theory.* Englewood Cliffs, NJ: Prentice-Hall.

Bandura, A., & Walters, R. (1963). *Social learning and personality development.* New York: Holt, Rinehart, Winston.

Beidler v. North Thurston School District (Thurston Cty. Super. Ct 2000).

Benfer, A. (2001). *Cyber slammed.* Retrieved July 7, 2001, from http://dir.salon.com/story/mwt/feature/2001/07/03/cyber_bullies/

Berson, I. R., Berson, M. J., & Ferron, J. M. (2002). Emerging risks of violence in the digital age: Lessons for educators from an online study of adolescent girls in the United States. *Journal of School Violence, 1*(2), 51–71.

Berson, M. J. (2000). The computer can't see you blush. *Kappa Delta Pi Record, 36*(4), 158–162.

Besag, V. E. (1989). *Bullies and victims in schools*. Milton Keynes, UK: Open University Press.

Bethel School District v. Fraser, 478 675 (S. Ct. 1986).

Beussink v. Woodland R-IV School District, 30 1175 (E.D. Mo. 1998).

Bjorkqvist, K., Ekman, K., & Lagerspetz, K. (1982). Bullies and victims: Their ego picture, ideal ego picture, and normative ego picture. *Scandinavian Journal of Psychology, 23,* 307–313.

Bjorkqvist, K., Lagerspetz, K. M. J., & Kaukiainin, A. (1992). Do girls manipulate and boys fight? Developmental trends in regard to direct and indirect aggression. *Aggressive Behavior, 18,* 117–127.

Bjorkqvist, K., & Niemela, P. (1992). New trends in the study of female aggression. In K. Bjorkqvist & P. Niemela (Eds.), *Of mice and women: Aspects of female aggression* (pp. 3–16). San Diego: Academic Press.

Black, H. C. (1990). *Black's law dictionary* (6th ed.). St. Paul, MN: West Publishing.

Borg, M. G. (1998). The emotional reaction of school bullies and their victims. *Educational Psychology, 18*(4), 433–444.

Borg, M. G. (1999). The extent and nature of bullying among primary and secondary schoolchildren. *Educational Research, 41,* 137–153.

Boyd, D. (2006, February). *Identity production in a networked culture: Why youth heart MySpace.* Paper presented at the American Association for the Advancement of Science, St. Louis, MO. Available May 31, 2008, at http://www.danah.org/papers/AAAS2006.html

Boyd, D. (2007). Why youth (heart) social network sites: The role of networked publics in teenage social life. In D. Buckingham (Ed.), *Youth, identity, and digital media* (pp. 119–142). Cambridge, MA: MIT Press.

Broidy, L. M., & Agnew, R. (1997). Gender and crime: A general strain theory perspective. *Journal of Research in Crime and Delinquency, 34*(3), 275–306.

Brown, B., & Merritt, R. (2002). *No easy answers: The truth behind death at Columbine.* Brooklyn, NY: Lantern Books.

Brown, L. (2003). *Girlfighting.* New York: New York University Press.

Brown, S. E., Esbensen Finn, A., & Geis, G. (2001). *Criminology: Explaining crime and its context.* Cincinnati: Anderson Publishing.

Burgess-Proctor, A., Patchin, J. W., & Hinduja, S. (in press). Cyberbullying and online harassment: Reconceptualizing the victimization of adolescent girls. In V. Garcia & J. Clifford (Eds.), *Female crime victims: Reality reconsidered.* Upper Saddle River, NJ: Prentice Hall.

Butterfield, L., & Broad, H. (2001, April). Children, young people and the Internet. *Social Work Now,* 18, pp. 5–11. Retrieved June 30, 2005, from http://www.cyf.govt.nz/SocialWorkNow_1246.htm

Calvert, S. L. (2002). Identity construction on the Internet. In S. L. Calvert, A. B. Jordan, & R. R. Cocking (Eds.), *Children in the digital age: Influences of electronic media on development* (pp. 57–70). Westport, CT: Praeger.

Carson, J. A. (2007). *Battling bullies: From being shoved in the hallways to cyberspace scares, teens bearing the brunt of bullies need understanding and help.* Retrieved May 31, 2008, from http://www.keyclub.org/magazine/0307ftbbull.asp

Carvel, J. (2002). "One in four teens" is victim of text message bullying. Retrieved April 15, 2002, from http://www.guardian.co.uk/mobile/article/0,2763,684555,00.html

Centers for Disease Control and Prevention. (2007). *Suicide trends among youths and young adults aged 10–24 years—United States, 1990–2004. Morbidity and Mortality Weekly Report,* 56(35), 905–908. Retrieved May 23, 2008, from http://www.cdc.gov/mmwr/preview/mmwrhtml/mm5635a2.htm

Cleary, S. D. (2000). Adolescent victimization and associated suicidal and violent behaviors. *Adolescence, 35,* 671–682.

Conn, K. (2004). *Bullying and harassment: A legal guide for educators.* Alexandria, VA: Association for Supervision and Curriculum Development.

Cooper, C. J. (2004). *Cyber venom: Adolescent bullying moves from the schoolyard to the Internet.* Retrieved October 16, 2004, from http://www.signonsandiego.com/uniontrib/20041016/news_lz1c16cyber.html

Cowie, H., & Berdondini, L. (2002). The expression of emotion in response to bullying. *Emotional and Behavioural Difficulties, 7*(4), 207–214.

Crick, N. R., & Grotpeter, J. K. (1995). Relational aggression, gender, and social-psychological adjustment. *Child Development, 66,* 610–722.

Dake, J. A., Price, J. H., & Telljohann, S. K. (2003). The nature and extent of bullying at school. *Journal of School Health, 73*(5), 173–180.

Davis v. Monroe County Board of Education, 120 1390 (F.3d 1999).

Devoe, J. F., Peter, K., Kaufman, P., Ruddy, S. A., Miller, A. K., Planty, M., et al. (2002). *Indicators of school crime and safety* (NCJ 196753). Washington, DC: U.S. Department of Education, National Center for Education Statistics and U.S. Department of Justice, Bureau of Justice Statistics. Available May 31, 2008, at http://www.ojp.usdoj.gov/bjs/abstract/iscs02.htm

Diener, E. (1980). Deindividuation: The absence of self-awareness and self-regulation in group members. In P. B. Paulus (Ed.), *The psychology of group influence* (pp. 209–242). Hillsdale, NJ: Lawrence Erlbaum.

Diener, E., & Wallbom, M. (1976). Effects of self-awareness on antinormative behavior. *Journal of Research in Personality, 10*(1), 107–111.

Duncan, N. (1999). *Sexual bullying: Gender conflict and pupil culture in secondary schools.* London: Routledge.

Durrani, A. (2007). *Bebo promotes safety online.* Retrieved July 24, 2007, from http://www.balderton.com/?q=content/bebo-promotes-safety-online

Edds, K., Lawhon, C., & Miller, S. (2006). *Part 3: Web threats; Anonymous Internet access can turn sites into bathroom walls.* Retrieved May 5, 2006, from http://www.ocregister.com/ocregister/life/atoz/article_1137010.php

Eisenberg, M. E., Neumark-Sztainer, D., & Story, M. (2003). Association of weight-based teasing and emotional well-being among adolescents. *Archives of Pediatrics and Adolescent Medicine, 157,* 733–738.

Emmett v. Kent School District No. 415, 92 1088 (W.D. Wash. 2000).

Ericson, N. (2001). *Addressing the problem of juvenile bullying* (OJJDP Fact Sheet #27), U.S. Department of Justice, Office of Justice Programs, Office of Juvenile Justice and Delinquency Prevention. Washington, DC: U.S. Government Printing Office.

Erikson, E. H. (1950). *Childhood and society.* New York: W. W. Norton & Company.

Espelage, D. L., Bosworth, K., & Simon, T. R. (2000). Examining the social context of bullying behaviors in early adolescence. *Journal of Counseling and Development, 78,* 326–333.

Facebook. (2008). *Statistics.* Retrieved January 17, 2008, from http://www.facebook.com/press/info.php?statistics

Farrington, D. (1980). Truancy, delinquency, the home, and the school. In L. Hersov & I. Berg (Eds.), *Out of school: Modern perspectives in truancy and school refusal* (pp. 49–63). New York: John Wiley & Sons.

Festinger, L., Pepitone, A., & Newcomb, B. (1952). Some consequences of deindividuation in a group. *Journal of Abnormal and Social Psychology, 47,* 382–389.

Finkelhor, D., Mitchell, K. J., & Wolak, J. (2000). *Online victimization: A report on the nation's youth.* Retrieved June 30, 2000, from http://www.ncmec.org/en_US/publications/NC62.pdf

Finkelhor, D., Turner, H. A., Ormrod, R. K., & Hamby, S. L. (2005). The victimization of children & youth: A comprehensive, national survey. *Child Maltreatment, 10*(1), 5–25.

Flaherty, L., Pearce, K., & Rubin, R. (1998). Internet and face-to-face communication: Not functional alternatives. *Communication Quarterly, 46*(3), 250–268.

Fried, S., & Fried, P. F. (1996). *Bullies and victims.* New York: Evans and Company.

Friendster launches fan profiles. (2007). *PRNewswire.* Retrieved September 27, 2007, from http://www.redorbit.com/news/technology/1081343/friendster_launches_fan_profiles/index.html

Garry, E. M. (1996). *Truancy: First step to a lifetime of problems.* Washington, DC: U.S. Department of Justice, Office of Juvenile Justice and Delinquency Prevention.

Gavin, T. (1997). *Truancy: Not just kids' stuff anymore.* Washington DC: Federal Bureau of Investigation.

Gebser v. Lago Vista Independent School District (5th Cir. 1998).

Girl tormented by phone bullies. (2001). *BBCNews.* Retrieved January 16, 2001, from http://news.bbc.co.uk/1/hi/education/1120597.stm

Gottfredson, M., & Hirschi, T. (1990). *A general theory of crime.* Stanford, CA: Stanford University Press.

Graham, S., & Juvonen, J. (2002). Ethnicity, peer harassment, and adjustment in middle school: An exploratory study. *Journal of Early Adolescence, 22,* 173–199.

Granneman, S. (2006). *MySpace, a place without MyParents.* Retrieved June 30, 2006, from http://www.securityfocus.com/columnists/408

Gruber, S. A., & Yurgelun-Todd, D. A. (2006). Neurobiology and the law: A role in juvenile justice? *Ohio State Journal of Criminal Law, 3,* 321.

Halligan, J. (2006). *Ryan Patrick Halligan.* Retrieved January 23, 2008, from http://www.ryanpatrickhalligan.org

Hass, N. (2006). *In your Facebook.com.* Retrieved January 8, 2006, from http://www.nytimes.com/2006/01/08/education/edlife/facebooks.html

Hawker, D. S. J., & Boulton, M. J. (2000). Twenty years' research on peer victimization and psychological maladjustment: A meta-analysis review of cross-sectional studies. *Journal of Child Psychology and Psychiatry, 41*(4), 441–445.

Hazelwood School District et al. v. Kuhlmeier et al., 484 260 (S. Ct. 1988).

Helmond, A. (2006, October 18). *Comments on Danah Boyd's article about MySpace.* Message posted to Masters of Media, Universiteit van Amsterdam, blog, archived at http://mastersofmedia.hum.uva.nl/2006/10/18/comments-on-danah-boyds-article-about-myspace/

Hempel, J. (2008). *New effort to protect kids online: MySpace joins with 49 states to step up efforts to keep kids safe from online predators.* Retrieved January 14, 2008, from http://money.cnn.com/2008/01/14/technology/hempel_myspace.fortune.index.htm?postversion=2008011413

Hinduja, S., & Patchin, J. W. (2007). Off-line consequences of online victimization: School violence and delinquency. *Journal of School Violence, 6*(3), 89–112.

Hinduja, S., & Patchin, J. W. (2008a). Cyberbullying: An exploratory analysis of factors related to offending and victimization. *Deviant Behavior, 29*(2), 1–29.

Hinduja, S., & Patchin, J. W. (2008b). Personal information of adolescents on the Internet: A quantitative content analysis of MySpace. *Journal of Adolescence, 31*(1), 125–146.

Holahan, C. (2006). *The dark side of Second Life.* Retrieved November 21, 2006, from http://www.businessweek.com/technology/content/nov2006/tc20061121_727243.htm

Hoover, J. N. (2006). *Kids vs. creeps: Concerns mount over online child predators.* Retrieved May 1, 2006, from http://www.informationweek.com/software/showArticle.jhtml?articleID=187001704

Hotaling, G., & Finkelhor, D. (1990). Estimating the number of stranger abduction homicides of children: A review of the available evidence. *Journal of Criminal Justice, 18,* 385–399.

Hudson, D. (2000, April). *Censorship of student Internet speech: The effect of diminishing student rights, fear of the Internet and Columbine.* Paper presented at the Telecommunication Policy and Law Symposium, Washington, DC. Available at the Freedom Forum Web site: http://www.freedomforum.org/templates/document.asp?documentID=14592

J. S. v. Bethlehem Area School District, 757 412 (Pa. Cmwlth. 2000).

Jangl is "first in" again: Launches SMS for Bebo's 40 million members worldwide. (2007). *Reuters*. Retrieved December 12, 2007, from http://www.reuters.com/article/press Release/idUS201587+12-Dec-2007+BW20071212

Jerome, L., & Segal, A. (2003). Bullying by Internet—Editorial. *Journal of the American Academy of Child and Adolescent Psychiatry, 42*(7), 751.

Johnson, M., Munn, P., & Edwards, L. (1991). *Action against bullying: A support pack for schools*. Edinburgh: The Scottish Council for Educational Research.

Johnston, D. (2007). *Students for Safer Schools*. Retrieved September 15, 2007, from http://www.jeffreyjohnston.org/journals.htm.

Jones, T. (2008). *A deadly Web of deceit: A teen's online "friend" proved false, and cyber-vigilantes are avenging her*. Retrieved January 10, 2008, from http://www.washingtonpost.com/wp-dyn/content/article/2008/01/09/AR2008010903367_pf.html

Jurkowski, T. (2005). *Bullying moves from school to cyberspace*. Retrieved November 7, 2005, from http://www.nbc-2.com/articles/readarticle.asp?articleid=4827&z=3&p

Kahn, R. L., & Antonucci, T. C. (1981). Convoys of social support: A life course approach. In S. B. Kiesler, J. N. Morgan, & V. K. Oppenheimer (Eds.), *Aging: Social change* (pp. 383–405). New York: Academic Press.

Kaltiala-Heino, R., Rimpelä, M., Marttunen, M., Rimpelä, A., & Rantanen, P. (1999). Bullying, depression, and suicidal ideation in Finnish adolescents: School survey. *British Medical Journal, 319*(7206), 348–351.

Kaltiala-Heino, R., Rimpelä, M., Rantanen, P., & Rimpelä, A. (2000). Bullying at school: An indicator of adolescents at risk for mental disorders. *Journal of Adolescence, 23*, 661–674.

Katz, L. (2005). *When "digital bullying" goes too far*. Retrieved June 22, 2005, from http://news.cnet.co.uk/mobiles/0,39029678,39190253,00.htm

Keith, S., & Martin, M. E. (2005). Cyber-bullying: Creating a culture of respect in a cyber world. *Reclaiming Children and Youth, 13*(4), 224–228.

Klein v. Smith, 635 F.Supp. 1440, 1441 (D. Me. 1986).

Klump v. Nazareth Area School District, 422 622 (E.D. Pa. 2006).

Kowalski, R. M., & Limber, S. P. (2007). Electronic bullying among middle school students. *Journal of Adolescent Health, 41*, S22–S30.

Kowalski, R. M., Limber, S. P., & Agatston, P. W. (2007). *Cyber bullying: Bullying in the digital age*. Malden, MA: Blackwell Publishing.

Kowalski, R. M., Limber, S. P., Scheck, A., Redfearn, M., Allen, J., Calloway, A. M., et al. (2005, August). *Electronic bullying among school-aged children and youth*. Paper presented at the Annual Meeting of the American Psychological Association, Washington, DC.

Kumpulainen, K., & Rasanen, E. (2000). Children involved in bullying at elementary school age: Their psychiatric symptoms and deviance in adolescence. *Child Abuse and Neglect, 24*, 1567–1577.

Kumpalainen, K., Rasanen, E., & Henttonen, I. (1999). Children involved in bullying: Psychological disturbance and the persistence of the involvement. *Child Abuse and Neglect, 23*, 1253–1262.

Lagerspetz, K., Bjorkvqvist, K., Bertz, M., & King, E. (1982). Group aggression among school children in three schools. *Scandinavian Journal of Psychology, 23*, 45–52.

Layshock v. Hermitage School District, 412 502 (W.D. Pa. 2006).

Leary, M. R., Haupt, A. L., Strausser, K. S., & Chokel, J. T. (1998). Calibrating the sociometer: The relationship between interpersonal appraisals and state self-esteem. *Journal of Personality and Social Psychology, 74*, 1290–1299.

Leary, M. R., Schreindorfer, L. S., & Haupt, A. L. (1995). The role of self-esteem in emotional and behavioral problems: Why is low self-esteem dysfunctional? *Journal of Social and Clinical Psychology, 14*, 297–314.

Leary, M. R., Tambor, E. S., Terdal, S. J., & Downs, D. L. (1995). Self-esteem as an interpersonal monitor: The sociometer hypothesis. *Journal of Personality and Social Psychology, 68*, 518–530.

Leckie, B. (1997, December). *Girls, bully behaviours and peer relationships: The double edged sword of exclusion and rejection.* Paper presented at the Australian Association for Research in Education, Brisbane, Australia. Retrieved May 15, 2008, from http://www.aare.edu.au/97pap/leckb284.htm

Leishman, J. (2005). *Indepth: Bullying; Cyber-bullying.* Retrieved March 30, 2005, from http://www.cbc.ca/news/background/bullying/cyber_bullying.html

Lenhart, A. (2007). *Cyberbullying and online teens.* Retrieved June 27, 2007, from http://www.pewinternet.org/pdfs/PIP%20Cyberbullying%20Memo.pdf

Lenhart, A., & Madden, M. (2007). *Social networking websites and teens: An overview.* Retrieved January 7, 2007, from http://www.pewinternet.org/pdfs/PIP_SNS_Data_Memo_Jan_2007.pdf

Lenhart, A., Madden, M., & Hitlin, P. (2005). *Teens and technology: Youth are leading the transition to a fully wired and mobile nation.* Retrieved August 2, 2005, from http://www.pewinternet.org/pdfs/PIP_Teens_Tech_July2005Web.pdf

Lenhart, A., Madden, M., Rankin Macgill, A., & Smith, A. (2007). *Teens and social media.* Retrieved December 19, 2007, from http://www.pewinternet.org/pdfs/PIP_Teens_Social_Media_Final.pdf

Li, Q. (2006). Cyberbullying in schools: A research of gender differences. *School Psychology International, 27,* 157–170.

Li, Q. (2007a). Bullying in the new playground: Research into cyberbullying and cyber victimisation. *Australasian Journal of Educational Technology, 23*(4), 435–454.

Li, Q. (2007b). New bottle but old wine: A research on cyberbullying in schools. *Computers and Human Behavior, 23*(4), 1777–1791.

Limber, S. P., & Nation, M. M. (1998, April). Bullying among children and youth. *Juvenile Justice Bulletin.* Retrieved January 20, 2006, from http://ojjdp.ncjrs.org/jjbulletin/9804/bullying2.html

Loeber, R., & Disheon, T.J. (1984). Early predictors of male delinquency: A review. *Psychological Bulletin, 94,* 68–99.

Lynn, R. (2007). *Virtual rape is traumatic, but is it a crime?* Retrieved May 4, 2007, from http://www.wired.com/culture/lifestyle/commentary/sexdrive/2007/05/sexdrive_0504

Magid, L., & Collier, A. (2007). *MySpace unraveled: A parent's guide to teen social networking.* Berkeley, CA: Peachpit Press.

Magnusson, D., Statten, H., & Duner, A. (1983). Aggression and criminality in a longitudinal perspective. In K. T. V. Dusen & S. A. Mednick (Eds.), *Prospective studies of crime and delinquency* (pp. 277–301). Netherlands: Kluwer Nijoff.

Makki, L. (2007). *Could Facebook follow in the foolish footsteps of Friendster?* Retrieved August 31, 2007, from http://web20.telecomtv.com/pages/?newsid=41790&id=e9381817–0593–417a-8639-c4c53e2a2a10&view=news

Manning, M., Heron, J., & Marshal, T. (1978). Style of hostility and social interactions at nursery school, and at home: An extended study of children. In A. Lionel, M. B. Hersov, & D. Shaffer (Eds.), *Aggresion and antisocial behavior in childhood and adolescence.* Oxford: Pergamon.

Marr, N., & Field, T. (2001). *Bullycide: Death at playtime; An expose of child suicide caused by bullying.* London: Success Unlimited.

Matsuoka, C. (2006). *Bullies going hi-tech.* Retrieved May 15, 2006, from http://www.kauaiworld.com/articles/2006/05/20/news/news02.txt

Mazerolle, P., Burton, V., Cullen, F. T., Evans, D., & Payne, G. L. (2000). Strain, anger, and delinquent adaptations: Specifying general strain theory. *Journal of Criminal Justice, 28,* 89–101.

Mazerolle, P., & Piquero, A. (1998). Linking exposure to strain with anger: An investigation of deviant adaptations. *Journal of Criminal Justice, 26*(3), 195–211.

McBrien, J. L., & Brandt, R. S. (1997). *From the language of learning: A guide to education terms.* Alexandria, VA: Association for Supervision and Curriculum Development.

McManus, T. (1998). Home Web sites thrust students into censorship disputes. Retrieved August 13, 1998, from http://partners.nytimes.com/library/tech/98/08/circuits/articles/13cens.html

Miller, A. (2002). *Mentoring students and young people: A handbook of effective practice.* London: Kogan Page.

Miller, P. M., Danaher, D. L., & Forbes, D. (1986). Sex-related strategies for coping with interpersonal conflict in children aged five to seven. *Developmental Psychology, 22,* 543–548.

Mills, C., Guerin, S., Lynch, F., Daly, I., & Fitzpatrick, C. (2004). The relationship between bullying, depression and suicidal thoughts/behavior in Irish adolescents. *Irish Journal of Psychological Medicine, 21*(4), 112–116.

Miniwatts Marketing Group. (2008). *Internet usage statistics: The Internet big picture; World Internet users and population stats.* Retrieved January 17, 2008, from http://www.internetworldstats.com/stats.htm

Morse v. Frederick, 127 2618 (S. Ct. 2007).

MySpace gains top ranking of U.S. websites. (2006). *Reuters.* Retrieved July 11, 2006, from http://www.usatoday.com/tech/news/2006-07-11-myspace-tops_x.htm

MySpace predator suspects plead not guilty. (2007). *KPTV.* Retrieved January 18, 2007, from http://www.kptv.com/news/10786493/detail.html

MySpace.com. (2008). *MySpace.com terms of use agreement.* Retrieved May 30, 2008, from http://www.myspace.com/Modules/Common/Pages/TermsConditions.aspx

MySpace.com subject of Connecticut sex-assault probe. (2006). *Associated Press.* Retrieved February 6, 2006, from http://www.foxnews.com/story/0,2933,183709,00.html

Nansel, T. R., Overpeck, M., Pilla, R. S., Ruan, W. J., Simons-Morton, B., & Scheidt, P. (2001). Bullying behaviors among U.S. youth: Prevalence and association with psychosocial adjustment. *Journal of the American Medical Association, 285*(16), 2094–2100.

National Children's Home. (2002). *1 in 4 children are the victims of "on-line bullying" says children's charity.* Retrieved September 1, 2003, from http://www.nch.org.uk (no longer online)

National Children's Home. (2005). *Putting U in the picture: Mobile bullying survey 2005.* Retrieved September 4, 2005, from http://www.nch.org.uk/uploads/documents/Mobile_bullying_%20report.pdf

Natvig, G. K., Albrektsen, G., & Quarnstrom, V. (2001). Psychosomatic symptoms among victims of school bullying. *Journal of Health Psychology, 6,* 365–377.

Neblett, M. (2007). *Rachael's story.* Retrieved January 26, 2008, from http://www.makeadifferenceforkids.org/rachael.html

New Jersey v. T. L. O., 469 325 (S. Ct. 1985).

Norris, P. (2001). *Digital divide: Civic engagement, information poverty, and the Internet worldwide.* New York: Cambridge University Press.

North High School. (2005). *Respect policy.* Retrieved September 21, 2007, from http://www.north.ecasd.k12.wi.us/respect/respect.pdf

O'Brien v. Westlake City School Board of Education (E.D. Ohio 1988).

Olsen, S. (2006). *MySpace reaching out to parents.* Retrieved April 15, 2006, from http://news.cnet.com/MySpace-reaching-out-to-parents/2009-1041_3-6059679.html

Olweus, D. (1978). *Aggression in the schools: Bullies and whipping boys.* Washington, DC: Hemisphere Press (Wiley).

Olweus, D. (1993). *Bullying at school.* Oxford, UK: Blackwell.

Olweus, D. (1994a). Bullying at school: Basic facts and effects of a school based intervention program. *Journal of Child Psychology and Psychiatry, 35,* 1171–1190.

Olweus, D. (Ed.). (1994b). *Bullying at school: Long-term outcomes for victims and an effective school-based intervention program.* New York: Plenum Press.

Olweus, D., Limber, S., & Mihalic, S. F. (1999a). *Bullying prevention program.* Boulder, CO: Center for the Study and Prevention of Violence.

Olweus, D., Limber, S., & Mihalic, S. F. (1999b). *Bullying prevention program: Blueprints for violence prevention; Book nine.* Boulder: Center for the Study and Prevention of Violence, Institute of Behavioral Science, University of Colorado.

Owens, L., Shute, R., & Slee, P. (2000a). "Guess what I just heard!": Indirect aggression among teenage girls in Australia. *Aggressive Behavior, 26,* 67–83.

Owens, L., Shute, R., & Slee, P. T. (2000b). "I'm in and you're out": Explanations for teenage girls' indirect aggression. *Psychology, Evolution and Gender, 2*(1), 19–46.

Parents: Cyber bullying led to teen's suicide. (2007). *ABC News.* Retrieved November 19, 2007, from http://abcnews.go.com/print?id=3882520

Pascoe, C. J. (2005). "Dude, you're a fag": Adolescent masculinity and the fag discourse. *Sexualities, 8,* 329–346.

Patchin, J. W. (2002). Bullied youths lash out: Strain as an explanation of extreme school violence. *Caribbean Journal of Criminology and Social Psychology, 7*(1–2), 22–43.

Patchin, J. W., & Hinduja, S. (2006). Bullies move beyond the schoolyard: A preliminary look at cyberbullying. *Youth Violence and Juvenile Justice, 4*(2), 148–169.

Poulsen, K. (2006). *Scenes from the MySpace backlash.* Retrieved February 28, 2006, from www.wired.com/politics/law/news/2006/02/70254

Prensky, M. (2001). Digital natives, digital immigrants. *On the Horizon, 9*(5), 1–2.

Prinstein, M. J., Boergers, J., & Vernberg, E. M. (2001). Overt and relational aggression in adolescents: Social-psychological adjustment of aggressors and victims. *Journal of Clinical Psychology, 30,* 479–491.

Requa v. Kent School District No. 415 (W.D. Wash. 2007).

Richmond, S. (2007). *Treat it like the village pub and you'll be fine . . . , honest.* Retrieved November 18, 2007, from http://www.telegraph.co.uk/connected/main.jhtml?xml=/connected/2007/11/18/dlnet18.xml

Rigby, K. (2003). Consequences of bullying in schools. *Canadian Journal of Psychiatry, 48,* 583–590.

Rigby, K., & Slee, P. T. (1993). Dimensions of interpersonal relating among Australian school children and their implications for psychological well-being. *The Journal of Social Psychology, 133*(1), 33–42.

Rigby, K., & Slee, P. T. (1999). Australia. In P. Smith, Y. Morita, J. Junger-Tas, D. Olweus, R. Catalano, & P. Slee (Eds.), *The nature of school bullying: A cross-national perspective* (pp. 324–339). London: Routledge.

Rivers, I., & Noret, N. (2007). *The prevalence & correlates of cyberbullying in adolescence: Results of a five-year cohort study.* Queen Margaret University & York St. John University.

Roland, E. (1980). *Terror i skolen.* Stavanger, Norway: Rogaland Research Institute.

Roland, E. (1989). Bullying: The Scandinavian research tradition. In D. P. Tattum & D. A. Lane (Eds.), *Bullying in schools* (pp. 21–32). Stroke-on-Trent, Great Britain: Trentham.

Roland, E. (2002). Bullying, depressive symptoms and suicidal thoughts. *Educational Research, 44,* 55–67.

Rosenberg, M. (1965). *Society and the adolescent self-image.* Princeton, NJ: Princeton University Press.

Seals, D., & Young, J. (2003). Bullying and victimization: Prevalence and relationship to gender, grade level, ethnicity, self-esteem and depression. *Adolescence, 38,* 735–747.

Sellers, P. (2006). *MySpace cowboys.* Retrieved August 29, 2006, from http://money.cnn.com/magazines/fortune/fortune_archive/2006/09/04/8384727/index.htm

Shariff, S., & Hoff, D. L. (2007). Cyberbullying: Clarifying legal boundaries for school supervision in cyberspace. *International Journal of Cyber Criminology, 1*(1).

Siann, G., Callahan, M., Glissov, P., Lockhart, R., & Rawson, L. (1994). Who gets bullied? The effect of school, gender and ethnic group. *Educational Research, 36,* 123–134.

Simmons, R. (2003). *Odd girl out.* New York: Harcourt.

Skinner, B. F. (1953). *Science and human behavior.* New York: MacMillan.

Skinner, B. F. (1971). *Beyond freedom and dignity.* New York: Knopf.

Slee, P. T., & Rigby, K. (1993). The relationship of Eysenck's personality factors and self esteem to bully/victim behaviour in Australian school boys. *Personality and Individual Differences, 14,* 371–373.

Smetana, J. G., Campione-Barr, N., & Metzger, A. (2006). Adolescent development in interpersonal and societal contexts. *Annual Review of Psychology, 57,* 255–284.

Smith, P. K., Mahdavi, J., Carvalho, M., Fisher, S., Russell, S., & Tippett, N. (2008). Cyberbullying: Its nature and impact in secondary school pupils. *Journal of Child Psychology and Psychiatry, 49*(4), 376–385.

Smith, P. K., Mahdavi, J., Carvalho, M., & Tippett, N. (2006). An investigation into cyber bullying, its forms, awareness and impact, and the relationship between age and gender in cyber bullying: A report to the Anti-Bullying Alliance. Retrieved May 30, 2008, from http://www.anti-bullyingalliance.org.uk/downloads/pdf/cyberbullying reportfina1230106.pdf

Smithers, R. (2008). Bebo named as best social networking site in survey. Retrieved January 4, 2008, from http://www.guardian.co.uk/technology/2008/jan/04/social networking.bebo

Soldier found dead after MySpace suicide note. (2006). *Associated Press.* Retrieved April 27, 2006, from http://www.msnbc.msn.com/id/12518853/

Sprint.com. (2005). *Acceptable use policy and visitor agreement.* Retrieved September 1, 2005, from http://www.sprint.com/legal/agreement.html

Striegel-Moore, R. H., Dohm, F.-A., Pike, K. M., Wilfley, D. E., & Fairburn, C. G. (2002). Abuse, bullying, and discrimination as risk factors for binge eating disorder. *The American Journal of Psychiatry, 159*(11), 1902–1907.

Surra, C. A., & Milardo, R. M. (1991). The social psychological context of developing relationships: Interactive and psychological networks. In W. H. Jones & D. Perlman (Eds.), *Advances in personal relationships: Vol. 3* (pp. 1–36). London: Jessica Kingsley.

Sweeting, H., & West, P. (2001). Being different: Correlates of the experience of teasing and bullying at age 11. *Research Papers in Education, 16,* 222–246.

Tattum, D. P. (1989). Violence and aggression in schools. In D. P. Tattum & D. A. Lane (Eds.), *Bullying in schools* (pp. 7–19). Stroke-on-Trent, Great Britain: Trentham.

Teens arrested after posting alleged firebombing video on MySpace.com. (2006). *USA Today.* Retrieved April 5, 2006, from http://www.usatoday.com/tech/news/2006–04–05-myspace-arrest_x.htm

Teens arrested over filmed beating: Girl "lured" to friend's home and attacked by 6 other girls, Florida police say. (2008). *Associated Press.* Retrieved April 8, 2008, from http://www.cbsnews.com/stories/2008/04/08/national/main4000740.shtml?source=related_story

Teens attracted to Internet social forum despite warnings. (2006). *Associated Press.* Retrieved May 8, 2006, from http://www.boston.com/news/local/vermont/articles/2006/05/08/teens_attracted_to_internet_social_forum_despite_warnings/

The Ophelia Project. (2006). *CASS: Creating a Safe School*™ Retrieved May 30, 2008, from http://www.opheliaproject.org/main/cass.htm

Thomas v. Board of Education, Granville Central School District, 607 1043 (2d Cir 1979).

Tinker et al. v. Des Moines Independent Community School District et al., 393 503 (S. Ct. 1969).

Trolley, B., Hanel, C., & Shields, L. (2006). *Demystifying and deescalating cyber bullying in the schools: A resource guide for counselors, educators, and parents.* Bangor, ME: Booklocker.com.

Tully, J. M. (2007). *The outer limits: Disciplining students without getting sued.* Retrieved November 3, 2007, from http://uacoe.arizona.edu/wren/documents/The_Outer_Limits_Disciplining_Cyber-Mischief_Without_Getting_Sued.pdf

Turkle, S. (1995). *Life on the screen: Identity in the age of the Internet.* New York: Simon & Schuster.

Underwood, M. K. (2003). The comity of modest manipulation: The importance of distinguishing among bad behaviors. *Merrill-Palmer Quarterly, 49*(3), 373–389.

Underwood, M. K., Galen, B. R., & Paquette, J. A. (2001). Top ten challenges for understanding gender and aggression in children: Why can't we all just get along? *Social Development, 10*(2), 248–266.

Usher, P. (2006). *Felony charges anticipated against Del Oro suspect.* Retrieved May 25, 2006, from http://www.auburnjournal.com/articles/2006/05/26/news/top_stories/05 blanchard_26.txt

van der Wal, M. F., de Wit, C. A. M., & Hirasing, R. A. (2003). Psychosocial health among young victims and offenders of direct and indirect bullying. *Pediatrics, 111,* 1312–1317.

van Tilburg, T. G. (1995). Delineation of the social network and differences in network size. In C. P. M. Knipscheer, J. de J. Gierveld, T. G. van Tilburg, & P. A. Dykstra (Eds.), *Living arrangements and social networks of older adults* (pp. 83–96). Amsterdam: VU University Press.

Vossekuil, B., Fein, R. A., Reddy, M., Borum, R., & Modzeleski, W. (2002). *The final report and findings of the Safe School Initiative: Implications for the prevention of school attacks in the United States.* Washington, DC: U.S. Secret Service and U.S. Department of Education. Retrieved August 29, 2003, from http://www.secretservice.gov/ntac/ssi_final_ report.pdf

Wang, J., & Chen, C. (2004). An automated tool for managing interactions in virtual communities: Using social network analysis approach. *Journal of Organizational Computing and Electronic Commerce, 14*(1), 1–26.

Wellman, B. (1981). Applying network analysis to the study of support. In B. H. Gottlieb (Ed.), *Social networks and social support* (pp. 171–200). London: Sage.

Willard, N. E. (2003). *Safe and responsible use of the Internet: A guide for educators.* Retrieved January 20, 2007, from http://www.csriu.org/onlinedocs/pdf/srui/entire.pdf

Williams, D. (2006). *Cyberbullying: One family's story.* Retrieved April 28, 2006, from http://www.tolerance.org/teach/printar.jsp?p=0&ar=669&pi=current

Williams, K., & Guerra, N. G. (2007). Prevalence and predictors of Internet bullying. *Journal of Adolescent Health, 41,* S14–S21.

Wisniewski v. Board of Education of the Weedsport Central School District (2d Cir. 2007).

Wolak, J., Mitchell, K., & Finkelhor, D. (2006). *Online victimization of youth: Five years later.* Retrieved October 26, 2007, from http://www.unh.edu/ccrc/pdf/CV138.pdf

Wolak, J., Mitchell, K., & Finkelhor, D. (2007). Does online harassment constitute bullying? An exploration of online harassment by known peers and online-only contacts. *Journal of Adolescent Health, 41,* S51–S58.

Wolke, D., Woods, S., Bloomfield, L., & Karstadt, L. (2000). The association between direct and relational bullying and behaviour problems among primary school children. *Journal of Child Psychology and Psychiatry, 41*(8), 989–1002.

Writer, G. (2006). *Cyber bullies: What you and your kids need to know now.* Retrieved July 11, 2006, from http://www.phillyburbs.com/pb-dyn/news/291-07112006-682108.html

Xanga. (2007). *Xanga safety features.* Retrieved December 16, 2007, from http://safety.xanga .com/category/safetyfeatures/

Ybarra, M. L., Diener-West, M., & Leaf, P. J. (2007). Examining the overlap in Internet harassment and school bullying: Implications for school intervention. *Journal of Adolescent Health, 41,* S42–S50.

Ybarra, M. L., Espelage, D. L., & Mitchell, K. J. (2007). The co-occurrence of Internet harassment and unwanted sexual solicitation victimization and perpetration: Associations with psychosocial indicators. *Journal of Adolescent Health, 41,* S31–S41.

Ybarra, M. L., & Mitchell, K. J. (2004). Online aggressor/targets, aggressors and targets: A comparison of associated youth characteristics. *Journal of Child Psychology and Psychiatry, 45,* 1308–1316.

Ybarra, M. L., & Mitchell, K. J. (2007). Prevalence and frequency of Internet harassment instigation: Implications for adolescent health. *Journal of Adolescent Health, 41,* 189–195.

Ybarra, M. L., Mitchell, J. K., Finkelhor, D., & Wolak, J. (2007). Examining characteristics and associated distress related to Internet harassment: Findings from the Second Youth Internet Safety Survey. *Pediatrics, 118*(4), 1169–1177.

Yu, L. (2007). *Bill would restrict kids' MySpace profiles.* Retrieved March 9, 2007, from http://www.yaledailynews.com/articles/view/20339

Zahn-Waxler, C. (2000). The development of empathy, guilt, and internalization of distress: Implications for gender differences and externalizing problems. In R. J. Davidson (Ed.), *Wisconsin Symposium on Emotion: Anxiety, depression, and emotion: Vol. 2* (pp. 222–265). New York: Oxford University Press.

Index